The Ngatik Massacre

Smithsonian Series in Ethnographic Inquiry
William L. Merrill and Ivan Karp, Series Editors

Ethnography as fieldwork, analysis, and literary form is the distinguishing feature of modern anthropology. Guided by the assumption that anthropological theory and ethnography are inextricably linked, this series is devoted to exploring the ethnographic enterprise.

Advisory Board
Richard Bauman (Indiana University), Gerald Berreman (University of California, Berkeley), James Boon (Princeton University), Stephen Gudeman (University of Minnesota), Shirley Lindenbaum (City University of New York), George Marcus (Rice University), David Parkin (University of London), Roy Rappaport (University of Michigan), Renato Rosaldo (Stanford University), Norman Whitten (University of Illinois), and Eric Wolf (City University of New York).

The Ngatik Massacre

HISTORY AND IDENTITY ON A MICRONESIAN ATOLL

LIN POYER

Smithsonian Institution Press
Washington and London

Editor: Karin Kaufman
Production Editor: Jenelle Walthour
Designer: Linda McKnight

Library of Congress Cataloging-in-Publication Data
Poyer, Lin, 1953-
   The Ngatik massacre: history and identity on a Micronesian
atoll/Lin Poyer.
          p.   cm.
   Includes bibliographical references and index.
   ISBN 1-56098-261-6 (cloth). — ISBN 1-56098-262-4 (pbk.)
   1. Ngatik (Micronesian people)—History. 2. Ngatik (Micro-
nesian people)—Ethnic identity. 3. Ngatik (Micronesian peo-
ple)—Social life and customs. 4. Massacres—Micronesia
(Federated States)—Ngatik—History—19th century. 5. Ngatik
(Micronesia)—History. 6. Ngatik (Micronesia)—Social life and
customs. I. Title.
DU568.N44P69   1992
996.5—dc20   92-37911

British Library Cataloguing-in-Publication Data is available

Manufactured in the United States of America
00 99 98 97 96 95 94 93   5 4 3 2 1

To my family, and in memory of my father;
also,
to the memory of friendships on Ngatik
and to the future of Sapwuahfik and its people.

Ong ahi peneinei oh ketemen en ahi pahpa;
oh
ong kompoakapahi nan deken Ngatik
oh ong mwehi kokohdo en wehn Sapwuahfik
oh mehn Sapwuahfik.

Contents

Contents

Maps and Tables

Maps

Tables

Acknowledgments

MY THANKS GO ABOVE ALL to the people of Sapwuahfik, who have generously shared their time, knowledge, and hospitality with me. *Kalahngan en kumwail koaruhsie!* Everyone I met helped me in some way. I wish to acknowledge the particular help (in alphabetical order) of the Nahior, Panuel, Pohl, Salomon, and Sehpin families. Mr. Luten Pohl was most generous in sharing a portion of his great knowledge of history and culture with me, and Mr. Sinio Nahior was a valuable translator and colleague. I also thank the officials who assisted my work (again in alphabetical order): Mr. Victor Edwin, Mr. Ewalt Inek, Mr. Carl Kohler, Mr. Goodyear Panuel, the late Mr. Mwoughty Salomon, and Mr. Elter Sehpin. I wish to say a formal thank you, *Kalahngan en kupwuromwail,* to the atoll's traditional leaders during my stay, former Nahnmwarki Seneres Nason and Nahnken Are Panuel. Additional help during my work on the atoll was given by Dave Poyer and Pilipet Nason (in mapping) and, from afar, by Roberta

Myers, Dave Lemke, and other friends. I thank my mother and brothers for their support while I was far from home.

I owe a special debt to the women of the Sehpin family, who fed me and kept me company, especially Morihda and Masdihna, and I would like here to remember the late Mrs. Etty Sehpin. I was made to feel at home on Pohnpei, and helped in many ways, by Vic and Norma Edwin, and by the Bahá'í community, especially Virginia Breaks.

I hope that those who are not mentioned by name will also accept my thanks for taking the time to teach me and to make me feel welcome on Ngatik. Many will find their words, or their experiences, in this book. Following a custom of academic writing, I have not used people's real names, in order to protect their privacy.

This is an appropriate place to acknowledge my teachers at the University of Michigan, especially Vern Carroll, Conrad Kottak, Roy Rappaport, and Aram Yengoyan. My early understanding of Sapwuahfik and of anthropology owes much to their insight. In addition, I thank the senior scholars of the Pacific, who so kindly shared with me what they had in their files about Ngatik and welcomed me to this beautiful research area, especially Saul Riesenberg and the late Jack Fischer.

My handling of the topics dealt with in this book has benefitted greatly from discussion with colleagues, particularly Jocelyn Linnekin and others in the ASAO symposium "Cultural Identity in Oceania," and those anthropologists and historians who have worked on Pohnpei, whose influence is evident in the pages that follow, especially Suzanne Falgout, David Hanlon, Francis X. Hezel, S. J., Michael Lieber, Glenn Petersen, and Martha Ward. Comments by William Merrill and anonymous reviewers greatly improved what I had written. Thanks also to Jay Yocis for his work on the maps, and to the helpful and professional editorial staff of the Smithsonian Institution Press.

This book is based on 1979–80 fieldwork funded by a National Institute of Mental Health Predoctoral Research Fellowship. Archival research in Honolulu was made possible by a 1985 Colby College Social Science Grant. Librarians at the Pacific Collec-

tion of the Hamilton Library, University of Hawaii, and the
Hawaiian Mission Children's Society archives in Honolulu were
helpful, creative, and persistent. I also appreciate the support of
colleagues and resources at the University of Cincinnati. I thank
my husband Robert Kelly for his careful reading and consistent
support.

Portions of this book have appeared previously in the *Journal
of Pacific History* ("The Ngatik Massacre: Documentary and
Oral Traditional Accounts," 20 [1985]: 4–22), *American Ethnologist* ("Maintaining 'Otherness': Sapwuahfik Cultural Identity,"
15 [1988]: 472–85), *Ethnohistory* ("History, Identity, and Christian Evangelism: The Sapwuahfik Massacre," 35 [1988]: 209–33),
Journal of Anthropological Research ("Egalitarianism in the
Face of Hierarchy," 49, no. 2 [1993]), and as chapters in G. White
and M. Lindstrom, eds., *The Pacific Theater: Island Representations of World War II* (1989, University of Hawaii Press), J. Linnekin and L. Poyer, eds., *Cultural Identity and Ethnicity in the
Pacific* (1990, University of Hawaii Press), and S. Gregg, ed., *Between Bands and States* (1991, Center for Archaeological Investigation, Southern Illinois University). I thank J. Stephen Athens
for permission to use two photographs, and the Bernice P. Bishop
Museum for permission to quote from John L. Fischer's notes.

Introduction

T HE ATOLL MUST HAVE looked much the same, that July day in 1837, as it did when I approached it 142 years later. Pacific islands are beautiful; perhaps atolls are the most striking because their emerald strip of vegetation appears on the ocean horizon with the suddenness of a magic trick. But the men who sailed through the narrow twist of a channel into what they called Ngatik lagoon that day in 1837 did not think about the island's beauty. They had seen many atolls and were probably tired of them. They were, in any case, not the kind of men given to exclaiming at views. And they had come to loot and destroy the island, not to appreciate its scenery.

The ship was the trading cutter *Lambton*, out of Sydney, Australia, manned by the classic motley crew of runaways, villains, adventurers, and entrepreneurs—the sort who abounded in the European population of the Pacific in the early nineteenth century. Any of those words could describe the *Lambton*'s master, C. H. Hart. Hart had roamed the Western Pacific for years, making his way by a mix of fair trade and sly schemes. Hart traded Islanders beads and knives, guns and ammunition, tobacco, cloth, and rum, driving a hard bargain for the bêche-de-mer, pearl shell, and tortoiseshell that he loaded aboard the *Lambton.* Bêche-de-mer, sea cucumber, went to China for soup. The Chinese paid well for it, but it had to be boiled and cured in a foul, messy job. Collecting pearl shell, like processing bêche-de-mer, was labor intensive (Hezel 1983:211). Tortoiseshell, from hawksbill turtles—that was the stuff. It was made into ladies' combs and mirrors, decorated boxes, and knickknacks. The Victorian world, Far East and West, was wild for it, and hawksbill turtles were being decimated to fill the demand.

It took time and hard work to find the turtles, though they were easy enough to kill once you located them. But what Hart had, or thought he had, on the atoll called by its inhabitants Sapwuahfik (but by Hart "Ngatik," and on navigational charts by a dozen other names) was a hoard of tortoiseshell without the trouble of work—except the work of taking it from the island's people, who would, no doubt, object.

They had objected when Hart's crew first found the treasure trove of shell, more than a year earlier. Two of the *Lambton*'s men had gone inland and discovered a cache of turtle shell, but the Islanders would not sell and resisted theft. In fact, a group of men chased the sailors down to the beach, and the crew escaped by quick oar strokes. The *Lambton* returned to island trading and a trip to New South Wales, but Hart did not forget the shell, nor the close call he and his crew had experienced. Greed and revenge took root, and in Hart's mind he marked Sapwuahfik for a return trip.

The *Lambton* sailed to the region again in mid-1836, arriving at Pohnpei Island in August, just after a group of whalers from the ship *Falcon* had been killed following an altercation with Pohnpei men. The Europeans in the area, Hart among the leaders, joined forces to take revenge, culminating in the murder of a Pohnpei nobleman. (By involving himself with these events, Hart made sure that his name went down on the list of persons to be investigated two years later by a British warship, HMS *Larne*, under Commander P. L. Blake. Blake was a thorough and principled investigator, cautious but relentless in his pursuit of evidence of criminal activity. Because of Blake we have a historical record of Hart's crimes.)

After the *Falcon* incident, Hart went back to business, sailing between Guam, Manila, and Pohnpei. Then, on the last days of June or the first days of July 1837, he made ready for his return to Sapwuahfik—where, he said, he wished to "trade quietly" with the natives—by making cartridges and taking on extra hands from Pohnpei.

When he arrived at the atoll, Hart tried to land where he had landed before, but this time he was met with hostility. Sapwuahfik men beckoned them ashore, indicating their intentions with a display of their own weapons. The people of Sapwuahfik had known from divination when the ship would return; they had been watching, and when they saw it appear on the horizon, they prepared for war, readying clubs and slings.

Hart thought better of an immediate landing, taking the crew to spend the night on another islet of the atoll. The next day he loaded them into the ship's boats for a straightforward assault. Despite the defenders' preparations, the battle turned against them. In two days of fighting, every Sapwuahfik man but one was killed or fled by canoe. Though one woman was accidentally wounded, the invaders did not make targets of women and children.

Soon after the *Lambton* sailed from the atoll—which, now that the native voices were stilled, would be called Ngatik for more than a century—it returned to leave a group of Pohnpeians and a European in charge of what Hart saw as his conquered domain. The plan was to operate Ngatik as a business, producing tortoiseshell. They would bring in more settlers, marry the widows and girls of old Sapwuahfik, and see how much money they could make in this pretty place. So survivors and murderers began a curious interaction that would eventually produce a new population and a unique culture. Sapwuahfik's history had come to an end. The story of Ngatik had just begun.

The Meaning of the Massacre

In a sense, what happened at that time and place is beyond recovery, and therefore the historical documents are of interest
only to the Pacific scholar. But the modern memory of the massacre matters more concretely. On one hand, it is a record of one
kind of European activity in the Pacific Islands, that of the avari-
cious trader, the ruthless opportunist. (Blake's search for justice
reminds us of more honorable European activities there.) That,
perhaps, is the meaning of the massacre to Western readers. To
people living on what is once again (since 1985) called Sapwuahfik, the massacre has a more immediate meaning, because it is
their local history, and because their modern identity depends in
part on how they understand that history.

I came ashore at Ngatik in June of 1979, prepared to conduct
ethnographic fieldwork in the classic mode—to understand as
fully as I could the life of this small island community. To get to
Ngatik, I had flown from Honolulu to Kolonia, Pohnpei, where I
spent a few weeks collecting supplies and meeting local officials
and Ngatik people on Pohnpei. Pohnpei is a high island, surrounded by a barrier reef but edged with mangrove swamp rather
than the cinematic beach one might expect. Its mountains catch
all the rain, it seems, in a thousand square miles of ocean. It
rains nearly every day, and the heat and humidity, emerald vegetation, rainbow flowers, and opalescent light combine to create
the sense of living in a gigantic greenhouse. Kolonia is a small
town by U.S. reckoning; but it came to seem to me, as it did to
atoll people, a treasure-house of urban amenities: stores, movies,
ice cream, television, and medical facilities. I visited Pohnpei
several times, including one stay of four and a half months.
Nonetheless, and despite my general familiarity with Pohnpei's
language, culture, and history, I do not really know much about
the people of the high island. This is important, because much
of what I say about Sapwuahfik makes sense only in light of
what they think of Pohnpei. My view of the residents of the high
island, then, is filtered through the opinions of the low islanders,
the atoll dwellers, the "outer islanders" as they are often called

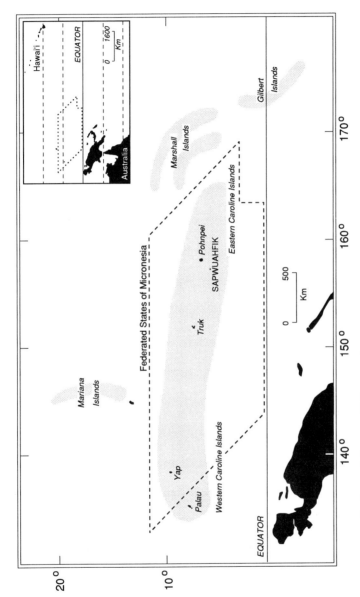

MAP I. *Federated States of Micronesia.*

5

in English. I lived and associated with Sapwuahfik people when I was on Pohnpei. I sometimes felt that we were hicks together in the big city, and when I left the high island for the atoll, it was with some of the relief of the small town girl leaving New York City behind. As you will see, that is only in part a fair description of outer islander feelings about Pohnpei.

Ngatik was sandy, palm-filled, sunny. By the time I was settled into a small house adjacent to a local family's home, I had begun to work. As I proceeded with the basics of learning the language, taking a household census, and engaging in exploratory talks with people about subsistence and social organization, I repeatedly encountered references to the past, to *ansouen mahs*, "the past," and *mehn mahs*, "the people of long ago." As I learned more of the atoll's history, I began to see that local knowledge of that history was part of the raw material of modern life. Ngatik's people regarded the ancient and modern people of Ngatik as markedly different and saw their contemporary way of life as strongly shaped by foreign influences, by their immigrant heritage. As people spoke to me of *tiahk en Ngatik* (Ngatik's custom), identified each other as, or as not, *uhdahn mehn Ngatik* (truly a person of Ngatik), and contrasted *stylen Ngatik* (Ngatik style) with the ways of Pohnpei or *wai* (foreign/American), I began to see the complexity of sentiment and structure that produced a distinctive community on Ngatik. It became clear to me that an important focus of the remainder of my work would be to understand what it meant to be *mehn Ngatik*.

My implicit contrasts were with the United States, where people have a habit of thinking of ethnically "mixed" people (i.e., people whose ancestors have their origin in several geographic areas, social "races," or even languages) as being marginal, interstitial, and usually, as the phrase goes, "searching for their identity." This was clearly not the case for Ngatik people. They were not in search of an identity; they confidently claimed one. Yet the peculiar slant the categories of my own culture gave to my initial responses eventually helped me formulate the questions that led to the analysis in this book.

I set out the puzzle for myself: How did the biologically mixed population in the chaotic situation of postmassacre Ngatik produce the culturally coherent community that I met in 1979–80? In retrospect, the question was not a legitimate one, phrased as it was in my own culture's terms, asking why the Ngatik case didn't fit my preconceptions. But pursuing it opened opportunities for me to explore notions of personal and group identity and, eventually, to turn a critical eye on the concepts of ethnicity that produced the question in the first place.

After I returned to the United States from twenty months of fieldwork, I reviewed what I had learned from the people of Ngatik about themselves. With the help of recent theorists in the study of society and history, I began to see how, on this atoll, history and identity took their shape from each other. In 1985–86, as if to confirm the direction of my analysis, the people of Ngatik affirmed their modern identity by officially reinstituting their atoll's aboriginal name.[1] When I visited Pohnpei briefly at the end of 1989 and the first days of 1990, I again found reference to the past to be an essential part of the changes and trends in Sapwuahfik community life. To understand what it means to be *mehn Sapwuahfik* in the 1980s and 1990s, I had to understand what *mehn Sapwuahfik* thought about the events of the 1830s.

Sapwuahfik Today

The Micronesian islands stretch over three million square miles of ocean between Hawaii and the Philippines. The area's largest islands are formed of volcanic rocks, clothed with rich soil and diverse vegetation. These are the "high" islands, including Guam and the Northern Marianas; the central islands of the Palau (Belau), Yap, and Truk (Chuuk) groups; Pohnpei; and Kosrae. The greater part of Micronesia's population lives on these high islands, where growing urban centers host government, medical, educational, and business facilities. But most Micronesian islands are much smaller, low sand atolls that form when land subsidence or rising water drowns a volcanic landform, leaving a ring or bar of coral barely above the ocean. This traps sand and debris until the sandbar builds into a habitable islet. An atoll results when several islets form around a relatively shallow central lagoon, protecting it from ocean waves and creating a distinctive ecological niche.

Sapwuahfik Atoll lies eighty-eight miles southwest of its nearest neighbor, the high island of Pohnpei, in the Eastern Caroline Islands (see maps). The atoll's total land area is .674 square miles (Bryan 1970); most residents live on the main islet (Ngatik Islet, .406 square miles) in households evenly spaced around the islet's edge. Each household consists of a residence house, a cookhouse, and, in most cases, a shed for boat or canoe storage. Land divisions in the late nineteenth and early twentieth centuries and subsequent inheritance have given every family access to land on both Ngatik Islet and one or more of the smaller islets. Although families often visit other islets to vacation or to harvest coconuts, taro, and pigs, and a few people prefer to live on Wad or Paina, Ngatik Islet is the focus of community life.

This main islet comprises several ecological and economic zones. Pigs forage and canoes are beached along the strip of sand bordering lagoon and ocean shores. A low coral-rock wall has been built around the circumference of the islet to keep pigs from wandering beyond the beach. From the beach to the fringe of trees at Ngatik's center is the main living area. A wide path, near which most people build their houses and cookhouses, encircles the islet just inland of the wall. Houses are made of wood, cement, or corrugated iron with metal, cement, or thatch roofs, and most have rainwater cisterns and outhouses nearby. Small cookhouses next to residences are more casually made of logs, lumber, and thatch. Living areas are neatly kept, with decorative lilies and plumeria gracing well-weeded paths and yards. Coconut palms, papayas, and bananas grow near houses, and chickens, dogs, and cats are kept here.

The forest proper begins behind the residence area, dominated by large breadfruit trees used for food and canoe logs. The forest is also the source of lumber and small quantities of fruits,

FIG I.   *Aerial view of Ngatik Islet, Sapwuahfik Atoll. Lagoon in fore-ground. (Photograph by J. Stephen Athens.)*

vegetables, medicinal plants, and other useful materials. A few families have cleared living space in the forest, despite a preva-lent feeling that spirits frequent the area. The forest surrounds cultivated taro gardens in the center of the islet. These gardens are deep-dug beds of rich, composted soil, cultivated and har-vested year around. Sapwuahfik people assert that these gardens have existed from time immemorial, and low dirt ridges in the islet's interior suggest they were more extensive prehistorically. (Smaller taro gardens, most dug more recently, exist in the inte-riors of Wad, Paina, and Wataluhk.) Walking paths cross Ngatik Islet's cultivated and uncultivated areas. The forest edge and clearings around forest houses are planted in bananas, manioc, and coconut.

With a 1985 population of 564 (Gorenflo and Levin 1992:12; 1979 fieldwork counted a de jure population of 567), Sapwuahfik is not overcrowded. In fact, Sapwuahfik people frequently ex-

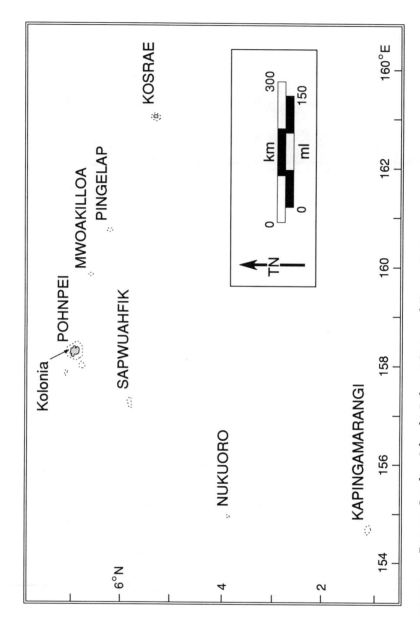

MAP 2.   *Eastern Caroline Islands, Pohmpei State and Kosrae State.*

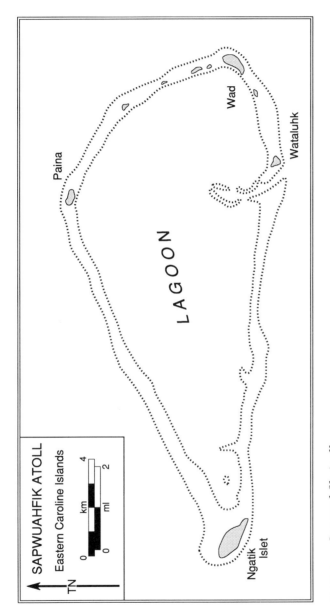

SAPWUAHFIK ATOLL

Eastern Caroline Islands

Paina

Wad

Wataluhk

LAGOON

Ngatik
Islet

TN

km 0 4

ml 0 2

MAP 3. *Sapwuahfik Atoll.*

FIG 2. *A Sapwuahfik woman cleaning taro, grown in gardens in the interior of Ngatik Islet. Residence house in background.*

press their pleasure at living on an island with plentiful space and abundant food. Households use their own land and labor to provide for their needs, combining vegetable and tree crops, domestic animals, lagoon and ocean products, and rice, flour, canned meat, and condiments purchased from the community-owned co-op store or one of several family-owned shops intermittently in business. Cash procures protein when fishing is poor, food for special occasions (such as bread for a wedding and rice for a child's birthday feast), and luxuries such as soy sauce, coffee, sugar, and candy. But the bulk of the everyday diet comes from gardens, trees, ocean, and lagoon.

The primary vegetable foods are numerous varieties of taro, breadfruit, and bananas, coconuts, yams, and purchased rice and flour. Taro (varieties of *Cyrtosperma chamissonis*, but also *Alocasia*, *Xanthosoma*, and *Colocasia* species) is the focus of gardening efforts, mostly, in my observation, by women with help from children. People say the gardens are men's to dig out and

FIG 3. *An outrigger canoe, used for fishing, rests on the lagoon shore. Note two distinctive traits of Sapwuahfik canoes: the* fedlatch *at each end and the pattern of light and dark, wide and narrow bands of paint.*

plant, and women's to weed and maintain. During the work of mapping landholdings on Ngatik Islet, an older man spoke of taro gardens as the *"gold" en Ngatik:* "For foreigners, money is gold, but taro garden land is the Ngatik people's gold." Coconut land and forest land are also valued. Every family on Sapwuahfik owns land, is intensely interested in the use and possession of productive land, and is willing to get into legal battles with relatives over the ownership of land.

Sapwuahfik's large lagoon is a readily available and plentiful source of protein. Though long ago, people told me, both men and women fished—Sapwuahfik women were famed for it—now men usually go out, using nets, spears, or lines. Women's fishing is for the most part gathering clams or catching octopus, though they can and do enjoy line fishing. It is not unusual for a woman to go lagoon fishing with her husband or brother. The ocean, however, is men's territory. Men take out motorboats or sailing canoes after tuna and other large fish, and dolphin. Ocean fishing peaks during the high-tide, high-wind season from October to December. June to August, with low tides and little wind or current, is best for lagoon fishing. When weather or manpower problems keep a household from enjoying fresh fish, purchased canned meat or fish substitutes. Pigs, dogs, and chickens make common special-occasion supplements to the diet.

Although all Sapwuahfik families depend on the productive capacity of their land and labor for subsistence, everyone recognizes the need for cash to purchase imported food, lamps, kerosene, flashlights, radios and batteries, medicines, cloth and clothing, stationery and school supplies, needles, thread, and soap. Cash comes from the sale of copra, occasional government wage labor, or one of the scarce salaried positions on the atoll, as well as remittances from family members working on Pohnpei. People occasionally sell pigs, fish, doughnuts, or bread to one another or to the school lunch program. By the late 1980s, producing seaweed for export was another option.

Sapwuahfik community life centers around the productive activities of the household, interpersonal kin relations, and the informal and formal sociopolitics of neighborhood, island, and church. Personal choices in residence, land inheritance, and daily activity are persistently bilateral; Sapwuahfik's matrilineal clans have little practical role beyond regulating marriages. Because of local endogamy, Sapwuahfik's small population and living area, the tendency for individuals to change residence fre-

FIG 4. *A children's footrace along the main path on an island holiday. The co-op store is visible in the background.*

quently, and the inclusiveness of kin ties, Sapwuahfik people are related by multiple social bonds.

Sapwuahfik's modern political organization is a mix of the traditional Pohnpei title system, imported to the atoll after the massacre, and institutions of electoral democracy introduced during the U.S. era in Micronesia. Today the two operate simultaneously under an unstated working agreement that traditional titleholders provide moral authority and elected officials make laws and enforce them. Actual decision making in the community involves a complicated interplay of both structures and relies heavily on community consensus. To understand Sapwuahfik's title system, we must briefly outline that of Pohnpei.

Pohnpei's traditional political organization consists of two ranked series of titles (*mwar*) in each of Pohnpei's five chiefdoms, culminating with the titles of *nahnmwarki* and *nahnken* (heading the *A* and *B* lines, respectively, to use Riesenberg's

[1968] terms). Following a widespread Pacific pattern, titleholders in the two lines have different obligations. The nahnmwarki
is the focus of power and ritual authority, whereas the nahnken
takes the role of "talking chief," communicating between the
nahnmwarki and his people and acting as chief negotiator and
public spokesman of the polity. Each Pohnpei title has historical
and religious meaning. Titles are normally held by men; a male
titleholder's wife holds a cognate title deriving from that of her
husband (there are a few separate women's titles, and women occasionally hold A- and B-line titles) (Riesenberg 1968:47–48).
Each of Pohnpei's chiefdoms is made up of *kousapw*, "sections,"
with their own sets of titles. At one time this produced a sort of
feudal arrangement, with holders of section titles controlling
land, labor, and local products in that section and in turn owing
allegiance to the holders of chiefdom titles, with the nahnmwarki ultimately controlling the land of the chiefdom.[2] Changes imposed by colonial administrations have drastically reduced titleholders' powers and rights, but the system itself remains vital.
Men of high title are also men of political and personal influence. On Pohnpei most men value titles, compete for titles, and
enthusiastically involve themselves in the complicated politics
of title inheritance. The statuses of nahnmwarki and nahnken
have no legal authority in the new national constitution, but
this does not negate the reality of their local influence.

The title complex is expressed publicly in two forms. One is
the elaborate display of respect (*wahu*), including honorific language and personal etiquette, tendered by persons of lesser title
to persons of higher title. This is seen especially at formal public
events, such as feasts given for special occasions. High-titled
persons are addressed and referred to by title, both publicly and
privately. Honorific language (*lokaian meing*, described in
Garvin and Riesenberg 1952) calls for an extensive separate vocabulary for different status levels. The body of title etiquette is
extensive, detailed, and complex, and must be studied assidu-
ously by someone who wishes to become a master of *meing* and
wahu.

Intentionally transferred to and modified for atoll life in the years following the massacre, Sapwuahfik's title system can be regarded as a simplified version of that of Pohnpei. On Sapwuahfik there is only one set of title lines (that is, Sapwuahfik is a single chiefdom), which does not play the important role in personal and political life played by titles on Pohnpei. The atoll's community life is by and large not managed by the traditional title system. Nonetheless, locality is an important component of Sapwuahfik's polity. Ngatik Islet is divided into five *kousapw*— Ewenedi, Pilendian, Liksarwei, Pwilinsokon, and Kepinamw— roughly equal in size, established under American administration as election units.[3] Section membership depends largely on current residence, but some people belong to sections in which they do not reside, because of either previous residence or personal preference. Each section (consisting of nine to fourteen households in 1979) elects a councilman to sit on the municipal council; in 1980 each also elected a representative to the island's school board. When islandwide projects are planned, tasks or contributions are often apportioned by section. The American term *neighborhood* is also a useful gloss, because people in a section often cooperate for public service projects, feasts, or religious services.[4] Land-tenure patterns—in which siblings share an inherited plot—tend to keep related families near one another, contributing to mutual assistance and informal interaction among neighbors.

Sapwuahfik's secular government consists of a municipal council and a separately elected chief magistrate. With the new constitution, the chief magistrate was renamed *Luhkenkolwof*, said to be an aboriginal Sapwuahfik designation. Election to these offices is by annual nomination and voting of all adults. The frequent council meetings are open to the public. Issues (usually budgetary matters such as taxes, wage work, and licenses) are discussed at large for days or weeks, then reviewed at meetings, where a decision is made. This is not necessarily the end of the matter, because people feel free to continue public discussion if they are unhappy with the official outcome. Community work and feasts are planned at such meetings, and occasionally divisive issues are subject to public referendum.

Religious activities are another important part of life on Sapwuahfik. People spend many hours in church-inspired meetings, feasts, song practices, and work groups. There are two major Christian denominations on the atoll, with just over half the people being Protestants and most of the rest Roman Catholic. In addition, by early 1990, a congregation of Seventh-Day Adventists had grown to several dozen. Teaching by Bahá'ís, Mormons, and other groups on Pohnpei suggest that these religions may also be represented on the atoll in the future. Although some small islands have tried to restrict missionary efforts by new denominations, Sapwuahfik people state that individuals should be free to change their religious affiliation.

Sapwuahfik Atoll is today a municipality in the State of Pohnpei, which along with the states of Chuuk, Kosrae, and Yap comprises the Federated States of Micronesia. Sapwuahfik's relationship with Pohnpei, traditionally multifaceted, faces new challenges because of the overlay of an American political framework. In the nineteenth century the number of Pohnpei's polities was frozen at five, the then-existing chiefdoms (*wehi*, also the term used for modern political units) of Net, Uh, Kiti, Madolenihmw, and Sokehs.[5] Established as administrative units by successive colonial regimes, today each *wehi* is represented in the legislature of the State of Pohnpei (Sapwuahfik elects one representative to that body). The city of Kolonia (1985 population 6,169 [Gorenflo and Levin 1992:12]), and each outer island atoll (Mwoakilloa [Mokil], Pingelap, Kapingamarangi, Nukuoro, and Sapwuahfik), comprise the other municipalities of Pohnpei State. By law, the outer island atolls are part of the State of Pohnpei in the same sense as the five *wehi* of Pohnpei Island and the city of Kolonia. In fact, however, the island of Pohnpei is a relative monolith in the politics of the state. The outer islands are not politically united and so have little voting power in the state legislature (see Damas 1985 for a view from Pingelap of outer island–Pohnpei political relations). Outer islanders rely on Pohnpei for economic and social services. A sizable population of Sapwuahfik descent lives permanently on Pohnpei, and most Sapwuahfik people travel there for business, school, health care,

or pleasure. Sapwuahfik is connected to Pohnpei not only historically—through immigrants from Pohnpei who resettled the
atoll after the massacre, and Sapwuahfik people who emigrated
to Sokehs in the early twentieth century—but also economically, politically, and culturally.

History and Identity

This book applies culturally oriented approaches to history and
identity to the study of Sapwuahfik. After the massacre, immigrants and survivors formed fragile new unions that became the
basis for the creation of a new society—an instance of the "invention of culture" (Wagner 1981) in its more literal sense. Over
the next decades, additional immigrants arrived from Pohnpei,
the Gilbert Islands (now Kiribati), the Mortlock Islands, Europe,
and the United States. When I conducted research a century and
a half after the massacre, I found the descendants of these survivors and immigrants knowledgeable about their island's history and assertive of their culture's contemporary strength. From
the chaos following the massacre, a distinctive and coherent
Sapwuahfik identity emerged. The book begins, then, in horror,
with the destruction of aboriginal Sapwuahfik culture, but ends
in an affirmation of a vital island community, aware of its past
and optimistic about its future.

The story of Sapwuahfik is compelling in itself. But this is
also a tale about history as a cultural product, how perceptions
of the past play a role in the social life of the present, and about
the relationship between local visions of the past and my ethnographic "vision" of modern life.

It is not new for anthropologists or historians to say that a
group's representation of its history may explain or justify modern practice, that the past is a "charter" for the present. What remains fascinating is how historical ideas prove so effective in
this ideological role. What makes history particularly potent in
shaping social action? The Sapwuahfik example permits us to
see how overlapping symbols, and the parallel structuring of

FIG 5. *Aerial view of Kolonia, Pohnpei. (Photograph by J. Stephen Athens.)*

these symbols in larger cultural domains, makes for the rhetorical, persuasive connection between history and contemporary social life.

Sapwuahfik and Pohnpei people are intensely interested in history. Ancient history—what scholars usually call legend or myth—is especially important to them, and someone well-versed in this sort of history hoards the treasure of such knowledge. Indeed, it is said that giving away what one knows is like giving away years of one's life. For that reason an outsider finds it difficult to collect information about the mythical past. Yet Islanders find even the more recent past fascinating. Sapwuahfik people attend to oral traditions, often comparing stories, evaluating their accuracy, and ensuring their transmission. Fortunately for my work, stories of the massacre and its aftermath are not classed as "secret-sacred" history (Falgout 1984a:51). Thus I ben-

FIG 6. *Canoes ferry people and goods to and from the interisland supply ship, which links Kapingamarangi, Nukuoro, and Sapwuahfik with Pohnpei. Ngatik Islet in background.*

efitted from the strong concern with the past, but I could ask about these stories freely.

In addition to their interest in particular accounts of the past, *mehn Sapwuahfik* hold a theory of history in the broad sense. The span of time they consider stretches from the mythical origins of clans (the era when spirits were dominant on earth) and biblical history to aboriginal Sapwuahfik and thence to the present. It extends to the future, most concretely in terms of problems of national independence and Sapwuahfik's role in regional politics. Although we know little as yet about unwritten philosophies of history, it is apparent that such a conceptual scheme is common. To some peoples, history is cyclic; to others, linear and progressive. Gellner (1964) differentiates evolutionary and episodic views of history (for a Melanesian example, see Mc-Dowell 1985). *Mehn Sapwuahfik*, I believe, see it in evolutionary terms, as a "tale of progress," a movement from premassacre "darkness" to the "light" of the present.

Viewing the Sapwuahfik vision of history as a story of "progress" is potentially problematic, because, as Robert Nisbet (1969) has effectively argued, the idea of progress as evolution is so basic to the Western notion of history as to be nearly inseparable from it, or, therefore, from the Western observer's conception of it. The apparent problem here is only apparent: the Sapwuahfik view of history is at most derived from, and at least strongly influenced by, Western historiography, and in particular certain evangelical Christian ideas of history.[6] Conversion to Christianity, formalized with the establishment of a church in 1890, changed Sapwuahfik ideas as well as life-style.

The study of local theories of history, including the infusion of elements of Western historiography, is relevant not only to local historical discourse but also to wider questions of culture—because notions of history may, as they do in the Sapwuahfik case, play an active role in shaping contemporary life. The massacre and Christian conversion are the key events of Sapwuahfik history. Memorializations of both are important today in constructing and maintaining a distinctive Sapwuahfik identity. References to massacre-era events and persons are a touchstone for understanding modern life: they explain facts of language, custom, kinship, personal appearance, land tenure, and material culture. Indeed, *mehn Sapwuahfik* are surrounded by tangible evidences of their history. Peoples' names and appearance recall their diverse ancestors; names of spirits inhabiting their islets recall the aborigines who named them; the distinctive *fedlatch-es* (angular pieces of wood at either end of the hull) on Sapwuahfik canoes echo the merging of indigenous and European seafaring traditions; and the men speak an English pidgin derived from nineteenth-century sailors' speech. This is the *habitus* (collective social practices, both material and cognitive; "custom") to which Bourdieu (1977) points us in understanding how implicit cultural propositions are reproduced from generation to generation.

Two points underlie my discussion of the relationship between the local perception of history and modern identity. First, a group's identity is not automatic, primordial, or "in the blood"; rather, it is constructed in a particular social context (in this case, in the regional sociopolitics of the Eastern Caroline Islands). Also, the specifics of identity—what people claim makes them unique—comes from the particular content of the local culture. Each culture has multiple potential symbolic elements out of which to construct a distinctive identity. Which are elaborated depends on both internal and external processes. For Sapwuahfik, these are preeminently the role of historical representations and the situation of *mehn Sapwuahfik* in modern regional and global politics.

Anthropologists and sociologists have studied group identity from the beginning of these scholarly disciplines. Webster's Third New International Dictionary defines ethnology as "a science that deals with the division of mankind into races, with their origin, distribution, and relations, and with the peculiarities that characterize them." Cultural anthropologists lost interest in "the division of mankind into races" several decades ago, but we retain our concern with what makes human groups alike and different. Instead of searching for some primordial essence that unites people as "races," we now analyze group identity in terms of social process and symbolic expression.

The current challenge in studying social groups is to understand how cultural ideas about identity and the social and material context of group life mutually shape the behavioral choices of individuals and communal social action. Each group affirms its distinctiveness in the context of neighboring populations. Although political and economic conditions organize these populations as bounded units, the cultural construction of sameness and difference provides the conceptual basis for group identity.

Both the expressive symbols of identity and the social structuring of group relations are essential to an analysis of distinctive communities.

"Ethnicity" as Theory and Practice

Like concepts of religion and kinship, ethnicity as a topic in social science has undergone critical scrutiny as social scientists try to separate its scientific meaning from ideas bequeathed by European culture. Ethnicity as a theoretical construct originated in the industrialized, pluralistic nation-states of Europe and North America, and nations derived from these. The vocabulary and theories of ethnicity were and are useful and appropriate in analyzing these societies. The sorts of explanations that were developed—how boundaries are maintained through social interaction, how ethnic identity is manipulated to maximize access to resources, how national character is reproduced in each generation—fit the cultural formulations of the groups under study. When the concepts of ethnicity are applied uncritically to other world areas, though, we risk obscuring social processes we are trying to illuminate. Group identity in other cultures may not resemble the ethnic activity that Western social scientists recognize in their own (Linnekin and Poyer 1990a).[7]

An indication of serious problems with the use of ethnicity in scholarly discourse is that social scientists writing about it employ a wide variety of definitions. All too often the term is left undefined, the writer assuming that the audience shares an unproblematic notion of what an ethnic group is. Or the effort to make a precise definition is abandoned in the face of the diversity of the phenomena being studied. The range of groups called *ethnic* indicates that the term can refer to shared biological ancestry, putative genealogical descent, historical ties to a symbolic homeland, shared language, religion, or appearance, minority status in a nation-state, or simply a recognition of sameness, a "primordial"—that is, inexplicable—sentiment.

The reason ethnicity makes social scientists turn cartwheels trying to define it is that it is not an analytical concept. It is, instead, a "folk" category—an idea used by a cultural group to explain something they perceive as important. European-derived cultures strongly embrace biological metaphors of "blood" and "race" to talk about what makes people alike and different. In the European and American nation-states, political and social activity has long been organized partly along lines of shared sentiment: groups organize themselves or are categorized by the wider society in terms of dominant ideas about "shared blood," "nationhood," and "race" (see, e.g., Anderson 1983; Isaacs 1975; Smith 1986). When Franz Boas emphasized that race, culture, and language are not necessarily covariant, he was countering the dominant local folk theory of how human beings were organized. That folk theory is still very much with us. In fact, with the expansion of European political, economic, and ideological dominance through colonialism, many non-Western peoples have used an ideological framework of ethnicity as an organizing principle for political action.

Ethnic group formation is an effective political strategy in part because the ideology of ethnicity is so widely understood in the late twentieth century. A glance through any American newsmagazine will demonstrate how the most disparate social conflicts, from Inuit whaling concerns to Sri Lanka's internal differences, are acceptably described as "ethnic" conflicts in a political arena. That is, disputes between groups within a nation-state are represented as conflicts between peoples who share ancestry and primordial sentiments of sameness.[8]

The fact that many groups find organizing under the rubric of ethnicity an effective political strategy should not, however, lead us to assume that all cultures share the Western concept of ethnicity. To the contrary, a growing number of case studies demonstrate that a community's self-identity can be based on quite different theories of human nature, social affiliation, and population differences.[9] What is seen as making "us" like each other and "them" different from "us" is an empirical question. To understand a sense of community, or group identity—or, the term I prefer, *cultural identity*—we must begin by asking about local folk theories of human life and human society. Out of these cultural presuppositions about the nature of humankind—and in the context of specific political, economic, and social situations—sentiments of sameness are created and, it may be, manifested in political action.

Cultural Constructions of Identity in the Pacific

Pacific Island communities are often described as relatively isolated, linguistically and culturally homogeneous populations. This has led some to pose them as unproblematic "ethnic groups," but reality refutes this. For one thing, Pacific Island societies vary a great deal in how homogenous, isolated, or bounded they are—and were, long before European contact. Islands with sizable populations, considerable political complexity, or both, such as Tahiti, Hawaii, New Zealand, and Yap—not to mention New Guinea—comprise polities and communities marked by linguistic and behavioral differences. Gender organization, social stratification, and religious and occupational specialization created differentiation in aboriginal polities. Communication and travel, including interisland voyaging and sea drifts, related populations through trade, tribute, conflict, exchange, and the diffusion of technology and ideas. There is no evidence that differences within and among Pacific populations constituted ethnicity in the sense in which it is usually used. Group identity was not superordinate, generated by intense boundary activity in a wider political context, or based on an ideology of shared blood or primordial sentiment (see Linnekin and Poyer 1990a and Howard 1990 for comparative discussions of Pacific identity).

But the changes that occurred in the Pacific as a result of European control have produced conditions in which ideas from ethnicity theory become useful in certain cases. In urbanizing colonial and postcolonial settings we see groups with different cultural characteristics obliged to interact and group affiliation frozen by the practices of colonial governments. Imposition of a

Western style of nonconsensual, adversarial politics, with its by-definition-limited scarce resources (political rewards) has also had an effect. Like populations elsewhere in the world, Pacific Islanders find that organizing as an ethnic group is one way to operate successfully in colonial and postcolonial sociopolitical systems (Chowning 1986; Keesing 1989; see Keesing and Tonkinson 1982 on *kastom* in Melanesia). In urban areas, and where Islanders and Islander social organization have been largely replaced by foreign populations and government, we now see an ideology of ethnicity as a superordinate category of identity that is in fact very much like that in Western society. Social scientists feel at home describing Maori nationalism, Hawaiian activism, and the Fiji coups in the same terms in which they discuss Northern Ireland and minority problems in the United States. The theory familiar from studies of European nation-states fits many situations in the modern Pacific quite well—but this is not because of the universal explanatory power of ethnicity theory. Rather, it is because the theory is being applied to cases that mimic, due to history, conditions in which the theory was originally generated.

European, American, and, especially in Micronesia, Japanese notions of race, blood, and innate characteristics are widely familiar and increasingly important throughout the Pacific. These ideas also exist in concrete form as political and social structures. Colonial and postcolonial governments have frozen group boundaries and used ethnic categories to define citizenship, political and economic rights, and minority status. Yet even where colonialism has dramatically transformed indigenous life and even where indigenous epistemology included ideas of shared and heritable substance, Islander concepts of identity differ from Western notions. Ethnographers of the Pacific have repeatedly described the permeable membership of island societies (e.g., Howard and Howard 1977; Marshall 1975; Nason 1975; Watson 1990). Islanders acknowledge physical differences among populations and recognize the claims of genealogical descent, but they tend to evaluate putative members of a community in terms of "how they act" rather than "who they are" in a biological sense.

27

Even in Hawaii, where culture has been profoundly affected by Euro-American categories and concepts, modern judgments of who is Hawaiian depend on genealogical evidence for access to government services but on evaluations of behavior when it comes to life in a local community (Linnekin 1985, 1990). On Pohnpei, descent, geography, and history are all sources of personal characteristics (Falgout 1984a:122–124). On Sapwuahfik, tracing a link to autochthonous or immigrant atoll ancestors is an important factor, but not a determining one, in community membership. It is behavior as a Sapwuahfik person that is the crucial criterion of identity.

As Pohnpeians, aboriginal Sapwuahfik people, and Americans and Europeans made up the postmassacre biological population of Ngatik, so these groups identify the context of modern identity. *Mehn Sapwuahfik* themselves, their Pohnpei neighbors, and the postcolonial economic and political situation (still powerfully influenced by the United States) constitute the field in which Sapwuahfik identity is played out. In merging with and separating themselves from Pohnpei, *mehn Sapwuahfik* use their historical affiliations to make either point: at some times and in some ways, they say they are "the same as" *mehn Pohnpei*. In other circumstances they assert, "We don't like their customs," and claim a distinct identity. Similarly, they conceptually ally themselves with certain American notions, according to the play of the range of aspects of Sapwuahfik identity on which they desire to call.

Self-conscious community definition is a permanent and ongoing process, and cultural units emerge, unite, maintain or dissolve themselves in local and regional matrices. The expressive mechanisms of Sapwuahfik self-definition possess meaning, and have power, only in the context of the regional interplay of local identities. These identities will become more rigid as Islanders are drawn firmly into the sociopolitical organization of the Federated States of Micronesia. As Sapwuahfik and other Eastern Caroline Islanders increase their involvement in the wider political and economic order, local cultural identity will take on structural characteristics of ethnic groups in nation-states (see

Linnekin 1990). The decade between my original work and my most recent visit saw Pohnpei's Sapwuahfik community becoming more active as a political group, forming associations, planning activities, setting goals, and managing politics in the city and state systems. The "ethnicization" of *mehn Sapwuahfik* is continuing—perhaps accelerating—under the impact of a postcolonial system that rewards competitive group strategies.

Because the name of this atoll is itself an index of destruction and domination, resurrection and cultural revival, I have used it self-consciously throughout the text. To reflect changes in the atoll's status with a minimum of anachronism, I retain the name *Ngatik* for the entire atoll in the context of the time between the massacre and 1985 (Ngatik Islet identifies the main islet only). *Sapwuahfik*, then, refers to the premassacre era and population of the atoll, and to the modern community. Readers should be aware of one consistent anachronism: I gathered most of my information in 1979 and 1980, when people spoke of themselves and of their aboriginal ancestors as *mehn Ngatik* (and indeed, the word *Sapwuahfik* was generally unknown). Though I use *mehn Sapwuahfik* in the text, I have not altered the usage of speakers in quotations from 1979–80. This seemed to me the only way to balance respect for the words in which they shared their knowledge with respect for their recent decision to adopt the identity of *mehn Sapwuahfik*.

CHAPTER ONE

Preludes and Contexts

NDERSTANDING THE MEANING of the massacre begins with knowing something about times before 1837, and about the circumstances that shaped the two groups that encountered each other on the shore at Ngatik Islet. The most challenging problem is to know what Sapwuahfik was like before the massacre. Of course, Hart and his crew also existed in a "premassacre" context, that of nineteenth-century European culture and society, in the particular form of the men who lived in and traveled through the Pacific Islands. So there are two preludes to the story: What were the circumstances of Hart's decision to attack? and what were the conditions of the people who met his attack?

When we seek to set Hart in his cultural context, we turn to the many sources familiar to historians of the Pacific: journals, letters, ships' logs, official inquiries (such as Blake's), and numerous other written accounts. Although some of these are derived from oral history, personal recollections, or rumors, our knowledge of the background to Hart's activities is essentially based on documents written by Europeans. Aside from the familiar problems of interpreting documentary sources, drawing Hart's context is a fairly straightforward task.

When we turn to shedding light on aboriginal Sapwuahfik, however, we confront two perspectives on the past. One is documented history: what literate visitors recorded about that atoll, and what anthropologists can deduce in general about aboriginal Micronesian atolls (properly ethnology, not history; but here, a part of historical reconstruction). The other is modern Sapwuahfik people's ideas about their aboriginal ancestors. Both perspectives are cultural products; neither is absolute truth. Nothing short of a time machine can take us back to the reality that was premassacre Sapwuahfik, but by carefully negotiating the trails of documentary and oral accounts of the past, we learn two sorts of things. First, we can try to reconstruct the threads of past social organization, material life, and cultural belief that form part of the fabric of modern Sapwuahfik life. Second, we can learn from their own words how Sapwuahfik people today think about their aboriginal ancestors, and how they feel about the events surrounding the massacre and its aftermath.

Europe in the Nineteenth-century Pacific

By the time Hart was engaged in the Pacific Islands trade, the early phase of European exploration had passed. Cook had established the nonexistence of Terra Australis and the existence of the more modest, but substantial, continent of Australia. Cook and other explorers, navigators, merchants, and whalers had given hundreds of islands European-language names and approximate locations on the map of the Pacific, which was becoming crowded with trading stations, rest-and-recreation stops for whalers, and strategic naval outposts.[1]

The major Caroline Islands were recorded on European charts by the late eighteenth century. But there are many tiny islands in Micronesia, European navigation and map making were still tentative, and communication among those who traveled the seaways was poorly developed. Sapwuahfik, like many islands, is mentioned occasionally in logbooks, published records, or government documents, located somewhat differently each time, appearing under many different names. Asking to know which European—or even which imperial power—was first to sight it is asking for unattainable certainty. Don Felipe Tompson is recorded as sighting the atoll in 1773, but some sources credit the famous navigator Quiros with a 1595 sighting. Even earlier is Alvaro de Saavedra, who noted an island in Sapwuahfik's general area during each of two attempts to cross the Pacific from the Moluccas, in 1528 and 1529. This might have been any of Pohnpei's outliers, though—sixteenth-century European navigators had a good fix on longitude but no way to determine accurate latitudes.

At any rate, Tompson was the first to misname the atoll. He thought it was the set of islands seen by Quiros, so he (re)named them Los Valientes. After that, Sapwuahfik picked up a string of designations: Islas de la Pasion, Valientes Islands, Raven Islands, Ravene (after Captain William Raven), Seven Islands, and every possible spelling of Ngatik: Ngarik, Ngaraik, Ngaruik, Ngaryk, Nateck, Nuteck, Nuttic. These all seem to be variants of *Ngafik*, which Sapwuahfik people today give as the aboriginal name for the largest, inhabited islet of the atoll.

Unfortunately, European visitors left little more information than this list of names. Half a dozen ships sighted the atoll but had no reason to visit it. It was not on any well-traveled European route. In the late eighteenth and early nineteenth centuries, passersby included Tompson's Spanish ship en route from New Guinea, Raven on a British storeship traveling from England to Sydney, American and European traders on their way to China, and a Salem trader on a bêche-de-mer cruise. Captain Benjamin Page, sighting what may have been Ngatik in 1798, left a typically minimalist description of a "small sand island."[2]

After Tompson, the next closeup view of the atoll is provided by the Russian captain Fedor Lütke, on a scientific expedition around the world with the sloop *Senyavin* and a supply ship. He cruised along Ngatik's shore in January of 1828 but could not anchor because of bad weather. The Russians saw some thirty Islanders on one islet and no evidence of habitation on the others. They noted an abundance of coconut palms on some islets, and breadfruit trees, but (oddly enough) saw no canoes and no anchorage. The bad weather prevented Lütke from sending a boat ashore, so the Russians tried to communicate by shouting and throwing knives and other objects to the Islanders (Lütke 1971 [1835]; von Kittlitz 1858).

Was Hart the first European actually to land on Ngatik? Almost certainly not, but historical documents are so fragmentary that it is hard to be sure who might have preceded him. The trading bark *Pallas* visited some part of the atoll in 1835; the men collecting bêche-de-mer on a beach were visited by two canoes with six Islanders. There was at least one other, more violent, encounter: men who accompanied Hart to Ngatik later reported that they found decayed pieces of a European boat and musket butts on Ngatik's beach during the *Lambton*'s first (1836) visit. Aboriginal women said four or five white men had come to the island in the boat some time earlier and been killed. These were probably survivors of an attack on the *Waverly* at Kosrae. Blake had no way of determining whether the unfortunates had drifted ashore or arrived with hostile intent, but he supposed that "if the latter, it affords some explanation of the reception given to the Lambton people on their first arrival" (Blake 1924 [1839]:666–67).[3]

Another bit of hearsay: When the *Clarinda* stopped at Ngatik in 1841, Captain Godby heard from John MacVie, a white man who lived there after the massacre, that MacVie had discovered the grave of fourteen murdered men (Godby 1845). Godby did not go ashore to investigate this rumor. (Of course, the men might have been Islanders murdered by Hart's crew; that soil saw many deaths between 1837 and 1841. Still, it could as well have been foreigners who arrived on Ngatik before Hart.) Whatever the Sapwuahfik people's earlier experiences with Europeans or other visitors, critical as they may be for an understanding of their feelings as they watched the *Lambton*'s boats draw near, it is beyond our ability to recover them.

Hart and his crew were opportunistic traders who circulated through Southeast Asia, Australia, and Micronesia, very much a part of the political and economic entrepreneurship that characterized Europeans in the Pacific at this time (Ralston 1978). They returned time and again to Pohnpei, which from the 1840s was a trading center and whaling stopover. Pohnpei's diverse beachfront population included a growing number of Europeans. Reports begin with an estimate of 25 on Pohnpei in 1835, rising to perhaps 150 in 1850; then the expatriate population dropped with the decline of whaling to about 14 in 1871 (Zelenietz and Kravits 1974). The tortoiseshell trade began in the area around 1833; this and the bêche-de-mer and copra businesses were soon overwhelmed by the influx of whalers. American and Portuguese deserters on Pohnpei in the 1830s to 1850s were mainly from New England whaling ships. Pohnpei also hosted Maoris and people from Rotuma, Tahiti, the Gilbert Islands, the East Indies, Palau, the Loyalty Islands, Hawaii, Mangareva, and Portuguese from the Azores and Cape Verde Islands. Historian David Hanlon describes Pohnpei beachcombers as common seamen, deserters from whalers, shipwrecked sailors, and a few "independent men" who left trading schooners for island life (Hanlon 1988:60–61). Blake thought many were Australian prison escapees, but Hanlon disagrees. Whatever a man's origin, he found Pohnpei in the first decades of the century to be a place where no questions were asked.[4]

As to Hart himself, his nickname might suffice: he was widely known as "Bloody" Hart. Perhaps the economy of the time pushed him to the very margins of what was permissible in order to make a profit on these penny-ante voyages.[5] He was certainly a man of ambition, willing to turn his hand to whatever opportunity offered, from tortoiseshell to the East Asia opium trade. (A missionary on Pohnpei credited him with setting up the first still there and teaching local people how to make liquor [Crawford and Crawford 1967:90 n.]). Hart cultivated people in

power, such as the Spanish official at Guam who credited him
with "the character of an honest man." His claim to own the
Lambton was not entirely clear, and perhaps not entirely legal,
but this remains unproved in the documents. Pacific historian
Francis Hezel (1983:120) describes him:

> The Sydney-born Hart had spent most of his life at sea at-
> tempting to build for himself, by fair means or foul, a wealthy
> trading empire that would enable him to lead the aristocratic
> life-style to which he had always aspired . . . [He] had for some
> years roamed the seas between Manila and Ponape, swindling
> whom he could and using more forceful means of getting what
> he wanted when necessary—and the latter seemed called for on
> Ngatik.

Premassacre Sapwuahfik

Historical documents, as we have seen, tell us very little about
aboriginal Sapwuahfik. If Europeans came ashore before Hart
and his crew, they left no records. What is apparent is that Sapwuahfik had virtually no engagement with Western culture before
1836; the very few contacts had been short and, it would appear,
mutually unsatisfactory. How, then, can we say what the place
and its people were like?

The following sketch of aboriginal Sapwuahfik relies on three
disparate sources. One is postmassacre documentary evidence,
from European visits to Ngatik after 1837, which provides useful
information if we assume that some of what is described might
be vestiges of aboriginal life. Also, we can make inferences from
Micronesian ethnology, assuming that Sapwuahfik lifeways resembled those of other central and eastern Micronesian atolls.
Because to date there has been no archaeological research on
Sapwuahfik, we cannot verify this assumption. The third source
is Sapwuahfik oral tradition.

Each source has obvious problems, as well as potential usefulness. I have relied on the first two most heavily for material

culture; oral tradition is my only source for aboriginal religious beliefs, ethos, and immediate premassacre events. Oral traditions are also the critical sources for understanding how Sapwuahfik people today interpret their aboriginal past.

When modern Sapwuahfik people talk about the ancient past, they do so in terms of history taught and learned orally, collected and analyzed by individuals interested in local tradition. In the absence of written documents and archaeological information, what we know about the specifics of the atoll's past depends on how that oral history has been preserved and managed by successive generations. Today people are keenly aware of the paucity of knowledge about aboriginal times. "The people of Ngatik have lost all that," one man told me regretfully. "Because foreigners used to come and carry away the people of Ngatik, come and massacre the *mehn Ngatik* of long ago. That is why, today, there is no longer anyone who truly knows the real history of Ngatik."

The scarcity of knowledge is due in part to the way it is transmitted in small-scale societies in which it has social and political value (see Borofsky 1987), but it is also the result of the break caused by the massacre. Some information was passed across that cultural chasm; much, inevitably, was lost. (It is not as simple as saying, What women knew was passed on, what men knew was lost. What was preserved depended on the personal knowledge of the women who both survived and stayed on the atoll, on their willingness to transmit it, and on the eagerness of younger people to learn it.) Contributions from Pohnpei, the Gilbert Islands, and Western sources began to enter the local corpus of knowledge immediately after the massacre, giving oral tradition additional resources but creating problems for both indigenous and outsider reconstructions of the aboriginal past.

What survives is impressive, sometimes amazing. For example, one account of the Kosrae hero-warrior Isokelekel's stop at Sapwuahfik on his way to conquer Pohnpei includes even the names of the two Sapwuahfik men who joined his expedition (one was from Ngatik Islet, one lived on Pikenkeleng). One of the men shot his sling at a canoe in the fleet, breaking an outrigger strut. Begging forgiveness and fixing the canoe, he asked to accompany the voyage. I marveled when I heard that tale, and my imagination pictured the massacre survivors, as elderly women, choosing among the fragments of their shattered culture those elements they felt were most important, those they wanted to see preserved. Was it like that? Did they have a poignant recognition of the entity we call culture, and of its fragility? Certainly the power of Micronesian commitment to oral history is made evident by the amount of material I was able to collect.[6]

One thing we can know about aboriginal Sapwuahfik with some certainty is the physical setting. Hart's plan of attack in 1837 and oral tradition indicate that then as now, people lived for the most part on the largest islet, keeping gardens also on one or several other islets, including Wad, the second largest. Local people say that the islets had a different appearance in ancient times. The abundance of coconut palms on Ngatik Islet is recent—its beaches were covered instead with scrub, as the smaller islets are today. Although in 1828 Lütke saw many coconut palms on some islets, intentional heavy planting of coconut began only after the European copra trade became established. The taro gardens, people insist, are in part natural and have existed since "the beginning," in contrast to those on neighboring atolls, which have been manually excavated. There were no paths in earlier times; people walked around the islet on the beach. There is general agreement that people used to live more on the oceanside than on the lagoonside of Ngatik Islet (the opposite is true today), but archaeology will have to establish whether this tradition refers to aboriginal or more recent times. The ancient people named areas of reef, land, and taro plots. Though some place-names used today are meaningful in the Pohnpei language (and so are probably recent), others seem to be remnants of the ancient language.

It is impossible to estimate the aboriginal population accurately. Testimonies Blake collected contain estimates of from 40 to 84 men killed in 1837—excepting those who escaped, this was the total adult male population of the island. As a very rough estimate, we can add equal numbers of men, women, and children to arrive at a total of 120 to 250. Atoll people today speak of ancient Sapwuahfik as having been heavily populated, and I think it might, at times, have had a much higher population than 250. One clue to this is the extensive taro gardens, many of which have not yet been returned to production. Another is simply the size of the atoll: given two sizable islets (Ngatik, .406 square miles; Wad, .144 square miles), a lagoon of 30.34 square miles, and plentiful fresh water, population would not be narrowly constrained by nature (although, as on all these atolls, people face occasional droughts). If so, why is the 1837 estimate so low? For one thing, Blake got his information from men who were being called to justice for their murders; they were likely to lean toward underestimation. For another, we do not know how many escaped the massacre by sailing away between attacks. Also, atoll populations fluctuated greatly because of destruction by storms (on nearby Mokil a typhoon near the end of the eighteenth century reduced the population to twenty-five to thirty survivors [Weckler 1949]). Finally, aboriginal populations throughout the Pacific suffered from introduced diseases; these might have reached Sapwuahfik despite the few direct contacts with Europeans.

Whatever the size of the population, it was distinct from that of nearby Pohnpei. Remnants of the ancient language indicate a phonology and vocabulary quite different at least from modern Pohnpeian, and no traditions link the two islands, close though they are, to a common origin. My primary consultant on traditional history insisted that "it was *mehn Ngatik* themselves who produced *mehn Ngatik*." Commander Blake, speaking of the Carolines in 1839, stated that "every Island also has its own language." He would have mentioned it, in his detailed report, had Ngatik and Pohnpei shared one. Blake also writes, "Nothing could be more striking than the difference of features and the exterior appearance of the Ascension [Pohnpei] and Nuttic Natives," but, alas, does not elaborate. Sapwuahfik people say their atoll was never under the political control of others, including the sometimes powerful rulers of Pohnpei. (Although there is a tradition that Sapwuahfik is one of the "gates" to Pohnpei.) So

Sapwuahfik was an independent polity, its people apparently distinctive in appearance and language.

It is important to point out that although the atoll had little
European contact, it was not in any real sense isolated. On the
day of the massacre, for example, there were at least two foreigners on Sapwuahfik: a man and a woman from the Marshall Islands. One presumes that they drifted there by canoe, and there
is evidence of considerable drift travel in this area (Riesenberg
1965). Some drifts ended in death, of course, at the hands of the
elements or an unwelcoming landing place, but sea drifts did
move ideas and people between islands.

More significant interaction came from deliberate voyaging.
Mehn Sapwuahfik speak of the aboriginal people as accomplished ocean travelers. Like other Micronesians, they navigated
by stars, currents, and prevailing winds. Judging by information
from the region, it is likely that people regularly sailed between
Sapwuahfik and the central Carolines, and to Pohnpei. Oral traditions recount several major planned voyages touching at Sapwuahfik. One describes the arrival at Sapwuahfik of a large fleet of
canoes from Yap on its way to attack Pohnpei. The Yapese were
brought into the lagoon by the spirits of the channel, where
Sapwuahfik people tricked them into surrendering and the fleet
was destroyed by magic. A tale already mentioned describes
Isokelekel's visit to Sapwuahfik on his famous journey from
Kosrae to attack Pohnpei. He sailed with a huge fleet of canoes,
and various Micronesian legends mention his visits to islands
along the way. (For traditional Pohnpei history on this topic, see
Bernart 1977; Fischer, Riesenberg, and Whiting 1977; Hanlon
1988:18–21.) Also, Marshall Islanders tell of the voyage by a
group of Tarawa people to Sapwuahfik and a battle waged
against it (Krämer and Nevermann 1938), and recount an attack
on Sapwuahfik led by a chief of Ebon (Erdland 1914, vol. 2 (1):
207; see also Riesenberg 1965). (In both cases, the sources use
the name Ngatik.) Again, archaeological research will help establish the extent and material impact of such interisland voyaging.

Common resources and the widespread nature of Micronesian atoll subsistence patterns suggest that the aboriginal material culture of Sapwuahfik closely resembled that of the Mortlocks, Mokil, and Pingelap. We would expect, and oral traditions confirm, the common precontact crops of the area: breadfruit, coconut, taro, banana, and pandanus; and perhaps also arrowroot, yams, and turmeric. The little meat in the aboriginal atoll diet was available from bats, rats, and birds. Fish, turtle, and shellfish have always been plentiful in the lagoon; people used hook and line, spears, clubs, basket traps, and nets to harvest them, and an old story mentions a coral fish weir. Food then, as now, had important ceremonial value, being given in tribute to leaders and exchanged in festive, ritual, or ceremonial contexts.

We would expect a division of labor similar to that on other Micronesian islands of the Eastern Carolines, with men responsible for agricultural work, fishing, carpentry, warfare, toolmaking, some cooking, magic, and ceremonial skills; and women responsible for textile work (baskets, mats, sails, clothing), roofing thatch, reef fishing, child care, midwifery, and some cooking. Occupational specialization was common in the region for canoe building, house building (especially for men's houses), fishing, tattooing, medicine, and divination.

Anneliese Eilers, writing for the German Südsee-Expedition, which visited the atoll in 1910, said that in precontact times men wore grass skirts, and women, grass skirts braided with coconut leaves. The skirts were made of hibiscus bast, banana fiber, and coconut leaves. Flower and feather wreaths were worn as headdresses, and pendants and large rings of conus shell and spondylus discs were popular. Tattooing, though not specifically reported for Sapwuahfik, was common in the Eastern Caroline Islands. It is reasonable to expect that some of the tools found by the Südsee-Expedition were of the type used on the atoll aboriginally (perhaps this is more likely for women's tools). This tool kit closely resembles that of other low islands: woven mats and baskets, tridacna-shell adzes of wood tied with coir (coconut fiber cord), coral-stone pounders, shell scrapers, dishes, troughs and spoons of breadfruit wood, calaphyllum-wood pounders for taro and breadfruit, breadfruit pounding boards, and nets knitted of coir rope with wooden forks (Eilers 1934). Although to his surprise Lütke saw no canoes when he approached Ngatik, Tompson, earlier, had seen some in the lagoon. We have no description of these. Aboriginal weapons were spears and clubs, and perhaps slings, though tradition assigns the hard, rounded stones occasionally found today to the slings of later Gilbertese immigrants.

I could learn of no surviving origin myth for Sapwuahfik. When I asked about the creation of the island, one man answered revealingly, "No one made the islands. I don't know who made them." The legend with the earliest setting tells of a couple, Liesuh and Daukfauso, who alone survive a flood. Their descendants repopulate Sapwuahfik. The descendants of Daukfauso produced Luhkensapwsapw, the first nahnmwarki of Sapwuahfik (the aboriginal term is said to have been *Wilesoyar* or *Wilehsoh; nahnmwarki* is a Pohnpeian word) and the man who established its chiefly clan, one segment of the aboriginal clan named Dipwinmen toantoal. This then is the mythical starting point for aboriginal social organization.

Stories of Sapwuahfik's earliest times are well stocked with spirit, and spirit-human, figures (Liesoh and Daukfauso are spirit-humans). The regional culture-hero Olpad is part of Sapwuahfik's legendary history; he left his mark in the form of a path and a well on Ngatik Islet. There were spirits, *eni*, which inhabited many parts of the reef and islets. Each islet was "owned" by a ruler-spirit, and some special places of worship where spirits lived can still be identified. Many of the spirits left Sapwuahfik when Christianity arrived, but the most important ones remain. It is said that some of these spirits "work" on Ngatik, protecting it—spirits of the land, the reef, and the lagoon. Particularly important are the female spirits who guard the channel, who prevent unwanted ships from entering Sapwuahfik's lagoon by, in their anger, causing adverse winds and a strong current. The spirits of Sapwuahfik in general, except those bush-spirits that attack people, are said to "guard," "protect," "care for" Sapwuahfik today, as they have in the past.

Sea turtles, which play a role in the 1837 tragedy, figure importantly in Sapwuahfik traditions of aboriginal belief. An informant described a ceremony of the ancient past in which *mehn Sapwuahfik* would catch turtles, collecting them in a fence until they caught one identified as distinctive. Singing a particular song, the people carried this turtle from house to house, then cooked them all in special earth ovens. Other accounts indicate the importance of sea turtles here, as on Pohnpei (Hanlon 1988:14–15) and elsewhere in Micronesia: the aboriginal people are said to have prayed to turtles and (as Hart's men discovered) to have kept turtle shell and other marine products in their temples.

John Fischer (1957) suggests a simple, two-line aboriginal title system (with sacred and secular lines of titles) on Sapwuahfik, Mokil, and Pingelap. He thinks that after mission contact this original system was abandoned in favor of the Pohnpei structure on all three Eastern Caroline atolls (180). (Of course, on Sapwuahfik, "abandonment" would date to the massacre.) Fischer also writes that on these atolls, eligibility for titles was passed from father to son, and there was no regular promotion from rank to rank. This is an apparent contrast with Pohnpei's matrilineal inheritance and ideal of step-by-step promotion in titles (Riesenberg 1968). Sapwuahfik oral tradition confirms Fischer in some respects, but aboriginal rules of inheritance are difficult to determine with confidence. Like other central and eastern Micronesians, Sapwuahfik people belong to exogamous clans, which were of greater social and religious significance in the past than they are today. Two of the eleven modern clans on Sapwuahfik are aboriginal; these, like the clans that originated with immigrants from Pohnpei and the Gilbert Islands, trace descent matrilineally. However, whether clan membership, property, and sociopolitical titles were inherited matrilineally or patrilineally is open to question.[7] Modern inheritance patterns on Sapwuahfik tend toward patrilateral bias in inheritance of land and some other property, and patrilineal influence is visible even in traditional titles (ideally inherited matrilineally). Sapwuahfik patterns, however, have been affected not only by imported elements of Pohnpei social organization but also by the influence of

43

European settlers on Ngatik and German and Japanese colonial legal pressure to enforce patrilineal land inheritance.

Discussion of the extent and form of aboriginal status differentiation is equally problematic. Oral traditions indicate status differences—for example, that high-titled people were buried at a holy spot on Ngatik Islet, whereas commoners were buried at sea. Reconstructing social organization is very difficult, however, because of the profound influence of the importation of Pohnpei's title system.

If Sapwuahfik was organized as other central Micronesian atolls were, a paramount leader reigned over the entire atoll, which would have been divided into sections, with holders of lesser titles in charge of each. Tribute was paid along vertical lines, with the highest chief considered to be the true owner of the land.[8] The chief redistributed products obtained through tribute. Nahnmwarki accepted first fruit offerings; traditional dances were danced for them, for example, at breadfruit season, and they imposed taboos and settled disputes. Law and order depended on severe punishment by the leaders; oral traditions tell of vengeance warfare and killings.

Although little verifiable information exists about the political organization of aboriginal Sapwuahfik, oral traditions give a coherent notion of what nahnmwarki-ship entailed. The precontact ruler is presented in these traditions and legends as ultimate holder of all land rights, as omnipotent ruler with control over the labor, produce, and personal lives of his subjects, and as possessor of religious and spiritual, as well as political, power over the population. The fruitfulness of the land and the safety and happiness of the people depended on the rectitude, the proper actions, of the nahnmwarki. Traces of this attitude remain, as when people today discuss the varying productivity of taro gardens in the reigns of recent nahnmwarki. Stories of the ancient nahnmwarki also convey sentiment: the nahnmwarki are respected and magically awesome in their powers; at the same time they are presented as dictatorial, despotic, and quick to act forcefully or violently to protect their interests.

Stories of ancient nahnmwarki judge good leaders as those

who though owning the land and controlling food resources shared food among the people. Turtles and turtle eggs, flocking seabirds, schools of fat fish—these were special foods directly under the nahnmwarki's control. A good nahnmwarki directed people to gather these, or apportioned those that had been collected. Likewise, after people worked their assigned plots and produced taro, a good nahnmwarki shared it out at a feast. A "bad" nahnmwarki might tell people who caught these special foods simply to toss them away, or would keep the taro gathered for a feast of his own. Tales of ancient times dwell on not only the power but also the morality of nahnmwarki, and the most moral are those who redistribute. The ideals of a nahnmwarki being generous with food, and the sharing of food equally by high-titled folk and commoners, are both important in Sapwuahfik life today. The first is part of the wider Micronesian ideal of the leader; the second is a self-consciously Sapwuahfik ideal.

Events Preceding the Massacre

Although oral traditions include some information about events and characters of the atoll's history before European contact, we limit our focus here to the late eighteenth and early nineteenth centuries. Oral traditions about the period immediately before the massacre set the stage, in terms of narratives, for that event. The next-to-last aboriginal nahnmwarki of Sapwuahfik was named Isoah. His successor, who ruled at the time of the massacre, was Sirinpahn. Both are remembered as *suwed*, "evil," or *sakanakan*, "bad," nahnmwarki, but for different reasons.

Isoah's notoriety arises from his selfishness. When there was an abundance of food, "he didn't want people to join in eating it." That is, he abused the nahnmwarki's privilege of control over food resources by imposing restrictions. For example, when the community caught and cooked turtles, he permitted only high-title holders to eat them, and he forbade anyone else to catch terns to eat. Therefore, "the people of Ngatik hated his cruelty." The story of Isoah continues:

45

The people of Ngatik, tired of Isoah's selfishness and cruelty, decided to kill him. They decided this in a meeting held one night, agreeing together to kill the Nahnmwarki on the following day. The Nahnmwarki's son, Sirinpahn, learned of the plan. He went to his father and told him, "Papa, look, I will become nahnmwarki." His father agreed, for otherwise, he knew, they would kill him. Isoah announced: "Tomorrow, a feast will take place. Sirinpahn will become nahnmwarki." Isoah no longer came among the people, but stayed elsewhere.

Sirinpahn, when he became nahnmwarki, acquired a long-lasting evil reputation by announcing that "there is no longer any marriage" and instituting a licentious game called "night of mats" or "night of women." One informant told me that this practice was instituted by Sirinpahn to amuse and distract the people, so they would not kill his father, the former nahnmwarki. Another explained that Sirinpahn, as a handsome youth, had been set adrift as punishment by the previous nahnmwarki. When he was gone, the reigning nahnmwarki was visited by spirits who warned him to step down, or he would be killed by Sirinpahn. When Sirinpahn returned, he stepped onto the throne without difficulty, and declared that sexual jealousy was no longer permissible.[9] Those who tell the story of Sirinpahn agree that the people enjoyed this licentiousness; in any case, they did not try to depose him. One account describes the institutionalized promiscuity in this way:

All the women, married and single, would gather in the meetinghouse in Ewenedi. They made a palm-frond mat, and covered over the sides of the meetinghouse with it. They gathered firewood, and in the evening they would light a fire in the meetinghouse and make garlands. The men gathered outside the closed-up meetinghouse and danced traditional dances. Meanwhile, the men would be sneaking up close to the meetinghouse.

Then the women would douse the fire, and the men would race to get the woman each wanted. There were, it is said, no spouses, no siblings, no clans. A man who valued his wife might run to her, but he was not to be jealous if another man was faster. "But we [that is, the men] wouldn't be jealous, for if we were jealous over it, it would be reported to Sirinpahn that I was the one who was jealous, and . . . [I] would be killed. That's how it was."

The man took the woman to his house, or to some other place, to sleep, then returned her to her husband or family in the morning. Then, the man would deliver cooked food to the husband of the woman he had slept with. "I [that is, a man] would be happy about it, because I didn't have to make food since they brought mine; [I would] eat it and, when it was night, I would go back to the meetinghouse—that was what they did then."

Another version describes women, wrapped in mats to disguise their identity, appearing as if on stage to the accompaniment of songs and dancing. This account traces Sapwuahfik's doom to a jealous husband's interruption of the song, "breaking" it and fulfilling a fateful prophecy. In all accounts of this time, it is said that Sirinpahn did not permit jealousy and insisted on indiscriminate licentiousness.

Sirinpahn's reign was brief. And in the eyes of Sapwuahfik people today who reflect on history, it was the evils of Sirinpahn's era that brought on the massacre of 1837.

Contexts of Written and Oral History

Just as the two groups that met on the beach at Ngatik acted on the basis of their cultural background and the immediate circumstances, so we can distinguish the contexts in which both oral and documentary accounts of the massacre are produced.

The documentary sources were created in a cultural context with its own rules of evidence, style of ordering and recording information, and notions of what constituted significance. At the far end of the transmission, those who gave testimony to Commander Blake had their own motives for speech and silence, their personal circumstances and constraints (of nationality, age, gender, rank, status, and personality) that shaped what they revealed to him. Blake (and others who recorded hearsay or eye-witness information about the massacre) was another "lens" fil-tering what was destined for preservation. At the nigh end of the transmission, we read Blake's report to the Admiralty in light of our own values, our own understanding of the nineteenth-century Pacific, and our own intentions. We can speak of written history as "factual," then, only if we recognize the profound complexity that underlies the construction of historical fact.

Oral tradition has its own distinct context. Its most obvious characteristic is flexibility of transmission: the story differs each time it is told. Beyond questions of changes in the narrative, there is also the social context of oral history—what determines how it is shared and transmitted. Finally, we have again the "lens" of the reader of oral narratives, after they have been translated, codified, and fixed in writing.[10]

Suzanne Falgout (1984a:13) writes that "Ponapeans understand the world in which they live today as the product of the past," which is known through oral accounts. On Pohnpei and Sapwuahfik, people speak of three genres of narratives—those considered sacred, powerful, and true; those true but not sacred; and fictional tales. *Poadoapoad,* sacred narratives or history, are held as property by clans and individuals within clans, imbued with supernatural power and known to be true. It is dangerous for unqualified narrators to recount *poadoapoad,* or for the proper person to tell them too casually, too often, or too completely. *Soaipoad* is legend, stories based at least partly on fact, but not exclusively held or possessed of power. *Poadoapoad* and sometimes *soaipoad* play roles in disputes about title succession, land boundaries and rights, and relationships among political entities. *Soai* are fictional stories told for amusement or to teach a lesson; *soai* is also used to refer to secular tales of recent (that is, not ancient) events (see Mitchell 1968, 1970 on Micronesian narrative; also Hanlon 1988:xvii).

On Sapwuahfik, certain spirit tales and surviving clan origin myths are considered *poadoapoad.* Otherwise, Sapwuahfik people retain few sacred narratives of aboriginal history. The older people who know these are highly respected for their familiarity with these potentially powerful matters. Sapwuahfik *poadoa-poad* are surrounded with some of the secrecy, awareness of power, and actual physical danger to the possessor and reciter that surrounds *poadoapoad* on Pohnpei. In Pohnpei epistemology, knowledge is power (*manaman*) in a concrete sense; revealing it casually or too completely can deplete the lifeforce of the teller (Falgout 1984a:135). Management of knowledge is a significant cultural theme, and historical knowledge is highly valued (Falgout 1984a, 1984b, 1985; Hanlon 1988; Petersen 1982a).

To non-Islanders, the most famous Micronesian historian is Luelen Bernart, a Pohnpei man whose written account of that island's past has been published with scholarly commentary (Bernart 1977; Fischer, Riesenberg, and Whiting 1977; Hanlon 1992). Bernart absorbs recent postcontact events into a history of the island from its mythical beginnings. His writing suggests that indigenous historians do not segregate recent history from ancient legend when they represent the past. On Sapwuahfik, similarly, I found that those most versed in traditional *poadoapoad* were also most familiar with details of the massacre and postmassacre periods. Yet accounts of more recent times are not sacred, and their retelling entails relatively little power or danger; they are not *poadoapoad* in the usual sense. Unlike many *soia* intended as didactic fiction, they are not bracketed with formulaic opening and closing phrases, and they are regarded as true. Sapwuahfik people usually refer to conversations about the early contact period as *koasoai en mahs*, "talk," "discussion," or "stories" about "long ago." It was relatively easy for me to collect historical accounts, because they are valued enough to be considered worth preserving but are not considered powerful knowledge in the Pohnpei sense. Massacre-era accounts are also somewhat insulated from the intentional editing of historical narratives that reveals and preserves the power of knowledgeable individuals (Falgout 1985).

I spoke about the massacre with almost every older person I interviewed, and taped eleven narrative accounts of it in the Sapwuahfik language (nine by adult men, one by an adolescent boy, one by an adult woman) during 1979 and 1980.[11] There is considerable variation in the amount of detail available to and given out by tellers of the oral tradition. One man can name the man in the ship's boat who fired the first shot, whereas others are able only to say that the massacre occurred and that Sapwuahfik men were killed. Of the eleven accounts, only four are relatively detailed, and I have relied on these in constructing the oral history of the massacre in the next chapter.

Oral traditions about the massacre are in complete harmony with the Western documents, as far as a simple recital of events goes. They also verify and are verified by the Western version. The most striking example of this is the oral tradition of the Sapwuahfik men hiding in leaf-covered holes in preparation for a surprise ambush, a detail given by only one narrator. Blake's report mentions that "pits were discovered on the beach four or five feet deep, and covered over with the wild 'Tara' leaf, which is immensely large." (Sapwuahfik people have had access to published or verbal versions of the Western sources; two informants mentioned having seen written accounts. Yet my evaluation of the body of oral tradition suggests that it retains independence in concept and information. For example, Riesenberg's 1966 account, which is known on Sapwuahfik, does not include the detail of the pits dug on the beach.)

The memory of the massacre is kept alive in the general population because there are frequent reminders of it. Why do the Sapwuahfik people speak English, have such varied personal characteristics, or own particular pieces of land? The answers, as local people see it, go back to the fact that the atoll was depopulated and then repopulated by immigrants. The results of the massacre are evident in daily life, and so everyone, including older children, has some knowledge of this historical event. There is a pervasive consciousness that Sapwuahfik's modern characteristics are rooted in the past.

Sapwuahfik people who are historically naïve—children, adolescent girls, and some women (especially those unrelated to any historically knowledgeable person)—can say only that "long long ago *mehn wai* ["foreigners," today used to mean Americans or Europeans] came and killed the people of Ngatik." Most adults and some adolescent boys, however, know somewhat more than this. An example of a general level of familiarity is the summary of the massacre recounted in an interview with a seventeen-year-old boy (my questions, as insistent interviewer, are in parentheses):

> He came with a group of men to fight with *mehn Ngatik*. That was his name, Captain Lao. I don't know the name of the nahnmwarki here, [at that time] if it was Aisikaya, or what. *Mehn Ngatik* fought with knives and such things. But they used guns. Guns. They fought [at the eastern tip of Ngatik Islet].
>
> (That's where the ship came?)
>
> Yes, the boat that the soldiers came ashore in. *Mehn Ngatik* ran to their boats, holding on to their knives. But the attackers simply used guns. They shot them, and after a while there was only one man who was able to catch the edge of their boat—what was his name? I don't know the name of the man who caught the edge of the boat. They shot him down. He was the only one who made it that far. The attackers went inland, they carried away the women. I don't know where they took them. [Name] is the one who knows the story.
>
> (They took the women?)
>
> I don't know if they took them or they decided to live here on Ngatik. They carried away the women.
>
> (None were left?)
>
> There were some left; probably there were some left.

This brief interview exemplifies several characteristics of an intermediate level of knowledge about the massacre. The young man is familiar with the story but reluctant to be pinned down on details, cautious and unsure about his own knowledge. Two of his details (the names of the attackers' leader and the premassacre nahnmwarki) are wrong, according to documents and accounts by older people. He is quick to refer me to someone more knowledgeable. He is not ready to push beyond the basic account to inquire into the ramifications of the event. The specific detail he gives (of the single warrior catching the edge of the attackers' boat) indicates, even had he not mentioned his name, the original source of this version.

Knowing details of the massacre story depends on access to older people who know more about history. This young man told me he learned about the massacre from his father's sister's husband, with whom he spends time fishing, working, and visiting. (However, the boy's classificatory brother [father's sister's son], though older and related to the same man as his wife's sister's son, has only a vague knowledge of the events. One's knowledge depends as much on how much and what kind of time one spends with one's knowledgeable relatives as on how knowledgeable those relatives are.) Historical knowledge does not come exclusively from relatives. I think it tends to, because of the time young people spend with older people, most of it is with kin. But groups of unrelated older men or women discuss history, usually in the form of telling stories, and others listen. Some discussions I heard were stimulated by my obvious curiosity, but people referred to other conversations they had had, and often the discussion would go far beyond what I could have understood or been interested in. Also, people's interest in and excitement about these topics was evident.

The few individuals considered historically knowledgeable—those to whom other people continually referred me and to whom they bring their own questions—acquired their knowledge informally, usually from older relatives. The emergence of an expert on history results from a combination of circumstances: the individual had access to the time and concern of an older person who knew history well, and had the motivation and capacity to learn and remember oral tradition. Older people with culturally important knowledge will plan for its transmission and choose someone to teach. On Sapwuahfik, stories of the massacre may be learned in the context of acquiring valued secret knowledge, but they are also learned separately and more casually. One man described the informal nature of learning oral history: "I would hear about it from my father. They didn't really tell me the story—but they would converse, and I would listen. At that time I didn't know much; I was just a boy. They would converse, and I would listen. And the old man, mother's father—he would tell tales. He would tell us stories, about those foreigners."

So a few people, because of their proximity to knowledgeable elders and a commitment to learning, become knowledgeable themselves. Even the best informed, however, recognize a loss in historical knowledge from the generation preceding them, because of how such knowledge is transmitted. For example, the seventy-year-old man acknowledged as the person most expert in local history could not answer my question about the earliest ancestor of his clan (an aboriginal Sapwuahfik clan). He said he regretted never having asked his adopted father, who knew such things, about clan history. All he had wanted to learn as a young man when his father was alive, all he had asked about, was traditional dance songs.

Such selectivity, as well as biographical chance and, since German colonial times, the diversion of formal schooling, has resulted in the loss of not only some of what little aboriginal tradition survived but also knowledge of the massacre itself and events after it. Because these stories are not valued as sacred knowledge, they are less likely to be at the forefront of what young people want to learn and what older people want to teach.

One important reason to analyze ethnohistorical material is to sort what Western scholars are interested in as descriptive history from the looser category of legend, carefully comparing written and oral sources in order to produce a narrative account of a certain place and time. Although I have done some of this in putting together the "double-sided" account of the massacre that follows, the goal of this book is not to write an official history of Sapwuahfik. Instead, I concentrate on the *ethno* of *ethnohistory* and ask questions about the meanings and interpretations, rather than the representations, of events. This is the aspect of history that is vital to a study of modern Sapwuahfik culture—the Sapwuahfik understanding of the massacre as a central fact of their history, as a tragedy in which they play the role of both victims and descendants of the murderers.

CHAPTER TWO

The Massacre and Its Meaning

*I*N 1838 THE BRITISH ADMIRALTY began to look into
C. H. Hart's activities on Pohnpei and Ngatik. Hearsay
and eyewitness testimonies were collected in Macao from
five of Hart's former crewmen, and Commander P. L.
Blake in HMS *Larne* was ordered to the area to investigate accusations against Hart for his actions on Pohnpei involving the
Falcon, and on Ngatik. Blake collected information from Europeans on Pohnpei (some of whom had taken part in the attack
on Ngatik), and in February 1839, he visited Ngatik and questioned two white men who had gone there to live after the massacre. (Taking the *Larne,* which had no flag hoisted, as a whaler,
the two men came aboard unsuspectingly; "their surprize was
perceivable," Blake comments, "on discovering their mistake.")
Admiralty dispatches, with sworn testimonies as enclosures, are
the primary documentary sources for the massacre. Although
constrained by contemporary concerns, the official report on the

attack is an attempt to be, in the legal sense, fair. There are also occasional references to the Ngatik tragedy in contemporary ships' logs and travelers' accounts.[1]

Chaotic conditions on Ngatik after 1837 and the rapid loss of the aboriginal language made the preservation of oral history hazardous, and accounts I use were collected nearly a century and a half after the event. Yet in some ways, the massacre is very close to contemporary life. I spoke with those who, as children, knew elderly aboriginal people who had survived the massacre. Sapwuahfik understanding of this pivotal event emerges from the oral history.

Ngatik, 1836: The First Encounter

It was the search for trade goods of value in Chinese and European markets that first brought Hart to Ngatik. James Sindrey, a twenty-year-old London native, had joined the ship at Pohnpei when it was four months out of Sydney on a trading voyage. Sindrey left the only European account of the *Lambton*'s first visit to Ngatik in testimony to the chief superintendent of British trade in Macao in 1838. He remembered the small cutter's crew as consisting of about fourteen Europeans and three Maori men.

The *Lambton* arrived at Ngatik early in the year 1836. It reached the atoll in late afternoon or evening, but the surf was too high to allow a landing, though Sindrey and several others made an attempt (the ship was off the reef, not inside the lagoon). The next day the ship's boat landed successfully with Hart, Sindrey, and four others, who took five unloaded muskets ashore with them. Sindrey reported that "the natives received them well; they began dancing and appeared to be contented." He estimated that they saw about forty men and three women.

Sindrey and an unnamed Pohnpei man (who had accompanied them, though Sindrey did not include him in his crew count) went "up into the bush" with two Ngatik people. The other foreigners remained with the boat.

After a short time, deponent [Sindrey] seperated from the Native of Ascension [Pohnpei] and all of a sudden he heard him call out, "Jim, take care of yourself, for the natives are getting their clubs and knives and coming to kill you." Upon this deponent looked about him and saw his best chance was to run through them to the boat. In doing so, they struck at deponent with a knife and struck him in the hinder part of the two legs with a Club. When deponent got to the boat, he found the Captain and the others loading their Muskets. The Native of Ascension had got to the Boat just before deponent; they then shoved off and went on board the Cutter, which lay about 4 Miles off; to the best of Deponent's recollection there were no shots fired that day at all . . .

Sindrey failed to mention the stimulus for the "natives" taking after him, which was that he and the Pohnpei man had left the boat to search for tortoiseshell (intending to obtain it by barter) and had in fact found some. When Sindrey got back, he told Hart it was in a "cookhouse," and he estimated he had seen 130 or 140 pounds of valuable hawksbill shell—but at the moment of finding it, he heard the alarm and had to run for the boat. If Sindrey omitted this information to mask the motive for the later attack, his intentions were subverted by his crewmate James Headley, who revealed it when being questioned by Blake. (Blake thought Headley mentioned it "inadvertently," and he accepted it as "a Key to the Motives" of the attack.)

Ironically, in light of Islander reverence for sea turtles, tortoiseshell also had a powerful attraction for those who sought their fortune in island trading. Hart must have been strongly tempted. Blake was no doubt aware that Pohnpei (and so, perhaps, nearby islands as well) was noted as a source of tortoiseshell (Riesenberg 1968:4). Hezel writes, "During the 1830s, Ponape was generally acclaimed by British captains to be the best island in the Pacific for turtleshell" (1983:126). The shell sold for five to six dollars a pound, and, due to the popularity of the trade, was already becoming rare around Pohnpei by the early 1840s (ibid.).

Most Sapwuahfik people today agree with Blake that greed
for tortoiseshell was the motive for the massacre. I collected two
oral accounts of the events of Hart's first visit to Ngatik; here is
the more detailed version:

> The ship came long ago. They came on shore from the ship and
> went to a house, which was called Windeniol. That was the
> Nahnmwarki's building, a large building, which used to be dec-
> orated with *liang* [a mollusk?] of all kinds, and tortoiseshell.
> They would make offerings of it, just as we offer money in
> church. Also, many huge canoes were kept in that building, and
> it was full of all sorts of marine organisms, shells and so on.
>
> A foreign man who came with the ship went and saw all
> this. He came, and wanted to take the things; he wanted to
> own them. But they said, oh, you cannot. They were afraid of
> their god; they worshipped their god. That man asked, but they
> didn't give him permission.
>
> There was a man who guarded that building, a strong man.
> He was the Nahnmwarki's "officer" or "policemaster" or such-
> like—a very strong and brave sort of man. He was the one who
> usually took care of that building.
>
> The foreign man just went and took the offerings. The
> guard forbade it. But it was no use, because that man just went
> and took it. He hit the guard with a club, really hit him,
> knocked him down. Well, the guard wasn't unconscious, so the
> foreign man ran outside the house. The guard also jumped up
> and ran after him, but couldn't catch him. That foreigner was
> really fast. He ran towards the shore to the boat, and raced off
> to the ship. At that the ship departed. They left.
>
> But the people of Ngatik turned to their personal gods.
> They used to foretell the future with coconut fronds. They
> said, that ship will return; it will come back.

The circumstances look quite different from this point of view.
The second oral account of the 1836 encounter supports this
interpretation, stating that the visitors refused to pay for the
tortoiseshell they wanted to take. Although only fragments of
the traditions remain, aboriginal Sapwuahfik people apparently
shared the wider Caroline Islands cultural emphasis on the sym-

bolic and religious importance of sea turtles. Turtles were closely associated with the privileges of high rank. Taboos and ceremony surrounded the killing and eating of them, and chiefly or-
naments were made from the shell. Although the second of the
oral versions describes the foreigners' actions in terms of bad
trade relations, it is evident that Sindrey and his crewmate in
fact threatened an important social and religious institution
when they invaded Windeniol. Although the *Lambton* departed
Sapwuahfik in a hurry, the Islanders were not complacent about
their victory. They turned to their personal gods in inquiry, foretelling the future in a complex play of coconut frond strips, and
they learned that the ship would return.

To establish a legal basis for criminal accusations, Blake needed to determine whether Hart had premeditated the murder of
the Islanders. He closely questioned those he interviewed as to
whether Hart discussed the tortoiseshell or his intentions toward
Ngatik during the following months, which the *Lambton* spent
in New South Wales and in island trading. Three crewmen testi-
fied that Hart "was always keen after the Shell," but Blake could
get no direct evidence that he intended to kill to get it. The only
man who asserted premeditation was William Marshall, whose
value as a witness was flawed by a bad reputation and prior quarrels with Hart. Marshall's testimony at Macao concludes:

> If Captn. Hart said that he committed the action at Nuttic in
> self defence, it is false, for I heard him say nearly twelve
> months before at Manila and afterwards at Guam that they had
> plenty of Tortoiseshell at Nuttic, and that they would not part
> with it, because it was their Maquhawee, but he intended to
> take it and kill every man on the Island; he further said he
> knew where they kept it for T. Lindrey [Sindrey] had seen it in
> the cookhouse.
>
> Maquahawee means in their language their God [*me
> sarawi*, Pohnpeian "that which is sacred"; Riesenberg, pers.
> comm. 1981].

Without more reliable witnesses, Blake could not prove premeditation. He concluded, "Whatever may have been the secret

broodings on that subject within Captain Hart's own bosom, I should think that he was not rash enough to avow them." In the end, Blake relied on circumstantial evidence to determine that Hart intended violence.

Pohnpei, 1836: The Falcon Tragedy

Nearly the whole crew had changed—though Hart was still master and Sindrey and his Pohnpeian companion were again aboard—when the *Lambton* set sail again from Sydney in mid-May 1836. They arrived at Madolenihmw Harbor in August, just in time for Hart to become involved in the events surrounding the wreck of the *Falcon*. The *Falcon* story is a separate tragedy; it is relevant to Ngatik's history because of the vindictive cruelty shown by Hart and other Europeans toward the Pohnpei people involved and because the *Lambton*'s second voyage to Ngatik took place soon afterward. (In fact, we probably owe Blake's investigation to Hart's actions here; whereas "the affair at Nuttic" might not have brought a ship of His Majesty's Navy to the scene, the combined accusations did.)[2]

The *Falcon* had come to Pohnpei to refit. It had been Hart, when the two ships met by chance at sea, who advised Captain Hingston to harbor at Pohnpei, that island "being nearer than Guam, a more snug harbor, a place where we could get refreshments very cheap, and get the work done peaceably, there being no grog" (according to John Plumb, of the *Falcon*'s crew). After completing repairs, the *Falcon* set out in early July but struck the reef. The crew saved much of the cargo and stores, but though they stood watch, lost some of it to Islanders.

Hingston had unwittingly stepped into an internal contest in Madolenihmw chiefdom between the Nahnmwarki and the *Wasahi* (the second title in the nahnmwarki line) (Hanlon 1988:50–51). Angered over thievery, Hingston confronted the Nanawah (a title of high rank) and unwisely shook him by the shoulders. The captain was immediately threatened with a spear but not harmed; however, Hanlon writes, "his physical abuse of a Pohnpeian chief, an unconscionable offense in Pohnpeian society, sealed his fate" (1988:54). Later that day the Europeans were attacked by a large force of Islanders, who killed Hingston and several of the crew. They then mutilated and mistreated the corpses, which the Europeans greatly resented.

The Wasahi came to the assistance of the *Falcon*'s crew and recovered the bodies. European support arrived when the schooner *Unity* (out of Hawaii, under an unrelated Captain Hart), and then the *Lambton,* sailed in. With these reinforcements and the assistance of a large Pohnpei faction, the Europeans took their revenge. They attacked with ships' guns and muskets; the Islanders defended themselves with spears and slings. They plundered and destroyed houses and searched out and killed the Nahnmwarki. Plumb says, "We made great havoc on our way, burning houses, and destroying Bread fruit, Cocoa nut, and Plaintain trees, besides their Cava [kava; Pohnpei *sakau*], which they value most." The Nanawah was captured and, after conference of the three captains, hanged with gruesome ritual. It was this execution, mimicking the ceremony of naval justice, that most outraged British officials and spurred the navy's investigation. Rear Admiral Sir Frederick Maitland wrote to the Admiralty: "This perhaps is one of the most extraordinary instances on record of persons perfectly unauthorized by Law sitting in Judgment over a fellow creature, condemning him to death, and deliberately carrying that sentence into execution."

And not merely a death sentence; the Europeans mocked and terrified the Nanawah, and disregarded his last wish to die at the hands of a Pohnpei man of rank. Giving us insight into the character of such crews, Blake writes that the circumstances "exhibit in a strong light, the cruel, the remorseless levity of seamen, when their passions have been let loose, and where they are uncontrolled by Discipline or Education."

Hart freely admitted his role in the hanging, stating that it had been done out of necessity, but there is evidence that he had repeatedly announced his intention to hang the Nanawah. Blake writes that "it is impossible to refrain from remarking on the boldness and high presumptuous tone of authority assumed by

Captain Hart on all occasions," and states that Hart was in "Chief Command" of the Europeans, in whom he inspired "terror . . . against the slightest infraction of his commands."

After the hanging, the *Unity* and the *Lambton* proceeded to Guam, transporting some *Falcon* survivors. According to Hart's own testimony, he reported the events to a Spanish official there. (This was the same official who later credited Hart with "the character of an honest man"; quite different from Blake's assessment.) Hart then carried gunpowder for the Spanish government in the Marianas before returning to the island trade, spending the months of August 1836 to June 1837 in visits to Guam, Manila, and, several times, Pohnpei.

Pohnpei, June 1837

On Pohnpei in June, again at Madolenihmw Harbor, Hart prepared to return to Ngatik. Some who had obeyed Hart in the *Falcon* affair were prepared to accompany him, and he hired more Europeans (from seven to eighteen men, depending on who is recounting)—though at fourteen hands, his crew was already complete. The additions were men who happened to be on Pohnpei: deserters, sick sailors left ashore, beachcombers, and petty traders. Also, Hart took possession of a large boat that had belonged to the *Falcon* and made and loaded a supply of cartridges. He arranged for the ship to tow canoes carrying fifteen armed Pohnpei men.

Ngatik, June–July 1837

At the very end of June or early in July, then, the *Lambton* set sail again for Ngatik. The crew attempted to land where the ship's boat had landed the year before, but did not or could not go ashore. The attackers went fully armed in boats and canoes, and the men of the island met them with hostility, "hanging around the bushing, with Clubs, slings, etc., in their hands, and beckoning them to come ashore." Hart's men fired a few musket shots but went no further. Instead, they retreated and spent the night on "a small Island to the Eastward," one of Ngatik's other islets. (Wataluhk is the first islet east of Ngatik, lying at the head of the only passage into the lagoon.)

Blake compiled a comprehensive rendering of the events that followed, combining testimony from several of the *Lambton's* crew. The commander never spoke with Hart, and we have no testimony from Hart about what happened at Ngatik. He had his chance—in 1838 he made a formal "Declaration" about his recent activities to the Spanish port captain at Manila. In this document he completely ignores Ngatik, recounting his involvement in the *Falcon* affair and his return to Manila, where he freighted gunpowder, then skipping immediately to January 1838, with the statement, "Your petitioner [Hart] proceeded to his trade of tortoiseshell among the Islands."

Other eyewitnesses make Hart's silence immaterial. On the day following their arrival at the atoll, according to Blake's report, the entire company went back to Ngatik Islet in boats "and commenced a general attack on the natives, routing and killing them in all directions. It is not denied *that every man was shot* under whatever circumstances he was found" (Blake's emphasis). That first day the attackers found pits that had been dug out on the beach, "four or five feet deep, and covered over with the wild `Tara' leaf, which is immensely large." These did not slow them down. They retired to the other islet to spend the night and attacked again the following day, "precisely in the same manner as before. *No man was spared* . . . The Natives had no means of defence whatever beyond their Clubs and Slings against a strong party of Europeans and others well provided with fire Arms. On the afternoon of the second day's attack, the latter had entire possession of the Island . . ." (Blake's emphasis).

Let us turn, at this point, to the oral history of these events. Forewarned by the gods' prediction, the Islanders were watching for the foreigners' return. Traditions describing the attack itself indicate that the men of Sapwuahfik were aware of and prepared for the threat. Despite their preparations, they were overcome—not so much by the simple difference in weaponry as by the psychology and accidents of battle:

> They foretold the future and they knew the date that the ship would come back. When it came, they went out and were watching for it, and there it was; the ship appeared on the horizon. They held a meeting about it, and they went and waited at Sapwenleng [the eastern point of Ngatik Islet]. They were going to fight with the people on the ship. But how could they? They were going to fight with clubs, with pieces of wood, but against guns—it couldn't be done.
>
> But there was a Marshallese man with them. He said, "Look, they have these things that shoot bullets, they will shoot us." That man had seen them before; there were foreigners who came to the Marshalls. The others said, "So?" And he said the Ngatik men should lie down on the ground, take palm fronds, and put them over themselves. They would be holding their clubs. The foreigners would come from the ship, on a boat, and arrive at the beach, coming closer and closer. When they got nearer, the Ngatik men would surprise them; they would attack.
>
> They prepared to carry out his plan. If they had actually done that—truly they would have succeeded, because those who came were not many, they were few.
>
> Well then, they went and hid themselves at Nimwensapw ["the end of the land"]. They went and hid themselves, and the foreigners came from the ocean. At low tide they pulled up their craft at the edge of the lagoon, and waited. They pulled up their boat, and they were afraid to come ashore.
>
> Those who were hidden got tired of waiting; the foreigners were slow in coming. But—truly they were stupid [or "foolish"; *pweipwei*] people. They said, some should go to the beach. And five boys went closer to the boat. They went and stopped close to where the boat was waiting. The boat came closer, bit by bit. The Ngatik boys walked out; they got almost to the boat, then they were shot. At the moment they were shot, they fell, all of them dead.
>
> Well, those who stayed on shore saw this—oh! Their broth-

ers were dead. They were angry and they ran, wanting to fight. Well then. That's the reason they lost. If they had just remained lying down, truly, they [would have won] . . .

They ran out to the boat, and some of them were shot, and they ran out into the lagoon, and still they shot them. Some ran inland, but the foreigners came on shore, and searched for them, and shot them down. At that time, there were many people here on Ngatik . . .

During or after the first day's attack, two or three canoes (Blake estimates twenty people) escaped. Blake states that they left from the northeast side of the islet and "have never since been heard of." One oral account sheds light on this. The speaker, himself a man of high title, presents the attack in terms of the fates of followers of each of three high title holders (he uses three Pohnpei titles: nahnmwarki, wasahi, and *dauk* are not aboriginal Sapwuahfik titles):

> Long ago, the first foreigner came, a man named Captain Hart. He came to war with Ngatik, and killed every person. He killed all the men. The Nahnmwarki and all his followers, he killed. Dauk, and all his followers, he killed. But the Wasahi [and his followers] they got in a canoe, they fled. They fled, and went to Lukunor [in the Mortlock Islands]. The people of Lukunor killed them; only one of them did they adopt. Descendants of the Ngatik people still live in Lukunor today.

Both oral and written accounts agree that the attacks, and the attempt to escape, destroyed the entire adult male population of the atoll. All the men on Ngatik were shot (one who survived the initial attacks was killed afterward), but only one woman was hit by a musket ball, "accidentally," Blake says. The testimonies Blake collected report variously that from forty to sixty men were killed. Blake takes fifty as a reasonable estimate. One hearsay report claimed as many as eighty-four victims.

When the island's defenders were dead, after the second day's attack, Hart went to find the tortoiseshell. In Blake's words, he repaired to the spot to possess himself of it, as is affirmed by Randall, Headley and Corgat, but what was his extreme disappointment when he found that, out of the 130 or 140 lbs. computed by Sindrey, not more than 20 lbs. of it were good? However he possessed himself of what was worth having, which from varied accounts is stated at from 18 to 30 lbs. and took it himself on board the Cutter.

The remainder, more than one hundred pounds, was commercially worthless green turtle shell, not the valuable hawksbill. Hart would have to find another way to make murder pay.

European Assessment of the Massacre

Information in the documentary sources, especially that critical to establishing criminal liability, is shaped by the circumstances of those providing it. The Admiralty report includes descriptions of the massacre that cover a range of culpability. William Rogers, a member of the attack party, leans toward understatement. Originally from Bristol, England, Rogers had joined the *Lambton* at Sydney in March 1836, after the ship's first trip to Ngatik. According to Rogers, on their arrival at Ngatik "the Natives decoyed the people into the bush, and then attacked them." Armed only with clubs and stones, they did not harm any of Hart's party. Rogers "did not see more than Five or Six Natives killed, but cannot say how many more [were] killed" in the first day's attack. The second day, he "cannot say how many Natives were killed; perhaps four or five." Rogers also echoed all the testimony collected by Blake, saying that he "will most solemnly swear that he knows nothing of any violence committed on the women of Nuttic."

On the other hand, William Marshall, who was not "actually concerned" with the attack but joined the *Lambton* later, presented hearsay evidence maximizing the magnitude of the tragedy (recall that Marshall was widely regarded as an unreliable character and nursed a grudge against Hart):

[The *Lambton*'s crew, "extra white men" and Pohnpei men] after three days' fighting and killing every man except one, whom they could not find, plundered the place of all the Tortoiseshell, Mats, Nets, and in short everything moveable, the females were ravished, some before the blood of their husbands was cool, and many of the youngest and best looking were distributed amongst the men and brought over to Ascension [Pohnpei] . . .

Other witnesses gave evidence between these extremes, presenting various estimates of the degree of threat posed by the Islanders and the number of men killed. All the Europeans except Marshall insisted that women had not been harmed. Blake attributes these firm denials to simple self-interest: "During all my enquiries, it was ever denied that the women were violently treated, since it cannot be expected that the parties actually concerned, who were my only informants, would acknowledge if it was so." Oral traditions I collected agree women were not killed but are silent on whether other mistreatment occurred.

Hart's professed intent was to trade with the people of Ngatik; he and some of his crew later presented the murders as a defensive measure. Blake repeatedly questioned witnesses as to Hart's "declared intentions" before they left Pohnpei; they responded that he "always said `he meant to trade quietly if they would.'" But, Blake dryly points out, "on no occasion did he further disclose his intentions as to what measures he should adopt in case of other contingencies." Although Blake began his investigation without opinion as to Hart's guilt or innocence, he concluded that the claimed intent to engage in friendly trade was irreconcilable with the evidence:

The Natives of Nuttic, if accounts be true, had already shewn a hostile disposition to the white men approaching their Shores: a repetition of the attempt therefore might naturally be expected to meet with the same hostile reception. The Island is small tho' the largest of the Group and the only one inhabited. Those Inhabitants were known to possess none but their native Arms, vizt., Clubs and Slings, not even Spears. They might have had treacherous designs or objects on the white man when they appeared; but there was no urgent reason why the latter, with the plea of *Trading*, should, whether from Avarice or Revenge, carry a forced invasion to their homes. Savages as they most undoubtedly are and with no other means of Defence but their Native Clubs and Slings, what other than a total annihilation of them could be expected from a strong armed force of renegade European Seamen, with excited passions and well supplied with fire Arms and Ammunition.

Despite quibbles over whether Hart had openly stated his thoughts after his first visit to Ngatik or declared his intentions on Pohnpei in 1837, his preparations on Pohnpei and his keenness for tortoiseshell speak for themselves. As Blake put it, "In short, I conceive that it is an absurdity to blink the matter further." He pointed out that although Hart openly announced his intention to go to Ngatik to "trade quietly," it was known that the *Lambton* had met a hostile reception on its last visit and that part of its crew had narrowly escaped being killed. When the crew again approached Ngatik, they were met with obvious hostility. What then of their professed intention?

> By way of inducing them to "trade quietly," he [Hart] retreats to compose his force in order to visit their unfriendliness with redoubled vengeance on the following day, which he effectually executes, and, with a strong armed gang of Renegade European Seamen, exterminates in a most murderous manner the entire male population of the Island . . .

Although Hart may have had tortoiseshell uppermost in his mind, Blake indicated that others of the crew considered vengeance as a reason to return to the atoll. That revenge was easily taken up as a motive is suggested by one crewman's statement that (in Blake's words) "a desire to revenge the treachery of the Nuttic Natives on the Lambton's first visit to them was talked of among her Crew, though with about two exceptions she had since changed the whole of them at Sydney [that is, between the first and second visits to Ngatik]."

That the crew—even those who had not been present—felt that the Ngatik people had been "treacherous" is typical of European rhetoric about Pacific Islanders during this era. Sapwuahfik accounts of the 1836 events, of course, present another assessment of who had been treacherous. But "treachery" was, for Europeans, so common a reason for killing Islanders that it seems to have been readily accepted, and later disseminated by Hart and his crew, as the explanation for their actions. Though Hart said nothing about Ngatik in his statement at Manila in 1838, he and certain members of his crew in later years reinterpreted (or, let us say, presented other versions of) their motives. Crewman John MacVie said in 1841 that the attack had been in revenge for the murder of two unnamed captains by the aboriginal people (Godby 1845:505–7). Lewis Corgat claimed in 1852 that Hart "had been attacked by the natives of these islands; and not being strong enough to punish them himself, he came to this island [Pohnpei] to obtain help" (Gulick 1932:90).

Captain C. H. Fretwell appears to have later encountered Hart in Hong Kong, and in 1892 he published the tale Hart gave when the two met on Fretwell's ship (Fretwell 1892:117–19). As Hart told it, the *Lambton* had been anchored off Ngatik at night (Fretwell does not name the island, but the reference is clear—unless Hart committed genocide twice). A lone white man approached in a canoe and told Hart that his ship had been wrecked, all his companions murdered by the natives, and he himself only spared "on condition that he would be their Chief." When Hart "heard of this treacherous conduct, he vowed vengeance, and landing next morning with some of his men, he shot every man on the island." In confirmation of this tale, Fretwell adds that he later became well acquainted with "Mr. Adams," the white man who roused Hart's sympathy. Because the name of Mr. Adams's ship is not included, and renegades (unlike ships) did not register their frequent name changes, it is not possible to unravel this yarn, except to say that it fails to match either documentary or oral history, save at one point: Hart "shot every man on the island."

Aftermath

The documents do not record how long the *Lambton* stayed at Ngatik after the attack. Blake says only that Hart returned to Pohnpei "shortly afterwards." When the ship left, several of the men, according to one witness, asked to remain. William Rogers stated that two of Hart's crew and five or six Pohnpei men were partially paid off by Hart with the extra (*Falcon*) boat and a few muskets, and stayed on Ngatik. Hart paid the rest when they reached Pohnpei (probably not in money, which was nearly useless in that part of the Pacific, but in trade goods reflecting the crew's values and the local market: tobacco, tools, muskets, ammunition, rum). Other eyewitnesses describe the resettlement as beginning after the *Lambton* returned to Pohnpei and, shortly later, set sail again, stopping at Ngatik on its way south to leave Pohnpei Islanders and at least one European. In either case, there is no documentary record of the period immediately after the massacre, until the *Lambton*'s return a month later.

The days after the massacre were filled with horror and confusion. Blake reports that "within a few days" after the massacre, several of the women of Ngatik "destroyed their young children and hanged themselves." This might have happened while the *Lambton* was still there; the self-destruction of women and their children went on intermittently for some time. In conversations with me about the massacre, many Sapwuahfik people showed their familiarity with stories of the women's intent to kill themselves by starvation or to impose that fate on their children. A few of the children, self-preserving in the midst of nightmare, escaped both attackers and mothers, fled into the bush, and hid until the madness passed. This account was given by a sixty-two-year-old woman whose knowledge of other massacre-related events was vague:

The foreigners came and shot inland and killed *mehn Ngatik*. Well then, *mehn Ngatik* were going to kill their sons. They probably did this so that there would be no more boys who would grow up, because the foreigners had carried away the men, because they would take away the men of Ngatik.

It is said that two boys escaped and ran into the forest. They went to hide. Their mothers searched for them, and it is said that they were going to kill them. They were probably what was left of the men.

They felt they ought to tie up their children so they would die, lest the foreigners come again, because they would take away the men and carry them off. The women said, "Let us tie up our sons so they will die." They weren't going to feed them. Well, they tied them up, three boys, who were probably the only ones left. They tied them up, but those boys moved while they were squatting, and got shells. They cut, cut, cut [she motions with her hands to show one boy cutting the cords behind the back of another]. And they ran into the forest and they went and ate. . . . It is said—they grew up!

Here is the story recounted by the man who gave the detailed narrative of the massacre presented above:

The group of boys was small because the women wanted to kill them. They would tie their hands so they would starve and die. Well, the boys would escape. One of them was rather smart, the Wasahi [the boy who later held the title Wasahi], Noah [his name]. He took a cowrie shell and put it behind his back. Because they had tied their hands like [he indicates hands tied together behind his back]. Well, he fooled his mother, that boy:

"Mother!"

His mother said, "What?"

"Where is Papa's taro scraper?"—that's what they used to scrape taro and ripe coconut; it was rather sharp.

The boy said, "Mother, bring it to me because I am going to die. I will go and scrape taro for my father to eat in heaven." [Here the narrator laughs at the boy's cleverness.] And his mother said, "Oh, thank you." She went and got it. Well, she was crying and she went away from him. Her son whispered to one of the others: "Hey! Come over here!" That fellow came over, and he did this [scraping with tool behind his back] and cut the rope. When he was free he took the shell in his hand and cut the rope [that held the others, until all three were free] and they ran.

Informants agreed on the women's motive: they intended to kill their sons to forestall their murder or abduction by Europeans in another attack. Although girls who survived the attack and remained on the atoll are mentioned in genealogies as ancestors, I found no stories about them. Other than these accounts of women's attempts to destroy their children, stories of postmassacre events deal with a slightly later period, after Europeans/ Americans and Pohnpei people settled on the atoll.

When the *Lambton* sailed away, only a portion of the survivors remained on the atoll to face the aftermath of the massacre in the place it had happened. Some women were taken on board the ship and brought to Pohnpei. As they denied rape, so the attackers denied kidnapping. Sindrey (who did not take part in the massacre but was on Pohnpei when the *Lambton* returned from Ngatik) says that the ship brought only "two or three Native Women and two or three boys;" he believed they were aboard "with their own consent." Rogers (presenting the narrative of minimization) says six women came voluntarily: "They were asked if they would go and they consented." In fact, he "heard Captain Hart say that he would not let them be taken against their will." Perhaps, seeing their lives destroyed around them, the women did leave voluntarily, hopelessly. It is hard to imagine any acceptable choices open to them. Those who went to Pohnpei apparently never returned. One (this from Marshall's hearsay report) was "presented" by Hart to the daughter of a Nahnken; she was, Marshall claims, treated as a servant, "barbarously." Some became part of Pohnpei families; others were scattered farther—oral tradition traces a boy to Fiji and a woman to the Bonin Islands, south of Japan.

And Bloody Hart? The British had missed their first chance to catch him, after Marshall made criminal allegations against him at Macao in 1838. The *Lambton* was in Hong Kong at the time, and when Hart heard of the charges he immediately set off for Manila—in order, as he said, to procure documents from the Spanish government that would justify his actions. Blake, who was then in Manila, expected Hart to return to British territory—which he apparently did not do. The investigation continued nonetheless, with the *Larne*'s information-gathering mission, and Blake's report was duly packaged up and sent off to England.

Meanwhile, there was some uncertainty in the eastern regions of the British Empire as to whether Hart could be arrested for committing crimes beyond the empire's one-hundred-mile limit; or, if he could, whether the arrest should be performed by the chief superintendent of British trade in China or "the Senior Officer of Her Majesty's Ships" in the region. The Opium War with England (1839–42), may also have interfered with legal procedures. In the end Sir George Gipps, governor of New South Wales, received two bulky packets of testimony on Hart's activities from Downing Street, with a letter from Lord John Russell: "Use your utmost endeavors to bring to punishment any parties, whom you have reason to suppose might be convicted either in the Piracy Court or in the Supreme Court of the Colony of such Atrocities as are described in the enclosed documents."

This provided a legal channel for prosecuting Hart—but only in New South Wales. It comes as no surprise that Hart seems never to have returned to his home port.[3]

The Meaning of the Massacre

In our first consideration of this topic, we need only see the broad outlines of how massacre-era events are represented and understood today, by considering the mixed perceptions the people of Sapwuahfik have of their ancestors—aboriginal, Pohnpeian, other Islander, and non-Islander. Elements of this indigenous historiography will be considered in more detail later.

Some ambiguity in their views of these ancestors results from gaps in the historical information available to them. A great deal of it, though, arises from the circumstances of the Sapwuahfik community today.

Ambiguity in valuing the past sets up a powerful symbolic focus for reflecting on the massacre and modern Sapwuahfik life. Although respecting and taking pride in the powers of the ancients, Sapwuahfik people also refer to them as heathens, "unenlightened," and "people of darkness" and condemn their evil behavior (such as Sirinpahn's licentious games): "In ancient times, people were not yet good. They were not yet enlightened. . . . Life was hard, because there was fighting! fighting! fighting! War! war! war! . . . It is almost as if we people, at the beginning, we acted like animals."

This is the same ambivalent attitude, in a wider context, as that revealed in traditional tales of the premassacre nahnmwarki. The theme recurs in narratives about more recent events, and in the form of modern social life. Admiration of the magical and practical knowledge of the aboriginal Sapwuahfik people and regret at its loss is balanced by rejection of heathenism and pride in the Christian civilization in which modern Sapwuahfik takes part.

In traditions about premassacre Sapwuahfik, and in comparisons of past and present, aboriginal Islanders appear powerful and well versed in magic, chants, songs, spirit lore, and practical skills such as navigation. This sense of the power of the "people of long ago" applies also to the magically astute generations just passed (that is, to older informants' parents and grandparents) and to the tremendously powerful spirit-humans of the legendary past. But even discounting supernatural tales of the very earliest times on Sapwuahfik (which informants cautiously prefix with "I don't know if it's true or not"), and looking only at the time between Luhkensapwsapw and Sirinpahn (the first and last aboriginal paramount chiefs), nostalgia for lost power and knowledge is evident. Most of this knowledge, such as spells for forecasting ships and controlling the currents, is considered lost forever. Some, though, is said to be potentially recoverable, such as the "Captain's Well," the water of which gives knowledge of ocean navigation. The location of the well was lost, it is said, two generations ago and has not yet been rediscovered. The power of the ancient people persists, though it is lost to their descendants.

Whenever Sapwuahfik people mention the change from the magical might of the past to magical powerlessness today, they phrase it as a voluntary loss—their ancestors *kesehla*, "discarded" or "threw away," magic when they accepted the "good news" of Christianity. The massacre and the introduction of Christianity occurred in quick succession. In historical perspective, we see the loss of all the knowledge of the "people of long ago" as involuntary. The surviving Sapwuahfik people, in the face of social disorganization, immigration, missionary endeavor, and European pressure, had little choice but to "throw away" what little they had preserved of the old ways.

Whereas the loss of other kinds of knowledge, such as the names of plants and animals and much traditional history, is seen as involuntary and very regrettable, people have mixed feelings about the loss of aboriginal magic. Although they are inclined (indeed, obliged) to see it as a virtuous rejection of paganism, they are also aware of their present-day vulnerability, because the people of some other islands are thought to use sorcery to inflict illness and misfortune on others, including Sapwuahfik people—who cannot protect themselves.

The image of "darkness" and "light" used in Sapwuahfik historical discourse is widespread. Stories of the ancient Sapwuahfik people speak of them as *rotorot*—uneducated, pagan, "unenlightened," as the early Christian missionaries would have said. Islanders use the opposite of *rotorot, marain*—light, enlightened, Christian—to refer to *mehn wai*, American and European foreigners. The local view of history encodes a paradox: it was the "enlightened" foreigners who were guilty of massacring the unenlightened, innocent aboriginal men. Sapwuahfik people, then, see their murdered ancestors in two lights—as unenlightened and as innocent victims of a crime. And there is yet another moral twist: though the aboriginal Sapwuahfik people were helpless victims of superior force, in modern Sapwuahfik eyes, they were also guilty of pagan immorality. Oral traditions about aboriginal life preceding the massacre focus on the evildoings of Sirinpahn, the atoll's leader at the time of the *Lambton* attack. Sirinpahn directed activity now regarded as immoral, leading some informants to conclude that the massacre was a punishment from God. So we can see the aboriginal people as *rotorot*, as innocent victims, and as guilty sinners; we can see the attackers as *marain*, as murderous attackers, and as instruments of a higher power. This can be portrayed in diagram form:

Aboriginal Sapwuahfik	**American/European foreigners**
rotorot	*marain*
unenlightened	enlightened
heathen	Christian
innocent	guilty
but "guilty"	but "innocent"

To follow the narrative pathway of the moral tale out another step, there is evidence that some *mehn Sapwuahfik* interpret the arrival of Christianity in 1889 as a repayment—by foreigners and in a sense by God—for the punishment of the massacre. The repayment continues to the present, as Sapwuahfik is protected from storms, war, and sorcery by outsiders.

Of course, both *mehn mahs* (people of long ago) and *mehn wai* who settled on the island—some of whom took part in the massacre—are equally part of modern genealogies. The foreigners are attackers, murderers, and also ancestors. The aboriginal people are the defeated, the losers—yet they are also ancestors, culturally as well as biologically. Sapwuahfik oral tradition represents the two groups ambivalently, each having admirable and contemptible attributes.[4] The local representation of the massacre is a complexly layered moral argument in which both attackers and victims share qualities of *marain* and *rotorot*, innocence and guilt.

CHAPTER THREE

Reconstructing Society

I SLAND PEOPLE TODAY CONSIDER the massacre to have been a complete destruction of aboriginal life. Yet modern Sapwuahfik is not a society assembled de novo from unrelated elements—not a Pitcairn Island. Several aboriginal women, three boys, and an unknown number of girls survived and remained at home. These were people whose knowledge, memories, habits, and personalities had been shaped by aboriginal culture. The survivors, and the first immigrants to join them, inhabited a world built by the aboriginal community: they ate from long-cultivated taro gardens and trees, and used houses, shrines, canoes, tools, and weapons made by those who had died or left. The atoll itself, with its named and known reefs, lagoon areas, fishing spots, shoreline, interior spaces, and sacred sites, retained their imprint. A few kinship ties remained: oral history claims that three of the surviving aboriginal women were "sisters" (*pirien*, sisters, cousins), that the mother of the aboriginal boy Aisikaya survived, and that Aisikaya's companion Noah still had a sister. To say aboriginal culture continued, albeit in different form, would be to undervalue the lives of those who were killed or scattered into exile. Yet Sapwuahfik/Ngatik was never left empty of human life, of social interactions and exchanges, of daily activities and sentiment. As soon as the massacre ended, cultural reconstruction began.

Not until several decades after 1837 do visitors report a population on the atoll, now called Ngatik, large and stable enough to be termed a community. Even in the first years after the attack, the few inhabitants managed to produce food, raise children, contract and break off ties of sex and friendship, and promote and settle quarrels. They experienced relations of mutual assistance, and of dominance and subordination. But before new social institutions could effectively forge a community, enculturate a new generation, organize life and make it worth living, the physical emptiness of the place had to be partly filled. The population grew slowly, first by immigration—an unstable, transient collection of individuals—then, starting in the late 1860s, by a steady increase in births, Ngatik's new native population. But it was not enough for people simply to repopulate the atoll. Some of them had to develop a sense of being at home there, a commitment to nurturing families and establishing shared understandings. Exploitative control by despotic outsiders had to be resisted or outwaited until their rule was replaced by a social order supported by the community at large. In short, a new culture had to grow.

A Note on Sources

This chapter summarizes 150 years of postmassacre history, using oral and documentary sources to outline the economic, demographic, and social changes that occurred as the population grew and a new society developed. It is, in part, a familiar attempt to "reconstruct" the past. I also try, by using oral history, to indicate the substance and tone of the stories of the past that remain relevant to modern Sapwuahfik—the characters still remembered, the stories still told. These are seldom the same characters or events recorded in documents. (Where they are, I have cross-checked oral and written sources.) Each sort of history has its own value; especially where written accounts come only from Europeans and oral ones only from Islanders, they are best seen as complementary.

Written sources for the first decades after 1837 consist primarily of unsatisfactory porthole glimpses by whaling and trading ships. Many ships' logs of the 1840s and 1850s mention supply stops at Ngatik, but the entries contain little information. At best, they estimate population growth and hint at the local economy. The corpus of tales I collected in 1979–80 includes many about the first years after the massacre, a period nearly without documentation. Genealogies also provided information about this era. Starting in 1874, American missionaries visited periodically, producing letters and progress reports. Like whalers, missionaries had definite reasons for visiting islands, and they indulged in their own rhetoric of description. After 1899, when Germany took control of the Caroline Islands from Spain and set in place an operative colonial administration, official accounts provide more detail about local conditions.[1]

Oral accounts highlight the dramatic: heroes and villains, treachery and murder. Historical documents tend to the uninformative: Stopped at Ngatik. Took on 18 hogs and 500 coconuts. Off at 4:30. If we assume that stories told about the past reflect cultural concerns, we can see Western preoccupation with business and moralistic evaluations, and local interest in personalities, interpersonal conflict, landownership, and genealogies. Recognizing that the sources do not provide an adequate narrative account of the early years of Ngatik's new society and culture, I will nonetheless attempt a first approximation of one.

From the Massacre to the Land Division

From the 1840s to the 1880s, life on Ngatik expressed the socioeconomic and political currents that pulsed through the

Pacific region, changing it from a European "frontier" to a map reflecting the relative greed and strength of imperial powers. Beachcombers and castaways with personal agendas tried to carry them out on isolated islands, constrained by the alliance or hostility of Islanders with their own plans. Whaleships and traders sailed the ocean as a giant watery bazaar, acting out their assumption that they had a right to exploit its natural resources and pursue "free trade" with Islanders. Warships of empires, especially of the British, cruised as the sole representatives, as they saw it, of civilization. Islanders themselves moved through the region, journeying deliberately for trade, sociability, and war, or drifting in sailing canoes, hired on as sailors in foreign ships or accompanying foreign lovers on their travels. Those who stayed home became selectively involved with beachcombers, traders, and mission teachers, or they avoided and even violently resisted such involvement. The tiny population of Ngatik met and dealt with all these agents of history.

THE FIRST YEARS

It seems from the documentary record that Hart took the notion of conquest seriously, however absurd it appeared even to contemporary exponents of law and order. He had definite plans for Ngatik; the atoll was not to be left desolate. As soon as he had killed the men, distributed women and children among his crew, and perhaps watched other women kill themselves and their children, Hart was resettling the place with his employees. Soon after the *Lambton* returned to Pohnpei, a group of about twenty Pohnpeians went to settle on Ngatik, under the charge of Patrick ("Paddy") Gorman, who had joined the *Lambton* as an extra hand when it attacked Ngatik. Later, Gorman again accompanied Hart to Pohnpei, bringing back Gorman's three wives, several other foreign men "with their Girls," and additional Pohnpei men and women to the atoll. Gorman told Commander Blake in 1839 that he and Hart had a formal agreement to enter the tortoiseshell business:

He [Gorman] stated that, as the Work was done by himself, and all the Nets, Canoes, Poles, etc., his own, he considered the half, which he agreed to deliver over to Captain Hart, as a Return to him for his having given him (Gorman) possession and made him Ishapow [*Isipahu*, a title of the Nahnmwarki of Madolenihmw on Pohnpei] of the Island; and he added that he thought, as Captain Hart "had conquered and taken the Island," he had a right to make whom he chose the Ishapow or head of it.

Gorman even produced papers, dated August 8, 1837 (a month after the massacre), in which Hart leaves Gorman "in full charge and possession of these Islands and all persons thereon" and coolly adds, "any person or persons molesting the same, I shall consider Felony." "To comment on these documents," Blake wrote, "would be absurd." The commander leaves us a vivid description of the new ruler of Ngatik:

It would be impossible to convey an idea of the Wild and savage picture, which this man presented as he appeared to me on board the "Larne." He had on a sort of narrow mat with a long Grassy fringe round his middle called a Wye-Wye and worn by all the Natives. His long hair hung clotted with Oil; he had several Wreaths of beads round his head, and was tattooed [*sic*] from head to foot.

Gorman was an extreme of the type, but numerous mid-nineteenth century Pacific travelers' accounts describe the renegade who "goes native" in appearance but ensures that the comforts and most of the vices of his past life stay with him. With most of the aboriginal population murdered or gone and the few new settlers under his control, Gorman did not hesitate to impose his will. One of his first acts was to shoot in cold blood the single male massacre survivor, a Sapwuahfik man who was either "bed ridden, who could not have lived many days" (according to William Marshall) or who—according to Gorman's testimony—had to be shot in self-defense. The Pohnpeians Hart left with

Gorman soon had second thoughts. A dozen of them secretly set sail one night for Pohnpei, though only half reached home.

Stories about the reign of the flamboyant Irishman are still told on Sapwuahfik. Gorman is said to have set himself up as king, appropriating food freely and having himself carried around the island on a litter. He insisted that the Islanders supply him with desirable fish and turtle on demand. Though apparently Hart stopped returning for his share of the tortoiseshell, Gorman had a successful few years as a beachcomber and petty trader, figuring ways to make the atoll pay from the supply trade and, perhaps, piracy.

A number of Westerners lived on Ngatik during these first years after the massacre, including men who, like Gorman, had come to the atoll on the *Lambton*. In February 1839, Blake found Gorman and James Hall ("Jem the Cooper," appearing in oral tradition as "Coop") as the only resident non-Islanders, but in May of that year a trading ship was boarded by four Europeans. In 1841 Captain Godby of the *Clarinda* met John MacVie (also McVie or MacGee), one of the "savages and pirates" who tried to attack his ship. MacVie's was a figure the captain would not soon forget:

> He was about 50 years old, 5 Feet 6 inch. large, gray beard, and pupil of one eye double the size of the other, he begged only a couple of empty bottles, and a little tobacco, which with he departed, wishing us a pleasant passage, and wishing to be reported to any ships as being prepared to supply them with hogs. A more dangerous, suspicious, or vile character in appearance I think I never saw; he confessed that he had left his own country for smuggling, and intended to leave his bones on the island. (Godby 1845:507)[2]

The bottles were probably for liquor. One of Gorman's projects on Ngatik was to set up a still (Hezel 1978:130).

The population during these first postmassacre years amounted to a few dozen: European and American men, Pohnpei men and women (perhaps mostly from Madolenihmw, where Hart had contacts), and Sapwuahfik women and children. Visiting ships identified the Westerners, sometimes by name, making them appear in the historical record as "sole proprietors" of the island and its people (Captain Pease's words on his 1846 visit to Ngatik in the whaleship *Chandler Price* [in Ward 1967:148]). Oral traditions identify several Islander men as figures of capacity and influence in the tiny community. Yet the European/American men might well have monopolized weapons and alcohol at first; by managing interaction with visiting ships, they controlled trade. They appear in written records because they are Westerners, but they appear as important figures in Ngatik's past because being Westerners gave them certain strategic advantages on the repopulated island.

Most of the Europeans and Americans were not permanent settlers. Trying to track their comings and goings through documents and oral accounts is a frustrating business. They were on the move by choice and out of fear of the law and personal enemies; they changed their names as often as they changed their residence. Castaways intermittently drifted ashore, whaleships often stopped at Ngatik during the season, November through April, and other ships stopped less predictably. Ships' captains had the habit of putting undesirable crew members ashore at the next port of call; they would just as casually pick up additional hands. To give a few examples: In 1840 or 1841, the brig *Friend* put a white man named John Rodwright ashore on Ngatik; in March 1844 the whaleship *William & Henry* shipped an unnamed man aboard at Ngatik; and in December of 1844 HMS *Vestal* was approached by three "natives" who wanted to be recruited (one wonders if they were Pohnpei men suffering under Paddy Gorman). In the early 1850s, castaways of the *Genii*, out of Sydney, had their boat stolen when they touched at Ngatik and had to stay until the next shipwreck rescued them. That was the *Sarah Mooers*, which went on the reef in December of 1852, stranding fifty-two passengers and crew (including ten women) for four months until they were picked up by passing whalers. Even after that, one passenger and two crewmen decided to stay on Ngatik rather than be rescued.

Many of the Westerners on Ngatik during these years ended

as murder victims. Paddy Gorman's fate is undocumented, though oral history says he was punished by a ship captain for exploiting the Islanders and later left Ngatik on a passing ship. George Williams and a man named Steward, who were working with Gorman, went to Pohnpei a few years later and tried to entice the wives of two New Zealand men to return to Ngatik with them. They were killed by the New Zealanders, and John MacVie was killed on Ngatik in a conflict over their property. An oral tradition describes the murder of George May, called "Little George," as he bathed; Cheyne confirms his death on Ngatik in 1853.[3]

European and American men appear in oral history as perpetrators or victims of violence, with the exception of a few who established lasting relationships with Islander women, so becoming ancestors of the modern population. Among these were an African American, William Brown, who in oral tradition fired the first shot of the massacre, then lived on Ngatik long enough to father or securely adopt a daughter, whose mother was a massacre survivor. (This may be the same black American whom Godby reported on Ngatik in 1841, who had been "all his life" in the English service and had been cook of a vessel [Godby 1845].) Other Western ancestors of the modern population were the above-mentioned Rodwright (perhaps the "Jack Roneid" of oral genealogies), an Englishman who fathered children by two Gilbertese women; "Mister Else [Ellis?]," a New Jersey carpenter whose Pohnpei wife Meram established the Dipwinmen pwetp-wet clan on Ngatik through their ten children; and the Scot James Frazer, who had only one child by his wife (a massacre survivor) but spent the last half of his life, some forty years, on Ngatik. Frazer introduced Christianity and literacy to the island's children.

It is easier to know something about the foreign men than about the women and children they lived with. Genealogies indicate ten or so aboriginal women and girls, survivors who remained on Ngatik. Few children were born in these early years—or, if born, few survived. This suggests the women's reluctance to commit themselves to life, or to these new men. Population estimates by European visitors do not distinguish aboriginal and immigrant women; for example, in 1844 Cheyne reports four "Englishmen" and twenty Pohnpeians on the only inhabited islet (Cheyne 1852:94–123). On the *Chandler Price's* 1846 visit, Captain Pease counted four "white men," a few women, and no children over the age of twelve. Visitors during this decade report the use of Pohnpeian and English on the island; it appears that the aboriginal language was not reestablished in families or groups. This may have been when English pidgin—which continues to be a speech form for men, at least—began.

At least one Pohnpei couple remained intact in the resettlement, but hardly any other Pohnpei men appear in genealogies of this early period. An exception is Ownahngi or Onani, who married an aboriginal woman, had three children, and plays a leading role in several oral traditions. Few of the Pohnpeians brought to Ngatik by Hart and Gorman to work appear in genealogies of the modern population, suggesting that they did not remain on Ngatik or did not bear or father children. As we shall see, Gilbertese and Mortlockese later added to the population mix, and a second wave of immigration by Pohnpei men established a Pohnpei demographic majority. Though Westerners continued to drift in and out, after the earliest postmassacre period they do not play leading roles in the drama of Ngatik's history.

THE RESTORATION OF ORDER

In the decades after resettlement, Ngatik seemed to outside observers to be a trading establishment. Westerners saw the depopulated atoll as an opportunity for profit and for the autonomy that kept petty traders and beachcombers moving at the margins of European imperial power. Gorman and his contemporaries sought to exploit the lagoon's tortoiseshell and bêche-de-mer. Then, from the 1840s to the early 1860s, Ngatik became a provisioning stop supplying wood and water, pigs, coconuts, yams, and fowl to whalers and traders. Later, following shifts in the international economy of the Pacific, copra production changed the face of the island.

A series of resident European and American men controlled the island's trade for many years while surviving aboriginal people and a growing number of immigrants contributed their labor to it. Other foreign entrepreneurs followed Hart's lead in importing Pohnpei people individually as workers and as wives. Shipwrecks and drifted canoes added temporarily or permanently to Ngatik's population.

By the mid-1840s efforts had settled into supplying whaling and trading ships. In 1839 Blake had called the hogs there "extraordinary fine" and acquired them by trading tobacco and "slop" clothing. Another visitor that year stated that there were plenty of pigs, coconuts, and yams to be had, making Ngatik "an eligible place to touch at" in the Carolines, though, because anchorage was not good, a ship's stay was limited (from the *Frances Charlotte's* visit, in Ward 1967:145). A sailing ship could not easily twist through the lagoon channel, so the oceanside of Ngatik Islet became its trading center. A ship would send a boat ashore, or wait for canoes or a boat to come off, staying only a few hours or overnight. Whalers would take boatloads of coconuts, hogs, yams, fowl, wood, and water—and in 1852 the *William Hamilton* took off a dog and four pups.

The atoll became established as a minor supply post for European ships, like Mokil and Pingelap, useful when Pohnpei was overcrowded or short of food, or when Ngatik was handier to a ship's route. The Pacific network of commercial maritime news quickly passed the word on good and bad supply spots—"bad" meaning in part those with a reputation for violence. During the 1840s and 1850s, Ngatik hosted a steady stream of customers. Whalers were the bulk of the business, because they often stayed out of their home port for years at a time; a few warships, island traders, and merchantmen on their way to Manila or Hong Kong also stopped.

The four Westerners who in 1846 appeared to Captain Pease to be "sole proprietors" of the island and of the women and children on it were assiduous entrepreneurs raising hogs for the trade. Indeed, they must have kept busy; ships took on as many as twenty hogs and twelve hundred coconuts at a time. There are records of twenty-three ships visiting the atoll between 1842 and 1852—and there were probably many more whose records have not survived. In season, whalers came frequently; one January day in 1848 saw three whaleships at Ngatik. After such a run on supplies, the next would-be buyer had to leave disappointed. The only trade goods mentioned in the ships' logs are cloth and tobacco. No doubt people on Ngatik also received other common Pacific trade goods—foreign food, knives and tools, contraband. Perhaps log keepers thought it unwise to record disbursements of liquor, muskets, and ammunition. There was constant agitation "at home," encouraged by missionaries and some naval and trading men, to control the distribution of firearms and alcohol throughout the islands. It was impossible, of course, to constrain trade on islands not under effective European control.[4]

By the mid-1850s, Ngatik's inhabitants were profiting from someone's skill to initiate the atoll's long-standing reputation for excellent shipbuilding. Oral tradition identifies a Pohnpeian and an American immigrant as carpenters; perhaps one or both oversaw production of a small schooner built at Ngatik, seen in 1855 in a Pohnpei harbor.[5] Oral tradition states that they also built whaleboats, steaming and bending breadfruit wood to produce long, broad boats that could be rowed or sailed.

Approximately fifty people lived on Ngatik in the mid-1850s, a small colony producing food for consumption and export, speaking English and Pohnpeian, many of the adults probably still potential transients. The log of the *Martha*'s 1855 visit speaks of a "village" on the oceanside shore of the main islet, where ships' boats would come to trade. There people lived in elevated houses of stone and lime mortar (described in the log of the *St. George*'s 1852 visit). Perhaps most significant as a symbol of social order and promise for the future, it was sometime in the late 1840s or early 1850s that a formal political order was established, with the three surviving aboriginal boys taking on traditional Pohnpei titles.

I have found no documentary sources to indicate how these titles were assigned, though oral traditions agree they were imposed from outside by an American or British "captain." An

1852 visitor mentions Ngatik's "future king," a boy of about eight years old, "half white" (not so, according to oral history) and wearing European dress (Munger 1967 [1852]:50). It is hard to know why a whaler or trader would take it upon himself to establish a line of Islander leadership, but there is no evidence that the commanders of the only three warships to visit Ngatik took any such action. One oral account states that a white man assigned the titles to "take care of" the Islanders after certain other whites had cheated them (probably a reference to Gorman or Lass, see below). Although his identity is lost, the story of how this official assigned the titles is well remembered. I here consolidate several oral accounts to provide a summary:

> When the Captain asked who was nahnmwarki of Ngatik, the people replied, "No one." He insisted that a "true" (that is, aboriginal) Ngatik man be nahnmwarki, not an outsider, whether European, Pohnpeian, or other Islander. There were only three surviving aboriginal males: Noah (then about seventeen years old), Pakieh (about thirteen years old), and Aisikaya (about eight years old).
>
> The Captain told the oldest boy to be nahnmwarki, but he said he couldn't—he didn't know how or what to do. So the white man wrote three titles (using the highest Pohnpei titles, nahnmwarki, wasahi, dauk) on three pieces of paper. (One version has him writing "number one," "number two," "number three.") When the papers were ready, the captain lifted them up and prayed to God to choose and give him the power to say who would be nahnmwarki. The boys then picked their titles, literally, out of his hat. The oldest boy chose first. Thus, Noah became Wasahi, Pakieh Dauk, and Aisikaya, the youngest, became Nahnmwarki.[6]

Thus Aisikaya became the first leader after the massacre. His figure dominates the atoll's history until his natural death about 1911. He guided its mixed population through internal conflicts, the challenge of missionary teachings, and confrontations with the German colonial administration. His memory is still green on the island. Stories of his wisdom and courage are told, the site of his house is known, and old men and women recall having seen him—a huge, blind, powerful figure—when they were children.

The provisioning-trade boom dropped off sharply in the 1860s. Whaling collapsed under the triple pressure of the growing scarcity of whales, increasing use of kerosene, and the Civil War in the United States, which kept many American traders at home. Ngatik's population began to grow more quickly as a number of stable marriages began to produce children. At some point, the "four white men" last appearing in a ship's log in 1846 lost control of the island trade. After the 1850s only one white man, James Frazer, remained, doing a small trade in coconut oil and tortoiseshell, sharing Ngatik with a few dozen Islanders. As the population grew, they cultivated Ngatik Islet, keeping the aboriginal taro gardens in the center of the islet, planting two sorts of breadfruit in the forest area and coconut palms along the beach. Ngatik had few visitors between 1855 and the 1870s; it was relatively isolated from trade and free of the demands of tyrannous foreigners—with one significant exception.

There was one final attempt to establish a profitable private plantation on Ngatik, made by a Captain Lass. Lass arrived with a boatload of Pohnpeians and a plan to set them to work extracting coconut oil on a commercial scale. This alternative to whale oil became newly profitable as whales grew scarce but before kerosene took over the market. It would be an exaggeration to call the event a repeat of 1837, but oral traditions describe Lass's visit as an attack on Ngatik with the intention of making a profit, and the similarities are too poignant to ignore. There is little about Lass in written sources—only that he ran a brig, the *Wailua,* on whaling and trading cruises out of Honolulu. The *Wailua* operated in Micronesia in the 1860s and was reported at Pohnpei April 2, 1862.[7]

Oral accounts of Lass's visit indicate that he brought Pohnpei men to Ngatik, intending to establish a commercial coconut-oil enterprise there and willing to fight to do so. The Islanders were by this time armed with guns. They had also, as one narrator said, "learned, and didn't fight." Perhaps for this reason there was no pitched battle, though there was violence. As one man told the story,

> when Captain Lass came, [the three boys, Noah, Pakieh, and Aisikaya] had become men. They were adults. And there were boys with them. They were about to have a battle. Captain Lass brought his soldiers from Pohnpei . . . He came and put them ashore; they were no longer going to do battle. They only killed one woman. They no longer warred, and he set them down here, put the Pohnpei men ashore, for he was going to go away and return.

Lass, however, abandoned whatever conquistador plans he may have had and never returned. His impact on Ngatik was significant nonetheless, because after he set his "soldiers" ashore, "they got married. They just stayed here and became *mehn sahpwet*, 'people of this land.' They got married and all died here, they never went back to Pohnpei. It is said there were many; it is not clear how many people, but it was many." It was enough to redress the sexual imbalance among adults, and the late 1860s and 1870s saw a surge in population as a number of couples began families of seven to ten children who grew to maturity. These decades also saw Ngatik shift from a trading post controlled or mediated by foreigners to a mixed population in control of its own resources.

POPULATION COMPOSITION AND GROWTH

It was a diverse group that went into the foundation of the new culture. In 1855 James Frazer sent a note to American missionaries on Pohnpei. He gave a census of Ngatik, said that he was teaching the children literacy, English, and Christianity, and asked for help. The missionaries, facing their own challenges, were in no position to do more than send school supplies and Bibles. Frazer's census is a benchmark from which to measure the growth of the population. It indicates a community integrated by marriages and starting to rely on the birth of children, rather than on immigration, for expansion.[8]

Frazer listed Ngatik's 1855 population as two white men, seven Gilbert Islands women, a man and a woman from Pohnpei, four Ngatik men, fifteen Ngatik women, and eight children, of whom a boy and a girl are "half white." Let us pause to consider this diversity and what it suggests about the community.

Pohnpei women had accompanied some foreign beachcombers to Ngatik after the massacre. Gorman and Hart also brought men and couples from Pohnpei to work on the atoll. Some of them literally escaped Gorman's tyranny; later, others probably moved to and from the atoll before a few began to establish families there. Pohnpei immigrants might have been encouraged to leave for Ngatik by the growing hard times in areas of Pohnpei, climaxing in 1854 with a devastating smallpox epidemic that left Pohnpei in mourning and undergoing severe social stress. Some were drawn by personal ties with foreign traders and beachcombers and the usefulness of these ties for access to imported goods.

Aboriginal women survivors established affiliations with Pohnpeian, Gilbertese, British, or American men. The Westerners who stayed on Ngatik immediately after the massacre fostered surviving children. James Hall told Blake they "took each of them four or five children under their care, whose Mothers had destroyed themselves, and whose fathers had been killed." The Westerners were not the only ones with generous impulses; oral tradition credits the Pohnpei man Ownahngi with fostering children. By 1855 distinctions between Pohnpeian and aboriginal had been sufficiently erased for Frazer to include adult aboriginal women, immigrant Pohnpei women, and older daughters of both to reach the number of fifteen women who "originated on the island."

In addition to early and ongoing Pohnpei immigration, there were two other significant arrivals in the first postmassacre decades. These are Mortlock Islanders from the west, who came as castaways on two separate occasions, and Gilbert Islanders from the east. As the presence of Gilbertese women in 1855 and

the absence of Mortlockese in genealogies indicates, the out-
comes of the two immigrations were very different. Information
about the arrival and fate of the two groups comes only from
oral accounts. Documents give no evidence of the origin of the
seven Gilbertese women listed by Frazer. Perhaps they were
castaways. There is a record of an 1838 drift voyage of one
woman from Ebon (in the Marshall Islands) to Ngatik; three men
with her died during the voyage of twenty-six or twenty-seven
days (Riesenberg 1965). Yet it is odd that Frazer lists no
Gilbertese men, several of whom appear dramatically in oral tradition. One knowledgeable informant specified that at least
some of the Gilbert Islanders came to Ngatik on a foreign ship.

Oral history indicates a period before the mid-1850s in which
the island operated not as a single social unit but as three distinct groups: British and Americans and their Islander wives and
children, who lived oceanside (oral traditions speak of "American town"); an alliance of aboriginal survivors, immigrant Pohnpeians, and several Gilbertese, living in another area; and a
group of Mortlockese who drifted ashore and established a separate community. This description makes the situation seem
more organized than it probably was. Oral traditions about this
period are accounts of mutual mistrust, treachery, and violence,
culminating in the massacre of the entire Mortlockese community by the aboriginal-Pohnpeian-Gilbertese alliance.

The outline of the story is that the Pohnpei man Ownahngi—an advisor to Aisikaya who appears in several oral traditions
about this era—suggested that they join with Mortlockese in
eliminating the American/European settlement. Other of
Aisikaya's followers opposed his advice, saying the Mortlockese
were in the majority and, if the threat of the well-armed foreigners was eliminated, would take over the entire island. With
Aisikaya's permission, and under the direction of a skilled
Gilbertese fighter, the Mortlockese were tricked and all of them
killed instead. There are also accounts of the later arrival of another group of Mortlockese, again a result of canoes drifting
ashore, this time at the islet of Wataluhk. These men were also
killed by trickery, and today the only trace of their arrival at

Ngatik is the dramatic tale of the sole survivor, the boy Ewo. Ewo, repeatedly identified in oral history as strikingly brave, killed the Englishman "Roneid" and was himself later killed in a courageous attempt to avenge the massacre of his kin.

Among the immigrant groups, only the Mortlockese were victims of wholesale murder—perhaps because they arrived as castaways, perhaps because they were feared for their numbers and their skill in the Carolinian martial art *bwang* (Lessa and Velez-I. 1978), perhaps because of the timing of their arrival and their relationship with the other immigrants. No Mortlockese appear in massacre-era genealogies of the modern Sapwuahfik population, though they were included as a group when informants listed the variety of peoples who resettled Ngatik.[9] In contrast, several Gilbertese men and women—perhaps because they drifted ashore in tiny groups, or came allied with Pohnpeians, or came aboard European ships—became part of the reproductive population and the folklore of ancestors.

The population increase of the late 1860s and 1870s is confirmed by the log of the 1872 visit of HMS *Blanche,* which provides an estimate of one hundred residents, including sixty children and one white man (who did a small trade in coconut oil, copra, and tortoiseshell). In 1874 a Christian mission ship made a first visit to Ngatik, "simply to `knock' to see if the people were ready for a teacher. We had none for them" (ABCFM: Doane to Clarke, 29 January 1874). Reverend Edward T. Doane estimated a population of seventy-five to one hundred, with "numerous" children, like Pohnpeians in stature and language but light in complexion. They grew breadfruit, coconut, sugarcane, bananas, and onions. The visiting Americans described religious practice on the atoll:

> A singular piece of masonry may seem a sacred pile. The base was some 12 feet square and raised, some five solidly laid with rude steps for ascending [*sic*]. Then on this another square of less dimension, some five feet square was laid, this again was crowned by a large square stone, while this was capped with one standing erect with a crown piece of concave coral stone. This structure is sacred. Prayers and worship are here made to

the island divinity, and the hill is free to anyone to ascend and offer his devotions. (Doane, letter in the *Friend* 23, no. 6 [1874]:42)

The marriages producing the first generation of new Ngatik people are all interethnic, with no perceivable pattern to the affiliations. Of the fourteen known earliest marriages, all but one had an immigrant partner. The exception is Aisikaya himself, who married a woman born on the atoll, the child of a Gilbert Islands man and a Pohnpei woman.[10]

Early ancestors of modern Sapwuahfik, then, are British and American men, Ngatik women and children, Pohnpei men and women, and Gilbert Islands men and women. No group clung to endogamy. Within a generation, they merged into a new Ngatik population, and narrators of oral accounts in 1980 spoke of this historical population as *mehn Ngatik.*

LAND DIVISION

Although oral traditions describe the population in earlier years as living in small nucleated villages according to origin, Ngatik began to operate as a single social system after the murder of the Mortlockese, after the death or disappearance of most of the Westerners, and as the three titleholding boys grew to manhood. The land of Ngatik Islet was apportioned for private ownership and the population organized into three mutual-assistance groups. Before the islet was divided among owners who took their families to live in the evenly scattered pattern visible today, people lived together in a settlement centered on the home of Aisikaya, the Nahnmwarki.

Although evidence is inadequate to date the event precisely, Aisikaya shared out the land of Ngatik Islet after the massacre of the Mortlockese and before 1890. The land division may seem to demonstrate Aisikaya's power as nahnmwarki, but at least one oral account suggests that there was some pressure on him from British or American residents to take this step. Information about these events comes only from oral history.

On other Eastern Caroline Islands—Pohnpei being the most relevant example—all land "belonged" to the nahnmwarki until in 1908 the German colonial government insisted on individual deeds to land and attempted to impose patrilineal inheritance of property. On Ngatik the early land apportionment occurred only on the largest islet, where the main taro gardens were and where people for the most part lived. Authority over the atoll's other islets was divided among the three highest titleholders, each heading a mutual-assistance group sharing resources of an islet or islets.[11] The mutual-assistance groups used the islets cooperatively for gardening, visiting, pig raising, and, later, for coconut palm plantings. (This tripartite division of the population is confirmed in a 1900 colonial report.) Not until about 1912 was the smaller islets' land apportioned to individuals.

Aisikaya divided the land of Ngatik Islet informally. One informant said he just indicated who owned each piece of land. Some accounts say that Aisikaya chose to whom he gave land; others, that it was divided equally among all the families. Another version is that it was apportioned according to how much work each did and how much land he could use. All agree that in the first division, only a few men (the versions range from five to nine individuals) owned all the land of Ngatik, so the first method of apportionment seems more likely—particularly as it is said that Aisikaya's gifts of land to two men (Ownahngi and Frazer) were directly linked to their services. Ownahngi was rewarded for helping Aisikaya deal with the Mortlockese plan to kill the Westerners, as well as (according to a man who now owns part of that original land grant) because Aisikaya "felt sorry for" him because he was a foreigner. Frazer was given land because of his good advice and guidance and for his help in educating the children. One man described Aisikaya's presentation of land to the foreigners as a pact: "Aisikaya said to them, if they would become real Ngatik people [*uhdahn mehn Ngatik*], then he would permit them to join in getting land, to produce their own food."

Most informants specified that their understanding of the history was that land was divided equally among the men who participated in the initial apportionment. One version describes the equality as intentional, with scattered pieces assigned to compensate for variable land quality; another has the land division as a lottery, with people pulling numbers in a random assignment of property. One informant, however, said all shares, except those of the Westerners, were equal. Westerners measured out the land and set up the boundary lines, dishonestly acquiring bigger pieces, with the result that their children inherited an advantage.[12] Land rights are often contested today, making accounts of initial landownership susceptible to alteration according to current issues.

The division of land into private ownership did not mean that it became fee-simple land. In tracing the history of land parcels, it is clear that most land was used jointly by a family. At the death of the nominal owner, it was divided, usually equally, among male and female, biological and adopted children. Land in the past, as now, was given as gifts, or, occasionally, purchased, though never by a foreigner who lived off the island. The atoll's land remains a precious resource for the community.

CHAPTER FOUR

Conversion and the Colonial Era

W HEN LOCAL PEOPLE summarize the atoll's past, they highlight the massacre and the establishment of Christianity as the two key historical events. Protestant missionary efforts in the Eastern Caroline Islands began in 1852 with the arrival of three American and two Hawaiian couples on Pohnpei and Kosrae, the Americans under the direction of the American Board of Commissioners for Foreign Missions (ABCFM) and the Hawaiians supported by the Hawaiian Evangelical Association. Like their counterparts in missionary organizations throughout the Pacific, these workers felt that their task was as much to civilize the Micronesians as to Christianize them—and that, in fact, the one was necessary preparation for the other. An early and primary interest of Protestant missionaries to Micronesia was to dismantle much of aboriginal society so that a Christian society could be established in its place.

Although devoting most of their time to Pohnpei and Kosrae,

the missionaries also made efforts to evangelize nearby atolls by visiting them, sending teachers from Pohnpei to establish schools and churches, and bringing outer islanders to Pohnpei and Kosrae for training in mission schools. The first three decades of missionary endeavor resulted in a patchwork of Christian, non-Christian, and anti-Christian areas on Pohnpei. Churches were also formally established on Mokil (in 1872) and Pingelap (1879) after years of intermittent missionary effort on these atolls southeast of Pohnpei. Ngatik did not receive a mission teacher until 1889; missionary effort was instead directed westward to the Central Carolines, with the Americans by the early 1880s expressing a desire to proceed quickly to Yap.[1]

It is curious that Ngatik received so little attention in the early period of Protestant expansion, because the American missionaries on Pohnpei were aware of the peculiar conditions on the atoll as early as 1855, the year James Frazer sent them a letter including "commendable" specimens of the writing of the island boys, whom he had been teaching for several years. The Americans sent him school supplies and Bibles, but no promise of a teacher. During the brief 1874 visit of the mission ship, the Americans offered to take some children to be schooled on Pohnpei, "but parents could hardly afford that, 'twas too far, and they had not mastered their distrust of the Missionary" (*Friend* 23, no. 6 [1874]:42). Despite this, some indicated a willingness to welcome a missionary teacher.

Though James Frazer, and perhaps others, had already introduced Christianity to Ngatik, formal missionary activity did not begin until the 1889 appointment of a Pohnpei teaching couple (*Missionary Herald* 85, no. 5 [1889]:190). As Christianity began to reshape the life of Ngatik's people, a new secular power was entering their lives.

The Spanish Era

Spain maintained itself as the reigning colonial power in the Caroline Islands from 1886 to 1899. The Spanish established a presence in Pohnpei in 1887 but did not attempt to extend their control to the outlying islands. Colonial tensions escalated to a Pohnpeian attack on the Spanish in 1887, forcing foreign traders to flee to Ngatik and Pingelap (Hanlon 1988:161, citing Westwood 1905:149). Other foreign men continued to make Sapwuahfik their temporary or permanent home, for good or ill. "Ocean Island Jack," a renegade involved with escaped Australian convicts and the 1852 massacre of the crew of the bark *Inga* died on Ngatik in 1881 or 1882; nine men from the British ship *Bothwell Castle,* out of New South Wales, spent nearly a year on Ngatik after a shipwreck on Christmas Eve 1884. The influence of these transients was diluted, though, by the natural increase of the atoll's population, which was nearing two hundred by 1890.

Ngatik's agricultural fertility was worked skillfully to produce more than adequate subsistence for the community, which traded vegetable foods, fish, pigs, and fowl with the remnants of the Pacific whaling fleet. In 1880 the *Helen Mar* took on eleven hundred pounds of pork, a dozen fowl, and eight bunches of bananas. The second mate of the *Palmetto,* visiting in 1881, states that "the natives speak quite good English"—perhaps indicating Aisikaya's skill, as the "king" paid a visit to the ship. But the economy, as well as the political life, of the Caroline Islands was being drawn into the developing order of global colonial economies. German trading firms had reached Pohnpei in the mid-1870s, and by 1880 four trading companies operated on the high island (Hanlon 1988:133–34). By 1887 Ngatik—like ten other islands in the Carolines—hosted a trading station of the Jaluit Company of Germany (U.S. Navy 1944). The Islanders probably dealt with other traders, German and Japanese, independents and representatives of the growing trade firms stimulated by European colonial expansion. The new trade centered not on Chinese but on Japanese and European markets. Its currency was not whale oil, bêche-de-mer, and turtleshell but, increasingly, copra.[2]

On Pohnpei, official Spanish encouragement of Catholicism intersected local political rivalries. Though Protestants were the earliest missionaries on Ngatik, Catholic mission work in the Caroline Islands had actually begun in the first decades of the 1700s with failed attempts to reach the Western Carolines from Spanish colonial outposts in the Marianas. Another unsuccessful early attempt was the 1837 visit of Father Désiré Maigret to Pohnpei. Effective Catholic missions were established in the Eastern Carolines in 1887, when five Capuchin missionaries arrived on Pohnpei (Hezel 1970).[3] Catholic missionary work was successful enough to make religious affiliation an important factor in turn of the century Pohnpei politics, culminating in the Sokehs Rebellion of 1910–11. Part of the local politics of the rebellion involved the religious affiliations of Pohnpei's chiefdoms. Sectarian conflicts, U.S.-Spanish antagonism, and Pohnpei military action against the Spanish resulted in the expulsion of the American Protestant missionaries from Pohnpei in 1890. They moved their school to Mokil and remained active in church work on Kosrae and the Eastern Caroline atolls.

Ngatik's first experience with intensive mission teaching came in 1889, when John Francis, a Pohnpei graduate of the missionary training school, and his wife (not named in mission records) were assigned to begin work there. The American missionary who accompanied the couple on their first trip to Ngatik describes the people as "well-dressed" and comments that they asked for gin and tobacco. The *Morning Star*'s captain thought their houses were "cleaner and better than any in Micronesia," they gave John Francis a "warm reception," and they appeared ready to give up their former religious practices, which missionary Frank E. Rand calls "quite different from that of any other island in Micronesia." Rand also provides a bit more information about postmassacre religious activities:

> The idol they worship is a stone placed on an altar, about fifteen feet high. This altar, which was built fifty or sixty years ago, under the direction of a woman who drifted there from the Gilbert Islands, consists of three platforms of solid masonry. The lower platform is 20 feet square and $5\frac{1}{2}$ feet high; the next one is 8 feet square and $4\frac{1}{2}$ feet high, and the upper one 4 feet

square and 3 feet high. The idol on this altar is a stone somewhat the shape of a man's body; it has a small round stone for
the head with a piece of coral the shape of a hat on the top. The
woman who planned the building of this altar was the priestess
for many years. At her death her son became priest. He seemed
very glad when he found I had brought them a teacher, "for
now," he said, "we shall learn how to read and write." (Rand
1889:262)[4]

After the arrival of John Francis and his wife, Ngatik became a
regular stop for the mission ship, which delivered supplies for
the teacher and visits from American mission workers. Frazer's
literacy efforts might have paid off in the use people made of the
sacred and secular literature sent to the atoll. One annual ship-
ment consisted of twelve geographies, twelve prayerbooks, fifty
copies of the Book of Samuel in Pohnpeian, twenty-five "question books," and twelve slates and pencils.

At year's end 1889, John Francis was working with 110
Christian adherents and an average congregation of 125, out of a
total population of 150. There was a school with 50 scholars, 44
actual church members (but no church building yet), and a re-
spectable contribution figure for the support of the pastor and
school supplies. The practice of Protestant missions in this area
was to have the local community house and feed the pastor's
family, and have the missionaries provide them a complete set
of clothes each year. Although this demand for local support produced hardships and tension in some places, Ngatik was never
castigated in mission records for being tightfisted. Following a
standard pattern of Protestant missionary activity, John Francis
was expected to school children and adults in the Pohnpei language, arithmetic, Christian moral teachings, and Bible study.
The mission worker's wife was to teach girls and women what
she had learned at mission school about American-style house-
keeping, needlework, and Christian family life.

When Sapwuahfik people today describe the advent of Christianity to their island, they agree that people were at first un-
willing to let foreigners remove their children to Pohnpei for

schooling. Later, however, Aisikaya is said to have directly requested mission teachers and assisted in the complete discarding of pagan religious practices, including magic. What was left of aboriginal religion fell rapidly into disuse, and the population of Ngatik added Western religion to the language, clothing, and housing customs they had already adopted. The population's especial familiarity with foreign ways may have smoothed the path for the adoption of additional Euro-American practices and concepts.

Conversion proceeded rapidly; Ngatik's church was formally established on February 13, 1890, within a year of Francis' arrival. Amid ceremony, the veteran missionary E. T. Doane examined candidates for membership, found himself satisfied, ordained two deacons, and ordained John Francis to celebrate the Lord's Supper (though not to receive members into the church).

The firm establishment of the atoll's political structure is evidenced by the list of founding members of the Ngatik Protestant church, which gives titles and names of the seventy-one Islanders who became Christians at this first formal opportunity. The list is headed by "Isipau Aisikaia" and his wife "Nahnalek Askina" (*nahnalek* is the wifely cognate title for nahnmwarki).[5] Thirty-two male and twenty-four female titleholders are listed, most as married couples. The list cannot reveal any of the dimensions of social or political behavior consequent to this title structure, but it is a striking indication of how detailed was the borrowing of Pohnpei forms.

The development of the Ngatik church was monitored by visits of the missionary ship *Morning Star.* On the *Morning Star*'s February 1890 visit—during which the church was officially formed—the ship's log claims it to be the first vessel ever inside the lagoon at Ngatik. Whether it was or not, it was to find that tricky channel a familiar one, as a succession of *Morning Stars* visited Ngatik once or twice a year until 1897, and irregularly after that. These one- or two-day visits of the mission ship brought mission personnel, visitors, travelers, supplies, trade goods, and news.

By 1892, of an estimated total population near two hundred,

all but six adults were Christians. Mission records for 1893 include the first mention of Ngatik students at the mission training school on Pohnpei. One of these is Edgar, who later took over the local church when John Francis and his wife returned to Pohnpei. (Edgar and his wife Jule, or Julia, appear near the bottom of the 1890 list of founding members of the church; their names are not accompanied by titles.) After the whaling trade ended, missionary letters are the sole source of written information about Ngatik in the last decades of the nineteenth century. These are frustratingly short of descriptive material, even when mission workers spent several days or even weeks on the atoll. Reports of the *Morning Star*'s visits in the 1890s indicate a population speaking both Pohnpeian and English, building wooden houses and whaleboats that drew praise from the visitors, exporting a good amount of copra, raising chickens and ducks and "native food." They indicate rapid establishment of a church, no protracted fights with "heathen" customs such as are described for islands evangelized earlier, "bright, intelligent" people, and substantial European-style buildings. Nearly all adults were Christians, who regularly contributed enough Spanish currency to support John Francis and his wife. They worshiped in a whitewashed church, learned and sang hymns with enthusiasm, occasionally backslid into using tobacco or desiring to revive "heathen dances," and let the "idol" that had been a focus of postmassacre worship go off on a *Morning Star* trip to a Honolulu museum. In 1897 missionary Francis Price spoke with an old white man from New York who said he had lived on the island for forty years. This remnant of an earlier era saw his two granddaughters baptized.

The people of Ngatik seem to have welcomed the Pohnpeian teachers and readily formed a church. Hints of difficulty come only from scattered comments in the mission record, as when John Francis's assignment is termed "a hard place" (*Missionary Herald* 85, no. 5 [1889]:190), with no reason given. The 1890 Annual Report of the Hawaiian Mission Children's Society (p. 9) notes "the marvellous change at Ngatik where after repeatedly refusing to receive a teacher, the people have now accepted the gospel, and are turning to the Lord with almost one heart." Speaking in Honolulu in 1894, Mrs. Frank E. (Carrie) Rand (a member of the Pohnpei mission station) said, "Ngatik people had until recently been hostile to Christianity, but now were warmly friendly" (*Friend* 52, no. 4 [1894]:25). These comments are phrased in ways typical of the missionary publicity of the period and are more of a formula for describing the progress of the work than a history of conversion on a particular island. In fact, no Protestant teachers were available for Ngatik prior to 1889, and no effort had been made to establish a church there.

Despite a lapse in 1893, when the people are described as "somewhat lukewarm" after a six-month absence by John Francis and his wife (*Friend* 52, no. 1 [1894]:5), mission teacher Mary Logan describes an active and Westernized Christian community in 1898:

> The teacher's neat little cottage was swept and garnished, the people had donned their best, the women wearing white for the most part, and dressing their hair in western style. . . . Many of them can speak English, so they crowded into the teacher's house, sang hymns, and entertained us in right good order. There are about 250 people on the island. They have an abundance of food, export a large amount of copra, and hence are well-to-do. There are many wooden houses . . . The church building has walls of plaster and reeds, has seats of foreign style, though home-made, rude but comfortable, and it is large enough for the people. (*Missionary Herald* 94, no. 7 [1898]:292)

Ngatik's prosperity suffered with a tidal wave that hit in 1897 and an eight-day "flood" in November 1898. The church, the gardens, and twenty-seven houses were destroyed, and the effects were noted by visitors for years afterward. A 1900 report states that the flood completely destroyed local subsistence and "they urgently need[ed] external help in order to feed everybody," estimating that it would be ten years before they regained independence (Hahl 1900; also Hassert 1903). Natural disaster was followed by the first of several changes in colonial rule.

The German Era

Germany purchased the Caroline and Marshall islands from Spain in 1899, incorporating their administration into the German New Guinea protectorate. The brunt of the effort of German authorities to build an economically productive colony was felt in administrative centers such as Pohnpei, where land tenure and customary social life were significantly altered as colonial officials began a program of land reform and modifications in the role of high titleholders. Working through indirect rule, Pohnpei Island was organized as a group of municipalities, each under its nahnmwarki and all controlled by the central German authority in Kolonia. The local situation was enormously complex and charged with potential for violence. The political goals of Pohnpeians, continuing Protestant-Catholic tensions, conflict over colonial policies, and the actions of German and Pohnpeian leaders culminated in the armed opposition of the people of Sokehs in the northwest of Pohnpei—the Sokehs Rebellion. This was suppressed by a German invasion, and ended with the execution of the Sokehs leaders and the exile of their followers. The colonial government then imposed dramatic changes on the rest of Pohnpei: redefinition and restriction of nahnmwarki's rights over goods and labor, and comprehensive land reforms including freehold and patrilineal inheritance.[6]

As during the Spanish era, outer islands were much less affected by colonial policy, though officials made regular efforts to extend some aspects of administration beyond Pohnpei, especially establishing a steady supply of trade goods and encouraging copra production. On Ngatik the early years of German rule were characterized by increasing access to trade opportunities, growing efforts to plant and harvest copra, and the imposition of taxes—all indicating the primarily economic significance of German colonialism. Several men went from the atoll to Nauru to work at digging phosphate. At least three German men—perhaps traders—became part of Ngatik families, fathering children whose descendants still carry their names and memories.

One of these men's wives lived in the home and cared for the children of Governor Boeder, who was killed in the Sokehs Rebellion.

The German plan was to see copra become a profitable export. An ordinance required adult men to plant an annual quota of coconut palms. It is not clear whether this was enforced on the seldom-visited outer islands, but older Sapwuahfik people recall a significant increase in copra production under German rule. Warehouses were filled with the dried coconut, and production was stimulated by the need for cash to pay taxes and buy increasingly available consumer goods. One man recalled that there were two small stores on Ngatik during the German era, owned by local men. Japanese petty traders, who had operated in the area for decades, were banned by German order from 1901 to 1908, but then resumed operations. Large German firms increased trade links with outer islands, especially in eastern Micronesia, but the continuing success of Japanese traders was one reason for Japan's interest in obtaining control of the islands. By World War I Japanese traders and commercial fishermen, though few in number, were carrying copra, bêche-de-mer, passengers, freight, and mail in a near-monopoly over central and western Micronesia (Peattie 1988).

Islanders recall the expansion of international trade networks in terms of copra sold and imports purchased:

It was *mehn wai* who said, "You should plant coconut palms . . . it's a tree that will surround your houses, and will produce desirable things, food and many kinds of things. Well, people planted it, and we made copra in German times, but we didn't heat-dry it. We dried it under the sun. We spread it out to dry, but the Germans didn't like that sort of copra. . . . In the German era, people weren't very careful [about how they dried it]. In the Japanese era, [quality] became a bit better; in the American era, even better.

Germans then replaced [the Spanish] and came to live on Pohnpei. Germans attended to Ngatik as well as Pohnpei. They brought things to sell from Pohnpei: cloth, food, rice, flour, biscuits—delicious! Their era was good. They brought things in large tin containers. There was no difficulty until the Germans and Pohnpei people fought.

By this time, ships were regularly using the lagoon channel (rather than remaining off the oceanside reef of Ngatik Islet), anchoring near shore and loading copra by boat. People spent their cash to pay taxes, support the church, and purchase imports, including cloth, which one elderly man remembers as heavy, thick sailcloth, worn as muumuus before women learned to sew at German-run boarding schools.

A 1900 report of the visit of the vice-governor of the German emperor in Pohnpei to Ngatik confirms the egalitarian arrangement of economic life and the important social role of the high titleholders:

They have three parties, which each has a kind of head person: Nanmwarki, Uajai [Wasahi], Tauk [Dauk]. The first one is also the head of all. The land is equally distributed among everybody; every inhabitant or every head of a household has a space for living and, in the taro swamp, a place for planting. The islands that are not inhabited are used by everybody; the rule says that every independent, male adult can take his turn in harvesting copra for the amount of 20 marks. This equals about one fifth of a ton. They regulate their community life with the help of several rules: e.g., nobody is allowed to wear a knife outside his house after 6 P.M. Trespassers are punished with a fine, which is to be paid to the Nanmwarki, who supervises this money. The money is used for the purchase of food for all. Succession is according to the maternal line.

The official goes on to state his "good opinion" of the people (estimating 240 inhabitants), and describes the well-maintained island: "There is no weed, grass is planted everywhere in a very careful manner, even the most remote spot is cared for. The taro swamp is surrounded by a wall" (Hahl 1900). Eilers 1934 includes a 1903 map by Krämer showing a population of 230 living in households distributed along the edges of the islet (not clustered into a village), the settlement pattern still seen on the island.

After the transfer from Spanish to German control, American missionaries had returned to Pohnpei as soon as political conditions permitted in 1900. A missionary who made a one-day visit to Ngatik on a copra vessel in 1901 reported the population at 225, with 75 church members and the "king" (Aisikaya) a Christian "who tries to help in everything." The people were described as fond of the local teachers who had succeeded John Francis and his wife—Edgar and "sweet and winsome" Julia, who held weekly women's meetings. The church destroyed in the tidal wave had been replaced by a larger one, made of blocks of coral stone and whitewashed, and the people had built a four-room house for Edgar and Julia (Foss 1901). Missionary activity was always subject to secular colonial policy: the German administration was neutral in regard to religious sectarianism, but it was nationalistic. In 1902 the governor forbade missionaries to teach any foreign language except German, a direct attack on the use of English as the most common foreign language in the area. The ABCFM began negotiations to transfer its evangelical interests in the area to a German missionary society, which was done in 1907. On Ngatik, though, the Protestant church and day school had become largely self-run and self-supporting, under the direction of Edgar and Julia. The 1905 typhoon and transportation problems prevented travel for a time, but when he visited in 1905, missionary Thomas Gray remarked on a "quite liberal" 1905–7 contribution to the American Board by Ngatik and Nukuoro (*Missionary Herald* 101, no. 8 [1905]:417). The Pohnpei mission continued to send books, supplies, and an official visitor once or twice a year.

While continuing to expand their influence, Catholic missions made the same international shift. German Capuchins began to arrive in the Spanish Capuchin missions in 1903. By the first decades of the twentieth century, Catholic missionaries had established schools and functioning parishes in the Central and Eastern Carolines (Hezel 1970).

A few Ngatik children continued to attend mission schools

on Pohnpei. German was added to the curriculum, though few on Ngatik learned to speak it fluently. The colonial government's need to teach some children German led to a memorable encounter between Aisikaya and George Fritz (governor of Pohnpei, 1908–9), in which the administration's insistence on removing a group of children to Truk for boarding school encountered strong resistance. Oral traditions about this encounter are threaded with disturbing echoes of the massacre. Failing to get agreement to take the children on his first trip to Ngatik, the governor threatened to "remove the Nahnmwarki and his followers" if they weren't given up when he returned. In one account, Aisikaya declared, "They will have to kill me on my kingdom, because I'm not going anywhere." Soldiers accompanied the governor on his return trip, the ocean became agitated with waves and strong currents (implying spirit activity), and in the end Edgar, Julia, and a group of children were taken away to Truk, where many of the children later died in an epidemic.

The government was forced to take a more direct interest in the outer islands by the devastating typhoon of April 1905, which hit several islands and created conditions requiring both short- and long-term famine relief. Oral histories today vividly recount the extent of the destruction:

The typhoon submerged this islet . . . waves came ashore, there was seawater in the taro gardens. It killed the taro. After the typhoon, trees were dead, the taro was dead. People ate papayas, pumpkins, and other quick-growing plants. They got the rotten taro, carried it out, flavored it with coconut milk and ate it. The taro garden was destroyed. . . . Only coconut palms and breadfruit were left alive.

Waves came from oceanside to over there [from one side of the islet to the other?]. No one died. It is said that a couple who were in their canoe were carried inland and spun into a tree in the forest. You looked at the taro garden—it was full [of water]—you couldn't see the taro. During the storm, people gathered at [houses on] the high places. . . . They were asleep in the house . . . They woke up in the morning and opened the door—all the coconut palms were lying down flat. [The wind was so strong they hadn't heard the trees fall.] No voice could be heard but the voice of the wind. There hasn't been such a typhoon since.

After the typhoon people reconstructed their taro gardens, but also increased their investment in coconut palms. The 1910 Südsee Expedition found that the number of palms had greatly increased and that food crops had been replanted. Many had been destroyed by the storm, and there was government support for greater commitment to copra production. The typhoon also somewhat altered land ownership. One informant explains: "The typhoon destroyed the taro garden, and it was all replanted. Those who worked hard [then] got bigger pieces of land. . . . Some just went back to the land they had owned before. But some just discarded their places, and others took possession of them."

Land ownership was also deliberately reshaped, under German instruction, when the hitherto communally used resources of the atoll's other islets were formally divided. This was about 1912; oral history reports that then-governor Kersting sent a letter ordering the further land division in order to encourage copra production. Land of the atoll's other islets—formerly used cooperatively by members of the three mutual-assistance groups—was allocated for individual ownership among males. The three groups continued to be active throughout the German and Japanese eras, working together and hosting large feasts.

The typhoon that had devastated Ngatik in 1905 also hit Pohnpei's other outer islands, and another storm two years later destroyed food sources on several Carolinian atolls. Their productive capacity was slow to recover. Following the earlier natural disasters, fourteen men, eighteen women, and children from Ngatik had volunteered to leave the still-recovering atoll to resettle on Pohnpei with government assistance (Hahl 1900). Now the German governor blended charity with policy by transplanting outer islanders to the land of the exiled Sokehs people on Pohnpei. In 1911–12, after the Sokehs Rebellion, the land of Sokehs Island on Pohnpei was distributed to immigrants from Mokil, Pingelap, Ngatik, and the Mortlocks—1,250 immigrants in all. These received official certificates of title and retained their land even after Sokehs people returned from exile in the 1920s. Paul Ehrlich quotes an elderly Pohnpei man remembering that "Ponapeans were generally prohibited from even setting foot on Sokehs Island" (Ehrlich 1978:207). Ngatik people who settled on Pohnpei maintained ties with home, and many of their descendants continue to link high island and atoll.

In addition to directed economic development and European education, the German administration was interested in documenting its colonial possessions. The Südsee-Expedition visited Ngatik in 1910, providing a description, including several photographs, of contemporary life (see Eilers 1934). By this time Aisikaya had abdicated due to blindness, giving his place to Nahior, former Isipahu (misidentified as Aisikaya's "son").[7] The report contains illustrations and descriptions of material culture, commenting that the variety of form in tools and crafts is a result of Ngatik's relative isolation from shipping, its diverse heritage, and its relative poverty (for example, people at times made vegetable-fiber clothing when calico was unavailable). The report gives Ngatik Islet, the only inhabited islet, a population of 250 at that time (some Ngatik families may already have moved to Pohnpei). A Jaluit Company trading post and a Protestant mission were both managed by Islanders. Eilers notes:

> At the instance of the German government, a well-maintained path around the whole island was designed. The houses of the natives are all well-constructed and white-washed. With the exception of the church, all houses are built of wood, the church is the only stone building on the whole island. Some houses have porches. All of them are constructed on stilts and most display the Ponape style. However, a few show quite a free variation. Even two-story houses can be found. The people maintain their houses have always been built in such a well-constructed manner.

Eilers comments on the rapid growth of the population following the massacre and states that three individuals alive in 1910 are considered "pure" and "original" Ngatik people; the rest

photo Krämer

Wohnhaus des Häuptlingssohnes.

Boot am Südstrande

photo Krämer

photo Krämer

Zweistöckiges Wohnhaus.

Wohnhaus und Kopraschuppen.

FIG. 7. *Four photographs by Krämer of Ngatik in 1910. Note the "well-constructed" houses and the fedlatches on the canoe. From Eilers 1934.*

"perceive themselves as Ponapeans." Commenting on the distinctive qualities of a material culture "richer and better" than that of Pohnpei at this time, Eilers writes, "We could not find much preserved from the original culture, but it seems to be the case that it is not so much that the European culture would take the place of the old culture, but that the natives are rather developing a new culture."

The Japanese Era

By describing in some detail conditions in the first decades of the reconstruction of Ngatik's social life, I do not discount the shaping force of more recent colonial impacts by Japan and the United States. Circumstances of the Japanese and American eras lay the foundation of the contemporary relationship between Pohnpei and the atoll, with political, economic, and cultural implications for the crystallization of a modern sense of Sapwuah-fik identity.

Longstanding Japanese interest in Micronesia found its opportunity with World War I, when Japan's alliance with Great Britain provided a reason for Japan to move against Germany in the Pacific. Japanese naval forces occupied German Micronesia in 1914; political control was officially sanctioned by League of Nations mandate in 1921. Japan governed the islands until Allied military conquest of the area in World War II.

Unlike German and Spanish administrations, Japan was vitally interested in its Pacific empire; as a result, the three decades of Japanese control saw enormous changes in island life. Japan's interest in the islands was primarily economic and, in later years, strategic. The lengthy Japanese administration attached Islanders more firmly to the international economy and entrenched them more completely in a colonial system than had Spanish or German rule. Japan established a complex and fine-grained administrative system in 1922, which extended civil rule to the village level and included isolated atolls as well as municipal centers.

The first decades of Japanese control in Micronesia saw the establishment of public schools, health services, public works, and an elaborate bureaucracy. Other major factors in social change were large-scale Japanese immigration, extensive construction of economic infrastructure, and increasing government control over local life. The greatest changes took place in the large islands of western Micronesia. In the Carolines, high islands, including Pohnpei, saw immigration, industrial development, urbanization, and an elaborate bureaucracy, especially during the 1930s. Life on atolls was transformed to a much lesser extent by the Japanese colonial presence, though even the smallest atolls had officials appointed by the Japanese government, access to a school, a young men's organization, and visits by traders, medical personnel, census takers, and other administrators, who demanded signs of respect from Islanders.[8]

Compared with earlier colonial administrations, the Japanese held to an even greater interest in economic development over spiritual conversion, setting up schools, increasing the availability of consumer goods, and further developing export markets (on Ngatik, for copra and shells). Ngatik experienced the early decades of Japanese control mostly in the form of increased visits by traders, growth in the amount and variety of purchasable goods, the assignment of local men as government representatives, regular censuses and announcements of government regulations, and widespread though nonintensive schooling. In the first decades of Japanese control, local religious practice continued as usual. In some areas Japanese Christian groups replaced European missionaries, and Shinto missionaries began work; Ngatik's Protestant church, however, was operating effectively on its own.

The shift to Japanese control reduced Catholic mission work. By 1918 all German Catholic missionaries had left, to be replaced in the 1920s by Spanish Jesuits and nuns (Hezel 1970), who established a Catholic church on Ngatik in the 1920s (it was two Spanish men, according to oral tradition, who arrived with Catholic teachings). I do not know what decision making surrounded the establishment of a second form of Christian belief on the atoll; when I asked, people told me simply that several families became Catholic and their children followed suit. Documentary sources identify Fr. Luis Herrera as the first Catholic missionary to visit Ngatik. In August 1922, accompanied by Ngatik people who had become Catholics on Pohnpei, Herrera traveled to the atoll on the Japanese steamer that served the outer-island route. Herrera records that the single Catholic family on Ngatik at that time was that of Silvester. He wrote, "Soon it became clear that the religious question was the single matter of interest on the island, and that Protestantism was fighting back furiously at those who came to challenge their hold on the island." Protestants on Pohnpei had sent a group to Ngatik on the same trip, including a Japanese pastor. In twelve tension-filled days, Herrera stirred excited religious discussion, baptized twenty girls, a number of boys, and some adults, including a man named Julio in whose care Herrera left the nascent Catholic community.

Despite rumors that the Japanese police would not let him return, Herrera went back to Ngatik in December, baptized four more adults and three children, and responded optimistically to questions about when the congregation could have a church. By 1926, a priest named Castro had also worked on Ngatik and a chapel had been built. Missionary visits to Ngatik continued throughout the next decades. The Catholic church became firmly established on the atoll, but religious affiliation remained a focus of social tension. In the early 1930s, Fr. Berganza reports that he baptized "the daughter of a man who for some time had been the pastor of Ngatik" when she was on Pohnpei. She went back to Ngatik, but her father was so angry with her that she had to return to Pohnpei. Reports number the congregation at 120 in 1936 and 198 in 1938, and by the late 1930s students from Ngatik were attending the Catholic boarding school in Kolonia.[9]

Ngatik's population stood at 295 in 1935. Involvement in the commercial economy increased as cash was needed more often: for taxes, medical treatment, steamship travel, and legal fines (e.g., for drinking liquor), but most of all to buy goods from Japanese merchants. During the Japanese era, Islanders traded

copra and fish for canned vegetables, fish, and meat, and for tobacco, tea, salt, flour, soap, perfume, knives, tools, and cloth.
The Nanyo Boeki Kaisha (South Seas Trading Company) became
well established and on its way to monopoly, and independent
Japanese traders and copra brokers were also active. Cash came
from the copra and shell trades and from increasingly available
wage work, primarily on Pohnpei, for stevedores, carpenters,
shipwrights, policemen, interpreters, teacher's assistants, domestics, and midwives.

Throughout the 1930s a shipping line ran three trips a year between Pohnpei and its southern outer islands. A second line connected Pohnpei with Mokil, Pingelap, Kosrae, and the Marshall
Islands. Groups of men on Ngatik and Mokil built Western-style
schooners. Regular shipping increased the predictability of
Ngatik's involvement with a cash economy and dramatically developed Pohnpei Island's role as a regional center. Pohnpei saw a
great influx of Japanese nationals; intensive development of agriculture (especially rice production); and construction of roads,
government buildings, wharves, and a municipal center at Kolonia that included waterworks and an electricity generating plant.
During the war, at the height of hostilities in November 1943,
Pohnpei was the site of a Japanese airfield and seaplane base, as
well as a center for supplies, fuel, and restaging troops.

The resettlement of Ngatik families in Sokehs and the new
opportunities for employment introduced by Japan greatly increased travel between Ngatik and Pohnpei and gave young men
(especially) and women from Ngatik an expanded range of personal acquaintances among Japanese and Pohnpeians. People who
remained on Ngatik knew a few Japanese as traders or visiting
representatives of the colonial government. Those who met
Japanese only through such sporadic contact today offer little in
the way of recollections of them. In contrast, men and women
who lived on Pohnpei during this time were usually there as employees of Japanese officials or businessmen, or, as war neared, as
laborers on military projects. They developed familiar relations
with Japanese and continue to tell anecdotes about those years.

Those who went to Pohnpei worked mostly as domestic laborers, living in storage sheds if they were live-in help, or sleeping in a large house that young Ngatik men built for themselves. When there was a bond of friendship between Japanese employer and Islander employee, it was expressed in prompt, good pay, the chance to learn Japanese, an account at a Japanese-owned shop, and even an illegal nightly bottle of liquor to be drunk alone and in secret. Some Islanders, including at least one man from Ngatik, were selected for special training with machinery. A few Ngatik women worked as domestics, and more did heavy work in the rice paddies. I heard mention of Japanese people with girlfriends from Ngatik, and more than a dozen Ngatik people born in the 1920s and 1930s have a Japanese father (products of about seven alliances). Everyone who worked with the Japanese became more knowledgeable about the use of money and industrial technology, the size of the world, and the diversity of cultural ways.

In speaking of the Japanese era, Ngatik people distinguished between the "good times" of the early years of Japanese presence and the "hard times" of the years of military buildup climaxed by war:

> In Japanese times, that's when I was a man, starting at about age eighteen [i.e., in the early 1920s]. There was a time, at the beginning, that it was very good, because there were friends, there were different kinds of work, and money, and things to buy weren't expensive, they were cheap. Well, so we worked, and time passed, and it was good. Time passed, and then came the time that we call *daidowa* ["war" or "dispute"; from the Japanese] when the war between America and Japan was about to take place. That was when we began to have difficulty, because they would come and take away the young men of Ngatik to go and work at their military installations. So, we went along to that place [Pohnpei] to make barracks, places to stay during the war, over there; we went along and did that until the war was done. I stayed until the time when American planes flew over, and they started the fighting, the war, on Pohnpei.

Japan's thirty-year educational and economic effort in Micronesia built a store of loyalty toward the Japanese. Islanders were aware of benefits Japan introduced, including opportunities for wage labor, trade, and travel (including travel to Japan), health facilities, and widespread education. At the same time, Islanders recognized the unequal treatment they received, and the colonial bureaucracy was strict in administering the law and controlling local life. Gradually, as war increased the pressures on the Japanese military government, the military's harshness toward Micronesians reduced Micronesian goodwill and caused most Islanders to welcome the American invasion. Writing from personal wartime experience in Micronesia, anthropologist John Useem pointed out the high prewar standard of living for Islanders under Japanese administration and commented that "Micronesians do not regard the Americans as liberators who saved them from an awful fate," because they did not resent Japanese limits on Islanders' opportunities, the "caste" system, and intrusion into traditional life (Useem 1945:100). On the other hand, he thought that Micronesians did not resent what they saw as inevitable wartime destruction by the Allies and were impressed with American kindness and generosity.

World War II

Ngatik people living through the years of war experienced very different circumstances, depending on whether they remained on the atoll or were on Pohnpei.[10] The great majority of Ngatik men who were young and mature adults at the time, and most of the women of similar age, spent time as laborers for the Japanese military administration. For the men, most of this labor involved constructing airstrips and other military installations on Pohnpei or elsewhere in Japanese Micronesia. Women worked in rice paddies, supplying the great quantity of food needed for Pohnpei's wartime population. The atoll was left with old men, some women, and children and youth.

As war approached in the late 1930s and early 1940s, Micronesian Christians came under pressure to demonstrate loyalty to Japanese ways and de-emphasize religious activities manifestly American in appearance. Small atolls such as Ngatik were under less close supervision, but like other Islanders, atoll people had little or no contact with Christian missionaries in the later part of the Japanese era and during the war. Local churches continued religious activities on their own. After the war, they enthusiastically renewed ties with Pohnpei churches and foreign missionaries.

Those who were laborers on Pohnpei during the military escalation recall the time as one of hard, endless physical labor. When U.S. air attacks began, work on airstrips and other military facilities became dangerous as well as backbreaking:

> [It was] hard, hard for us; because we are not *mehn wai,* and we were afraid, for we didn't know what we would do. We waited to die. That's what we did. Because they brought bombs, and dropped them, brought guns, and shot them. Apparently, we were stupid [naïve]—we hid ourselves around in holes, or in rocks, or in trees and suchlike. We were all the time trembling.

When things became unbearable, many people stopped working and left the area under attack. Calling on kin or other ties, they sought the relative safety of the rest of Pohnpei Island. The pressure of strict Japanese military discipline and wartime laws, conscripted labor, food shortages, and bombings put everyone on Pohnpei into unusual social situations. The forced encounters in work groups, the crowding of Kolonia, and visits to the countryside to escape bombings compelled Ngatik people to expand their personal relations with other Islanders, especially people of Pohnpei. Many of the ties formed at this time continued after the war in marriages, adoptions, and business relationships.

By the end of hostilities, Islanders on Pohnpei were low on food. The disruption of trade meant that they were living in rags and had reverted to coconut oil lamps and traditional cooking methods. Hard times during the war on Pohnpei are remembered in sharp contrast with experiences of the same years on Ngatik Atoll.

The most important fact remembered about the war years on Ngatik is that the atoll was not hit by U.S. bombs. The explanation for this given by at least two individuals is that certain local people, knowing the English spoken on Ngatik since the massacre, wrote messages on the beach to which American pilots responded. In one story, a man wrote on the sand, "No Japanese on this island," and the Americans, flying over Ngatik after a bombing run on Pohnpei, spared the atoll. Another account describes a woman spelling out a message with coconut fronds, asking the Americans to "help this island," and others describe people writing requests for soap, cloth, and cigarettes.

The "help" Ngatik got from Americans went beyond preservation from bombing. According to numerous eyewitnesses, the atoll actually benefited from the presence of American planes in the area. In place of bombs, Ngatik was bombarded with packages of food, clothing, tobacco, and chocolate dropped into the lagoon by navy planes, there to be picked up by Islanders. Ngatik's good luck is explicitly contrasted, in stories of the war years, with Pohnpei's hardship, as in this man's poignant recollections of his feelings as a contract laborer on Pohnpei:

A time when I really thought I was going to die, when I was truly afraid, was during the war. We *mehn Pohnpei* [the speaker is a Sapwuahfik man who is a long-term resident of Pohnpei] were along doing the work. Well, when the airplanes came and dropped bombs, it was hard. I was very much afraid, I thought that I would die, that I was really going to die. That was a time of praying, or hiding, going to hide yourself somewhere—it was really difficult. That was when the hard time was closest. Because airplanes came and dropped bombs and things—*pa-pa-pa-pa!* American airplanes, too! A man of war came—*boom!*

Who could be tranquil? There was no one who could feel at ease. It was as though everything had happened to us except death. There were many dead. Guns killed some. Bombs fell, and killed some but not others. That was the time that I can tell you, I really thought I was going to die. That was the time that was really difficult, because we were on Pohnpei. But on Ngatik—no, it was good. They would come to Ngatik and drop cigarettes, food tins, six-pound tins [of meat]. That's really something, eh? It was upside down. [They would] go to fight on Pohnpei, but come here and drop cloth, tins of meat, cigarettes. [On Ngatik] people were smoking, but on Pohnpei cigarettes were scarce. . . . That's really a laugh, isn't it?

I've also been afraid of the ocean, I've been in difficulties where I was afraid. But that fear wasn't as strong as in the time of the bombings. There've been situations where I've been afraid, but I thought I could get out of them. But that, I thought I could not get out of.

Where Pohnpei received explosives dropped by Americans, Ngatik received gifts; where people on Pohnpei were suffering dire want from shortages of food and clothing, Ngatik's people were walking around fully clothed and replete with tinned corned beef, thanks to the U.S. Navy. Navy pilots even landed in Ngatik's lagoon on occasion, trading with people and directly renewing Ngatik's ties with the United States—ties that had lapsed during the German and, especially, the Japanese eras. Several women recalled times when seven, nine, twelve planes would fly over, and American military men would stop at Ngatik to rest, giving away candy and other gifts. The fact that Ngatik men spoke some English—the pidgin that was one legacy of the massacre—made such interaction rewarding rather than frustrating for both sides, and Ngatik people used these opportunities to learn about America.

Ngatik men who were on Pohnpei when the victorious U.S. military moved in also found their English useful—and a marker distinguishing them from *mehn Pohnpei:*

When Americans arrived in Pohnpei, when the Navy captured Pohnpei, all the *mehn Ngatik* went and conversed with the Americans.

(But Pohnpei people couldn't?)

They couldn't, that's right! They would ask, "Who is Ngatikese?" And [then say], "Come here, come here!" and the *mehn Ngatik* talked with the Americans; they discussed all kinds of things. They very much liked it, that *mehn Ngatik* knew English. That's the reason that, when cigarettes were scarce, all the *mehn Ngatik* would walk around with their pockets, their trousers full of cigarettes. They would give us a carton, as a gift. We are the ones who gave cigarettes to Pohnpei people, made it easy for them. Truly, they [Americans] were nice.

But today, with schools, *mehn Pohnpei* have surpassed *mehn Ngatik*, very much surpassed them in knowing English.

The stresses of the war years led Islanders to welcome the transfer of control to the United States after World War II:

[During the war] We lived under the law of the Japanese, so we could just die, until the Americans came, and the Japanese surrendered, and we were free. Under U.S. rule, if you wanted to work, you worked; if not, you didn't. It was up to people what they did. There were those among the Japanese, of high station, who didn't want to destroy people's feelings, and who knew the laws of freedom, but they couldn't act that way. But Americans set people free to do what they wanted to do.

World War II thus reinforced the special ties Sapwuahfik people feel they share with Americans, who, along with other English speakers, were instrumental in attacking and resettling the atoll in the nineteenth century. Ngatik people felt a kinship with the American servicemen who arrived in the area in the course of the war, and Ngatik men on Pohnpei benefited from being among the few local people who spoke English. A sense of affiliation with Americans, lost since postmassacre settlers and missionaries had left, was revived.

The American Era and Independence

As territory was taken from the Japanese, Islanders came under U.S. Navy administration as a United Nations Strategic Trust. American goals for Micronesia were and are primarily strategic, but also (especially after the 1952 shift from military to civilian rule) included creation of political structures modelled on democracy in the United States and changes in educational, health, and consumption standards. Beginning in 1963, a major shift in American policy brought enormous increases in economic aid flowing into the islands (Peoples 1985). Ngatik's postwar (1948) population of 222 grew to 442 by 1969, reflecting changes in living conditions and economic organization. The new budget of the 1960s instituted education and public health programs and greatly expanded the civil bureaucracy. Money came to Islanders through government employment, at wage and salary levels much higher than previous standards. Cash circulated in the local economy in purchases of goods and food imported from the United States, Japan, and Australia.[11] Ngatik's bureaucratic ties to Pohnpei deepened, as government funding, grants, direction of educational and health services, and, to a lesser extent, church administration was funneled to the outer islands through offices in Kolonia, the district center for the Pohnpei District of the Trust Territory. High school on Pohnpei, and, for a few youths, college in Hawaii, Guam, or mainland United States became routes to government employment or elective office, for which knowledge of English and familiarity with American culture were considered advantageous. As during the Japanese era, people found that travel to work on Pohnpei or beyond was the best source of cash income; petty entrepreneurship on Ngatik took advantage of the increased cash flow that reached even to the outer islands. The postwar scarcity of goods was followed by a large increase in the consumption of imports, especially building supplies and food, though Ngatik people continued to rely on gardens and the lagoon for their subsistence.

Critics of American policy in Micronesia argue that this vast outpouring of cash into the islands has been misdirected, because it has been limited largely to fueling people's ability to purchase imports. Very little has been done to improve the capacity of local economies to develop the islands' natural resources or introduce productive industry (Peoples 1985). Although Micronesians' standard of living—their access to purchased commodities—has risen, the productive capacity of the islands has remained stagnant, or even decreased. Journalists and travelers comment with amazement on the prevalence of canned tuna in the stores and spaghetti and pizza in the restaurants of cities such as Kolonia—where fresh-caught fish and local vegetables cannot be purchased. This is a "dependent" economy, in which nearly all manufactured goods and an increasing proportion of food are imported rather than locally produced. Micronesians do not lack the capacity or resources for production, but cash flowing into the islands has been expended on personal consumption, because U.S. policy directed economic aid into wages and salaries rather than into more concrete and long-term forms of development. The problems of a dependent economy were discussed in negotiations concerning the relationship between the U.S. and Micronesian peoples conducted in the 1970s and 1980s.

Central Micronesia remained a U.N. Trust Territory under U.S. administration until at the end of the 1970s negotiations and plebiscites set it on the path to a new political status as the Federated States of Micronesia (including an area from Yap in the west to Kosrae in the east) in "free association" with the United States. The 1986 establishment of the independent new nation places Sapwuahfik firmly in the administrative hierarchy of an elective democracy, as part of Pohnpei State in the Federated States of Micronesia. As part of the preparation for these changes, the people of Sapwuahfik wrote a constitution in 1985, and on October 18 formally celebrated the return to the atoll's ancient name.

CHAPTER FIVE

Cultural Identity in Context

THE SOCIETY BORN AFTER the 1837 massacre continues today as a unique, vital, creative construction.
Modern Sapwuahfik identity depends on local history
both symbolically and pragmatically. *Mehn Sapwuah-*
fik today maintain themselves as a cultural community by expressing their distinctiveness in comparison with others near
and far—most notably *mehn Pohnpei* but also other outer islanders, other Micronesians, Americans and other foreigners.
They express their distinctiveness, and continually re-create it,
in contemporary social action. Individual choices of action respond to personal circumstances and local and regional politics.
Yet the choices are framed by Sapwuahfik understanding of their
community's history.

Between the 1840s and the turn of the century, Ngatik was
an unstable polyethnic society. People lived in separate groups
on the main islet, according to ethnicity: there was an "American town," a Mortlockese settlement, a Pohnpeian–aboriginal–

Gilbert Islander area. Recalling the islet's size, it is no surprise that they were in constant contact. The groups were quite small—several families each—and there are stories of violent conflict between individuals. Accounts of the destruction of the Mortlockese and other tales of this time emphasize group affiliation—the separate villages, the conflicts, the repetition of the violence of the massacre (with former victims as new perpetrators). Many stories focus on individual action and group support and frequently include moral evaluations of the qualities of groups and individuals.

One can see in the oral history of this era the objective basis of a concern with community identity. Several distinct groups interacted in the postmassacre environment, but only in occasional dramatic events did they act as groups. Beginning with the attackers living with surviving aboriginal women and fostering their children, crosscutting ties immediately generated social interactions of the most intimate sort—countering the production of plurality and locating plurality at the level of the individual rather than society.

As identities were negotiated, so were rules of social life, economic practice, religious belief. The groundwork of political order was laid when an unidentified ship's officer randomly assigned Pohnpei titles to the surviving aboriginal boys, giving the atoll a sketch of Pohnpei's complex political hierarchy. Thus the historical charter for Sapwuahfik's "traditional" sociopolitical order is rooted in chance. For nearly half a century social order depended on the spontaneous generation of law by three individuals, especially by Aisikaya, using an imported framework. The importance of Pohnpei culture in the rebuilding of Ngatik's society appears at its inception: Pohnpei men are among the immediate postmassacre immigrants; the three surviving boys are given Pohnpei titles. Yet heterodoxy in the atoll's use of Pohnpei's cultural forms also appears as a possibility early on: who should succeed the aboriginal men who were Wasahi, Dauk, and, most of all, Nahnmwarki? The advent of Christian teachings, and the church as an encompassing social institution, supported the integration of the atoll's population through intermarriage. By the end of the century the "Ngatik" community appears in documents as a coherent society.

Sapwuahfik accounts of their past center on stories about the characteristics of individuals and groups and about relationships among them. Tales about aboriginal Sapwuahfik people, immigrant *mehn Pohnpei*, Europeans, Americans, and Gilbert and Mortlock Islanders who drifted ashore form the corpus of oral history. In formulating Sapwuahfik's past as a history of immigrants, it is likely that *mehn Sapwuahfik* draw on Pohnpei's historical philosophy, in which the mythical creation of the high island itself and the origins of its clans are traced to outsiders (Hanlon 1988:4–8). Local historians see Pohnpei's past as a continual, successive incorporation of peoples and cultures from beyond its shores. David Hanlon characterizes modern Pohnpei as "a resilient, flexible, though internally divided cultural order accustomed to the selective incorporation of foreign goods and influences. Indeed, Pohnpeians today refer to this continuing tradition with the phrase, *Pohnpei, sapw en alemengi*, `Pohnpei is a land of borrowings'" (Hanlon 1988:199).

Sapwuahfik accounts of immigrant groups describe their specific characteristics in the context of postmassacre Sapwuahfik. Oral history identifies social formations brought by waves of Pohnpei immigrants, Gilbertese skill in martial arts, and American/European religion, literacy, and technical knowledge. In the same way *mehn Sapwuahfik* describe the history of their community by exploring the qualities and relationships of indigenous and immigrant populations, they explore and express their community's modern identity through ideas about the characteristics and relationships of neighboring groups.

Who Is Mehn Sapwuahfik?

On Pohnpei and on Sapwuahfik, *Ih mehn ia?* is a common question when someone is being identified: "He [or she] is a person of where?" This means not only, as an English speaker would say, "Where is he from?" but, more to the point, "Where is he of?" A person's place of origin tells where his land and his kin are, what titles he is eligible for, where his language was learned and his physical and social skills developed.[1]

Sapwuahfik people and their Eastern Carolines neighbors recognize minor phenotypical distinctions and variations in dialect, food customs, and material culture as Sapwuahfik *style* (the local word, an English borrowing). But individual identity does not rely on these; people recognize that such traits can be misleading indicators of group affiliation. Furthermore, intimate contact with other populations has been an element of Sapwuahfik life since the atoll was resettled, resulting in a large body of traits shared with other Islanders, especially *mehn Pohnpei*. What makes someone *mehn Sapwuahfik* has more to do with social relationships and individual behavior, and such identification is not necessarily unique or unchangeable. The variability of who is Sapwuahfik, and under what circumstances, is related to how criteria of citizenship are called into play.

Determining who is *mehn Sapwuahfik* involves many of the criteria used on other Micronesian atolls (Marshall 1975; Nason 1975; Flinn 1990). Genealogy or descent, residence, land rights, language, life-style, and shared values all figure in establishing personal identity. The criteria are flexible in action; situational factors both within and beyond individual control play a part. A person has a certain limited freedom to push his or her identity one way or another (given enough of a genealogical or situational base on which to make an argument). In the same way, the community has some leeway in ascribing citizenship to its putative, or potential, members.

Most people base their identification as Sapwuahfik on genealogy, though no Sapwuahfik person today is "truly Sapwuahfik" in the sense of being fully descended from indigenous Sapwuahfik ancestors. As one woman told me, *Dene sohte uhdahn mehn Ngatik*, "It is said, there are no true Ngatik/Sapwuahfik people." Descent is an important factor in determining identity; genealogical claims to community membership depend on whether one's parents are considered to be *mehn Sapwuahfik*— though that classification involves criteria other than parents' ancestry. Of 278 adults considered *mehn Sapwuahfik* residing on the atoll in 1979, all but 31 have parents considered *mehn Sapwuahfik*. (Of those 31, 10 have a non-Sapwuahfik mother, 11 have a non-Sapwuahfik father, and 10 were adopted from other islands.) Sixty-four percent of Sapwuahfik adults described both their mother's parents and father's parents as *mehn Sapwuahfik*. The diverse ancestry of this population is an extreme example of similar settlement and migration processes throughout Micronesia (e.g., Marshall 1975; Nason 1975).

Three examples from 1979–80 demonstrate the variability in genealogical claims to Sapwuahfik identity. (The examples use pseudonyms for living persons.) The first example is that of Deborah, a woman whose father is *mehn Mokil* (Mwoakilloa). Her mother's father is considered *mehn Sapwuahfik* and her mother's mother, *mehn Mokil*. In a casual conversation, I described Deborah as *mehn Mokil*. The man I was talking with disagreed, saying,

> "Deborah is *mehn Ngatik*—Aaron's daughter gave birth to her, and so mixed her blood."
>
> "Is her mother *mehn Mokil?*" I asked.
>
> "Her mother is Aaron's child, by a Mokilese woman."
>
> "But *mehn Ngatik* call Deborah a Mokilese woman."
>
> He explained, "Because she only came three or so years ago."

The flexibility of Deborah's identity is explicitly recognized; her decision to live on Sapwuahfik and maintain close ties with Sapwuahfik relatives gives her a credible claim to Sapwuahfik identity, but she is frequently referred to as *mehn Mokil* on the atoll.

In the second case, that of Stephen, the diversity of ancestry is more striking:

Sowel (*mehn Ngatik*) = Kawed (*mehn Gilbert*)
|
mehn Pohnpei = Nadoh
|
mehn Germany = "*mehn Ngatik*"
|
Stephen

Stephen has spent most of his life on Pohnpei, where he holds a title. He visited Sapwuahfik as a child but went to school on Pohnpei. When people ask, I queried, do you say you are *mehn Ngatik* or *mehn Pohnpei?* "*Mehn Ngatik*," he replied—his mother's mother's father was "*uhdahn* [truly] *mehn Ngatik*," and his mother was *mehn Ngatik*. (In my understanding, however, Sowel was one of the first postmassacre immigrants to the atoll from Pohnpei.) Like his mother, he speaks both Pohnpei and Sapwuahfik dialects. This man serves as a link between islands, assisting Sapwuahfik people on Pohnpei.

The third example, the case of Robert, illustrates the bilateral tracing of genealogical claims to identity:

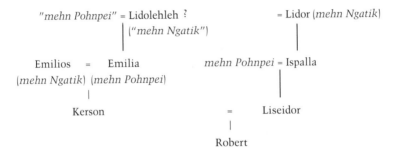

Robert told me that his grandfather Emilios was *uhdahn mehn Ngatik* because his grandfather's mother was *mehn Ngatik* (though he identified his grandfather's father as *mehn Pohnpei*). It is interesting that this man, although describing himself as *mehn Ngatik*, identified his mother as *mehn Pohnpei* because her father was *mehn Pohnpei*. Incidentally, information from other informants identified Lidolehleh as an early immigrant from the Gilbert Islands, and whereas some of his descendants say Emilios's father was Pohnpeian, others name him as Noah, an aboriginal survivor.

The diversity of genealogical paths to contemporary identity is emblematic of the modern Sapwuahfik view of the atoll's past. The historical processes of immigration and intermarriage that produced the modern population are well recognized. Sapwuahfik people are "mixed," or "half-caste," they say—often using the English words, demonstrating the "mixture" of language as well as "blood." Although the reality of a blended population is affirmed, the specifics of the historical melting pot are left unexamined. For example, Mortlockese are mentioned as a component of the early blended population, though they do not appear as ancestors in genealogies. Sapwuahfik people commonly speak of their *mehn wai* descent, despite the fact that relatively few English and American men of the massacre and post-massacre era left descendants. And the large component of Pohnpei ancestors of the modern population is sometimes affirmed, sometimes minimized, in the wider context of Sapwuahfik-Pohnpei relations. For Sapwuahfik community identity, historical components of the ancestral population have symbolic significance when used to refer to modern circumstances. For individuals, however, specific genealogical pathways are a key to affiliation with the Sapwuahfik community. Because of this, descent can become a contested field for interpersonal relations.

Ascriptions of identity are often used in daily life. People on Sapwuahfik are addressed or referred to, for example, as *mehn Sapwuahfik* (prior to 1985, as *mehn Ngatik*), *mehn likin*, "outsider," *mehn Mokil* (Mwoakilloa), *mehn Kirinis* (Kapingamarangi). Such ascriptions make a person's identity, or that of an ancestor, of immediate contemporary relevance. Adults teasing children and friends joking with each other will call on the other's foreign ancestry (which everyone has) to make their jest. So a noisy child is laughed at: "What is that, a Mokilese girl?" This is not simply a reference to the reputed rowdiness of Mokilese women, for the child has a Mokilese ancestor. As another example, a man whose biological parents are Mortlockese but who came to Sapwuahfik as a small child is teased about Mortlockese customs, such as wearing ear decorations (see Lieber 1990 for a similar pattern on Kapingamarangi).

Such teasing plays a role in socializing individuals into awareness of the critical importance of gossip and public opinion in small-island communities. It is part of a wide Oceanic pattern of socialization through teasing and shaming, aimed at adults as well as children. A woman who married onto Sapw-

uahfik as a girl and has lived there for fifty years is invariably referred to as "that Kapingamarangi woman," reflecting her relative lack of integration into the community. In contrast, a thir-
ty-year-old man from Pohnpei, of Mortlock/Filipino descent,
who married a Sapwuahfik woman and has lived quietly and
worked diligently on Sapwuahfik for less than a decade, is seldom pointed out as foreign. "Of him, people would say, you are
truly *mehn Pohnpei*, but now you are *mehn Ngatik*." Didactic
ascriptions of identity encourage people to adhere to Sapwuahfik
standards of behavior: to be generous, helpful, and loyal to kin,
to work hard in food production and crafts, to foster positive
feelings in the community and dampen jealousy or ill-will, to
avoid displays of pride.

Reference to the genealogical aspect of identity also may be
used to explain personal traits. As an explanation of his physical
appearance, one man is sometimes referred to as a "Negro,"
which puzzled me until a check of his genealogy showed an
African American sailor as a nineteenth-century ancestor. Similarly, the fishing skill of a man raised on Sapwuahfik from baby-
hood is attributed to his Kapingamarangi parentage. Genealogical attributions of characteristics occasionally extend beyond
the personal, as when a woman indicated that members of a matrilineal clan share some sort of identity when she complained
about a family's handling of a feast. "They're *mehn Tarawa*,"
she said (the clan ancestor was a Gilbertese immigrant), "they
have a different way of thinking from *mehn Ngatik*."

The political potential of such innocent explanations of behavior is always present. Because all are *mehn Sapwuahfik* (and
this must go without saying for the comments to work), community members deliberately use genealogical aspects of a person's self to shape social situations. Ascribed identity that is
neutral or humorous in one context can become a weapon when
circumstances change, and then public ascriptions of identity
can be potentially serious and damaging. At times of intense political activity, during an election campaign or when a conflict
arises over community resources, they are one of many weapons
available to the skilled politicians of the atoll. The reason once

given for not re-electing a chief magistrate was that he was not truly Sapwuahfik—a reference to his ancestry. Political infighting for weeks preceding the decision actually involved questions of family status, personal effectiveness, ties with the Pohnpei political establishment, and the distribution of favors. Ascription of identity as a political weapon is not consistent. One young man was removed from his position as radio operator with the public excuse that he "isn't truly *mehn Ngatik*"; he had been adopted to Sapwuahfik as a baby. His replacement, however, had also been adopted onto the atoll. The complexity of explicitly political uses of identity ascriptions became apparent to me when, several weeks later, the deposed radio operator described a speech the Nahnmwarki had made some time before. In this speech, the Nahnmwarki commented that it wasn't good for *mehn likin* (outsiders) to do official municipal work, ostensibly referring to several well-educated and capable young men adopted onto Sapwuahfik as children. However, the young man offered the opinion that the speech had been ghost-written by the Nahnken and was in fact a roundabout way of criticizing the Nahnmwarki himself for marrying an outsider. The Nahnmwarki's marriage to a Mortlockese woman was widely spoken of as bad for the community.

The Sapwuahfik Constitution (*Kou Pahson en Kovorment en Wein Sapwuahfik*), written in 1985, codifies the definition of *mehn Sapwuahfik*. Its provisions distinguish the qualifications for Luhkenkolwof (chief magistrate) from those for membership in the municipal council or judiciary of the atoll. Whereas the latter two require that the candidate *wia towe mehlel in Wein Sapwuahfik*, "be a valid citizen of Sapwuahfik municipality" (my translation), one requirement for the position of Luhkenkolwof is *ipwdi wia towe mehlel*, "birth makes valid citizenship." (All positions require residence of no less than five years on the atoll; a judge must also have been a Sapwuahfik citizen for at least twenty-five years.) In 1989–90 I discussed this distinction with two men who had taken part in writing the constitution. The men had been political rivals, and their differing interpretations suggest the salience of ascriptions of identity in community politics. One told me that the constitution defines citizens (*tohnwehi*) as those who are *inting Sapwuahfik*, "written at Sapwuahfik," that is, registered there exclusively for purposes of voting and government benefits, and restricts Luhkenkolwof to those *pwildak en Sapwuahfik*, "native" or "aboriginal" (Rehg and Sohl 1979). He stated that this excluded those adopted onto the atoll from being Luhkenkolwof, though anyone could be a citizen regardless of parentage. The other man rejected *pwildak* as an interpretation of the constitutional provision, saying the document limited the position to those who were either born on Sapwuahfik or had a Sapwuahfik mother or father and were *inting Sapwuahfik*. The provision attempted to encode what is felt to be of some relevance to the community: identifying who is and is not *uhdahn mehn Sapwuahfik*. Yet the phrasing, combined with the variety of existing genealogical and behavioral pathways to Sapwuahfik identity, focuses the concern without resolving it. As a model of increasing "ethnicity" with growing involvement in nation-state organization would predict, genealogy is becoming more significant in group affiliation. Yet although Sapwuahfik people express sharpened concern with membership and boundaries as their political life becomes more tightly connected to state and national structures, nongenealogical aspects of identity continue to be salient in community life.

Possessing an ancestor identified as Sapwuahfik is obviously a powerful claim to Sapwuahfik identity. But although a foreigner with a Sapwuahfik ancestor can come to the atoll with that claim and be treated as an honorary community member during the visit, the tie does not automatically include rights to land, kinship obligations, or involvement in local affairs. A genealogical link must be accompanied by appropriate social behavior if a person is to be considered truly Sapwuahfik. Long-term residence on the atoll is especially important (though not sufficient) to constitute Sapwuahfik identity. Several people adopted onto Sapwuahfik as babies, who have lived there all their lives, are still frequently referred to as *mehn Kirinis*. On the other hand, some who were born and have lived on Pohnpei, save perhaps for occasional brief visits to the atoll, are Sapwuahfik without dispute by selective application of other criteria. In these cases, descent is important to situation-specific claims of atoll identity—initiating a request for personal assistance, for example. Despite the importance of the genealogical claim, people with no genealogical ties to the atoll come to be considered Sapwuahfik by appropriate social behavior following adoption or marriage into the community.

Sapwuahfik's early population history is largely one of immigration. Today immigrants arrive not in waves but as individuals being adopted or marrying onto Sapwuahfik. Non-Sapwuahfik people who come to the atoll may become (*wiala*) *mehn Sapwuahfik*. This can happen through adoption, when a baby or young child is brought to Sapwuahfik, raised on the atoll, and receives land there from his adoptive parents. (Of ten adults or children in 1979 who had been adopted to Sapwuahfik from other islands, five were from Kapingamarangi, two from Nukuoro, and the other three from Pohnpei but of mixed [Pohnpei/Mortlockese, Pohnpei/Kosraean] descent.) Only one child of a Sapwuahfik family permanently residing on the atoll had been formally adopted off the island; she lives with a Pohnpei family with business connections to her Sapwuahfik parents. Adoption to Sapwuahfik relatives living on Pohnpei, though, is more common.

A change of identity also can occur with in-marriage on a case-by-case basis. Thus to the young man mentioned above, who had married onto Sapwuahfik only recently, people would say, "You are truly *mehn Pohnpei*, but now you are *mehn Ngatik*." It is in this sense of shared life-style, though much diluted, that people sometimes told me I had "become a Ngatik woman." Some people choose not to make the transition. Deborah, the woman in the first example above, who had the genealogical right or option of being Sapwuahfik was, because of her choices in language, church affiliation, and personal relations, generally spoken of as Mokilese. Sapwuahfik living on Pohnpei, or on other islands, may similarly "become" other identities. When I enquired about distant relatives, I was sometimes told the informant didn't know anything about those peo-

TABLE I

Ethnic Composition of Marriages, by Generation

Generation	Sapwuahfik = Sapwuahfik	Sapwuahfik = Pohnpeian	Sapwuahfik = Other Foreigner	Foreigner = Foreigner	Total
+4	0	3 (33%)	3 (33%)	3 (33%)	9
+3	8 (33%)	8 (33%)	6 (25%)	2 (9%)	24
+2	51 (81%)	7 (11%)	5 (8%)	0	63
+1	75 (56%)	40 (30%)	19 (14%)	0	134
0	87 (51%)	43 (25%)	41 (24%)	0	171
−1	30 (33%)	28 (31%)	33 (36%)	0	91

Notes: This table counts ties verbally described as marriages, and other alliances that produced at least one child. Units counted are unions, not individuals. Those born on Sapwuahfik are counted as "Sapwuahfik" for the next generation. A cross-generation union is counted in the older generation. Those adopted to Sapwuahfik as children are counted as "foreign" when they marry. The population is *mehn Sapwuahfik* resident on Sapwuahfik in 1979–80, and those on Pohnpei who were unambiguously listed in genealogies as *mehn Sapwuahfik*.

The +4 generation is the group living on the atoll immediately after the massacre. The marriages of the -1 generation were incomplete in 1979–80; statistics for this generation are affected by the increasing number of *mehn Sapwuahfik* resident on Pohnpei.

ple; they had *wiala mehn Pohnpei*, "become *mehn Pohnpei*," or another identity. Most were cases of marriage with foreigners, though a few had deliberately emigrated.

Interethnic marriages of course have a history going back to the massacre. Table I indicates a consistent increase in outmarriages, more noticeable in marriages with foreigners other than *mehn Pohnpei*, and a corresponding decrease in the percentage of total marriages contracted by Sapwuahfik people that are ethnically endogamous. The data in the table are not restricted to Sapwuahfik living on the home atoll, however, and the greater number of outmarriages occurs between Sapwuahfik people in more or less permanent residence on Pohnpei and non-Sapwuah-

TABLE 2

Marriages of Sapwuahfik Atoll Residents, November 1979

Sapwuahfik = Sapwuahfik	Sapwuahfik = Pohnpeian	Sapwuahfik = Other Foreigner	Sapwuahfik = Adopted-to-Sapwuahfik	Total
83	2	6	10	101
(82%)	(2%)	(6%)	(10%)	

fik people (compare Table 2, which shows the composition of atoll residents' marriages).

Decreasing atoll endogamy with increasing commitment to Pohnpei is one aspect of the thinning out of identification with the Sapwuahfik cultural community seen in people of Sapwuahfik descent residing elsewhere. The shift in identity can be abrupt—as when an individual marries a foreigner, say an American, and moves far away, thus forcefully and dramatically breaking all ties except those of communication and occasional gift exchange. But such cases are rare. For most people who are transformed from being *mehn Sapwuahfik* to "having become" members of some other group, the movement occurs over a number of years, requiring a generation or even two to pass before ties with Sapwuahfik are matters of genealogical record and memory only.

Although elsewhere in Micronesia access to land plays a central role in determining identity, this does not seem to be the case on Sapwuahfik. All those considered Sapwuahfik do not have effective rights to atoll land. In particular, many Sapwuahfik people residing permanently on Pohnpei do not, including descendants of families that moved to Sokehs in the early years of this century. Others have sold their atoll land. But in 1979–80, all plots of land on Sapwuahfik, with a single exception, were held by those considered to be *mehn Sapwuahfik* (a few plots are owned by churches). (Some people with rights to land are nonetheless not considered *mehn Sapwuahfik* in every context; for example, the Kapingamarangi people adopted as babies have rights in the land of Sapwuahfik adoptive kin, but may be commonly identified as Kapingamarangi.) Access to land is closely related to maintenance of personal ties with the atoll for Sapwuahfik people living elsewhere.

Using the Sapwuahfik dialect of the Pohnpei language is one behavioral marker identifying *mehn Sapwuahfik*. On Pohnpei, or on Sapwuahfik when dealing with government officials of any background or other foreigners, most Sapwuahfik people speak Pohnpeian, considered more formal. On the atoll, Sapwuahfik people may use *lokaian meing*, "high," or "respect" language in church and in public speeches, though only a few atoll people are comfortable with it. Ordinary conversation and school classes are in Sapwuahfik dialect. The use of the dialect when away from the atoll is a self-conscious distinguishing characteristic of those who consider themselves *mehn Sapwuahfik*. Men and women who speak both dialects fluently are interlocutors (in several senses) between the two populations. Sapwuahfik men use among themselves an English "pidgin" (as they call it) modified from nineteenth-century sailors' speech. They see this as distinctive of their community, and until the American-era introduction of English-language schooling (as a result of which many other Micronesians speak English more fluently than most Sapwuahfik men), it was a source of pride.[2]

It is evident from this discussion that no single rule defines an individual's Sapwuahfik citizenship, nor is there any consistent "content" defining the identity. To be *mehn Sapwuahfik* is to an extent to choose to be so through one's social acts, providing the community accepts that choice. Given that a person has some claim to being *mehn Sapwuahfik*, certain choices of action will confirm this identity, and others will invalidate it. These choices are made in a wider social context, because being *mehn Sapwuahfik* exists only in contrast to being some other identity. Sapwuahfik people are conscious of their place in the geographic and political setting of the Eastern Carolines, and they define a regional set of marked identities of which Sapwuahfik is but one.

The Regional Context of Sapwuahfik Identity

Sapwuahfik people participate in a set of nesting identities at different levels of inclusiveness. They recognize a common identity with all Pacific Islanders as distinguished from Europeans and Asians. *Tohndeke,* "inhabitants of islands," share a common subsistence life-style, close family ties, and patterns of gift giving and resource sharing not found among non-Islanders. Sapwuahfik people also share with the other atolls in the state a feeling of distinction from Pohnpei. The lifeways of the people of these "little lands" are seen as very similar. There is a sense of alliance, and I think the political implications of this word are increasingly appropriate, with the citizens of the outer islands as conceptually opposed to Pohnpei Island proper.

The outer islands of Pohnpei State have a precontact history of only sporadic interaction (through trade, accidental voyages, and military expeditions) with one another and with Pohnpei. The premassacre population of Sapwuahfik, according to a contemporary observer, differed from that of Pohnpei in language and in "features" and "exterior appearance" (Blake 1924 [1839]: 667). Grouping Pohnpei Island with nearby atolls into a colonial administrative district began during Spanish control of the Caroline Islands in the nineteenth century. It was in the context of Spanish, German, Japanese, and American administrations that the people of these islands entered into sustained interaction.

The constitutional category of Pohnpei State, of considerable practical import, is matched in significance by an uninstitutionalized distinction between Pohnpei Island (its municipalities conceptually merged) and the five outer islands of the state—a distinction which, with great difference in the content of the two categories, is held by the members of each. Immigrants and visitors from all the islands meet on Pohnpei, especially in the urban area of Kolonia. Since the establishment of foreign political control, and especially since the 1960s, the populations have come into ever more frequent contact with each other, with consequences for each group's perception of itself and its neighbors (Lieber 1984, 1990).

To explore Sapwuahfik ideas about their neighbors, I added to my informal interviews and observations a set of focused interviews based in part on the "Ethnocentrism Field Manual" (in LeVine and Campbell 1972). I obtained fairly consistent stereotypes of the populations most familiar to Sapwuahfik people. The descriptions tend to support Michael Lieber's (1990) conclusion, in a discussion of regional identities from the Kapingamarangi perspective, that local ethnic imagery reflects the current sociopolitical concerns of each group. More explicit symmetry between the political concerns of Sapwuahfik people and their descriptions of other cultural groups would probably be given by Sapwuahfik people permanently resident on Pohnpei, who were not adequately represented in my interviews. Atoll Sapwuahfik descriptions of their neighbors highlight attributes considered important in social interaction. In characterizing their neighbors, Sapwuahfik people point out the subsistence work, the sexual division of labor, the productivity of land, clothing and personal appearance, sociability (how peaceful or prone to fighting people are, hospitality customs), distributive and feasting behavior, and presence or absence of sorcery practices.

When speaking about themselves, Sapwuahfik people describe their atoll as very productive in contrast to neighboring atolls, and they list local food specialties. Sapwuahfik women are noted for fishing and weaving; the canoes are "beautiful" and the fastest in the area because of sail and hull shape. *Mehn Sapwuahfik* do not commonly distinguish themselves in terms of dress or personal appearance. They describe themselves as kind to visitors, generous, peaceful, not given to speaking ill of other peoples. They also mention the argumentativeness of *mehn Sapwuahfik*, boys' and men's drinking and women's laziness. And they note what others say of them: that they eat cat and shark, like to fight because of their "Gilbertese blood," and are expert sorcerers, due to the renowned magic of ancient Sapwuahfik. (The last two are examples of generalizations about Sapwuahfik ancestors in contemporary contexts.) Sapwuahfik people view themselves as both peaceful folk and fighters. They often express their sense that they are people of goodwill, cooperative and helpful, but they also relish the fear others may have of their fighting ability and supposed—but denied—skill as sorcerers (compare similar ambivalence on Pulap [Flinn 1990]).[3]

Sapwuahfik people see themselves, then, as outer islanders, affiliated with other outer islanders in distinction from Pohnpei. They also see themselves as Micronesian outer islanders, more similar to Mwoakilloa and Pingelap than to Nukuoro and Kapingamarangi, and as southern outer islanders, sharing certain practical concerns with the two Polynesian atolls, apart from Mwoakilloa and Pingelap. Although these small-island identities may be cited by individuals in particular situations, or by politicians for pragmatic purposes, the most significant context of Sapwuahfik identity is that of the relationship of Sapwuahfik to the high island of Pohnpei.

Pohnpei as Conceptual Other

Throughout the Pacific, "metropole" high islands are of great importance to the inhabitants of neighboring atolls. Pohnpei (with a 1985 population of 26,198 [Gorenflo and Levin 1992]) plays a central political and economic role in the Eastern Carolines. The material context of Sapwuahfik's relationship with Pohnpei shapes the situations in which Sapwuahfik actors create Sapwuahfik identity. Although the atoll has adequate gardens, pigs, and fish for self-sufficiency, Sapwuahfik, like other outer islands, depends on shipping from Pohnpei for much-desired foreign goods, especially imported food, cloth, soap, gasoline, and kerosene. The local elementary school and, less completely, the churches, are governed by higher echelons of these institutions on Pohnpei. Control of state and federal government information channels and budgets appears to outer islanders to be in the hands of those on Pohnpei (though recent concerted political activity by outer islanders may alter this). Pohnpei power in state politics gives predominance to Pohnpei ideas about proper behavior and provides a motive for Sapwuahfik individuals who wish to conform to Pohnpei cultural practice. On the other hand, Sapwuahfik's relative independence gives them a certain material ground on which to state their cultural distinctiveness. People repeatedly told me that if the supply ship stopped coming, they could manage without difficulty by returning to remembered substitutes for imported goods.

There is as well a certain cultural dominance related to the "big island"–"little island" tradition found also in other areas of the Pacific. Although there is no evidence that Pohnpei ever exerted hegemony over nearby outer islands on the order of the "Yap Empire," older people on Sapwuahfik have a distinct sense of the proper sort of relationship that should obtain between big and little islands. One elderly man spoke with disapproval of Pohnpei adopting a Sapwuahfik variety of tuber. "Things should come from the big land to the small one," he said. "A small island shouldn't be sending things to the big island." But, as we shall see, the things a big island does send to an atoll are not necessarily welcomed or accepted.

In discussing the conceptual contrast of Sapwuahfik with Pohnpei, I must add the caveat that it is misleading to represent Pohnpei Island as consisting of a single "traditional" culture, though I use that phrasing for convenience. Precolonial Pohnpei displayed considerable internal variation, and archaeology, oral traditions, and ethnology indicate significant prehistoric as well as historic changes (Hanlon 1988). As *mehn Pohnpei* say, *Pohnpei sohte ehu*, "Pohnpei is not one" (Hanlon 1984).

SAPWUAHFIK CONNECTIONS WITH POHNPEI

In addition to political-economic ties, the historical relationship between Sapwuahfik and Pohnpei has profoundly shaped modern Sapwuahfik culture, which could be seen as a localized version of that of the high island. The discussion of traditional status and feasting, religious beliefs, and sorcery presented in the next chapters outlines crucial distinctions drawn by Sapwuahfik people between their customs and "way of thinking" and those of Pohnpei. This sense of distinction is being increasingly challenged by contact, as Sapwuahfik people find themselves more frequently involved with *mehn Pohnpei* (and to a lesser extent with other Islanders and foreigners).

No Pohnpei people live permanently on Sapwuahfik, and bonds of marriage or adoption between the two islands are infrequent. But the high island, a center of government (now hosting the capital of the Federated States of Micronesia) as well as a traditional force in the region, is a focus of activity for the outer islands of Pohnpei State. Sapwuahfik people often travel to Pohnpei for medical treatment; to deal with government, legal, or church business; to make major purchases, visit family, or accompany a relative doing any of these—or simply for the pleasurable novelty of travel. "*Mehn Pohnpei* are another sort of people," a man told me as we stood on the deck of the supply ship leaving the lagoon. "I don't want to see only Ngatik people." A few Sapwuahfik youth attend the regional high school in Kolonia, and others visit Kolonia for its urban excitement. Sapwuahfik people are able to move easily between the atoll and Pohnpei because of the large inventory of shared culture: Pohnpei's language, customs of interpersonal etiquette, and social organization are similar to those of the home atoll.

In material terms, then, Sapwuahfik is politically and economically subsidiary to Pohnpei, tied to it also by constant visiting and a limited network of interpersonal bonds mediated by the small population of Sapwuahfik ancestry living permanently on Pohnpei. It would not be accurate to speak of Pohnpei "absorbing" or "dominating" Sapwuahfik, because life on the atoll proceeds for the most part without reference to Pohnpei and an ethic of potential economic self-sufficiency is still, at this point, viable. There are no material conditions that create a consistent source of strain between the two.

People of Sapwuahfik descent who live permanently on Pohnpei provide visitors with hospitality and information. Two

Kolonia neighborhoods in which several Sapwuahfik families live are known as Sapwuahfik areas. The part of Sokehs settled by Sapwuahfik people after its original inhabitants were dispossessed is also thought of as a Sapwuahfik area, though many of the Sapwuahfik families have sold or leased their land and now (like some recent arrivals from the atoll) live scattered throughout Pohnpei. These permanent residents of Pohnpei do not plan to return to live on the atoll. They often own land on Pohnpei, intermarry with other groups, and provide a constant trickle of people who no longer consider themselves, and are no longer considered to be, *mehn Sapwuahfik*.

Sapwuahfik people living permanently on Pohnpei do not form a distinct physical community, as do the Kapingamarangi people in Kolonia (Lieber 1977a, 1990) and the Pulapese on Truk (Flinn 1990), nor are they as dispersed as the Nukuoro people on Pohnpei (Carroll 1977). The several Sapwuahfik areas are informal and, as the shift away from Sokehs shows, impermanent. Only in the past few years have *mehn Sapwuahfik* begun to organize a church, a clear marker of a functioning, separate community on Pohnpei. Casual meetings maintain personal ties among atoll people on Pohnpei, but feasts sponsored by *mehn Sapwuahfik* are the only formal occasions that encourage Sapwuahfik solidarity. Funerals and commemoration feasts (marking the first anniversary of a death) of people with Sapwuahfik ties who die on Pohnpei are the most frequent and well attended of these. At such a death, genealogical ties are traced for the privilege of attending, and so the ties are maintained.

Sapwuahfik people living on Pohnpei work for businesses there or for the government; they may operate a small store, do some fishing, or, if they live outside of Kolonia, farm. Sapwuahfik people say that *mehn Pohnpei* sometimes "discriminate against" or have "prejudice" against them (using the English words), citing the use of insulting terms and the teasing of Sapwuahfik children and adults for their dialect, their English pidgin, their ignorance of honorific etiquette, and other stereotypes of Sapwuahfik people. Bascom stated in 1965 that *mehn Pohnpei* regarded Sapwuahfik as "historically, culturally, and linguistically related" yet, "curiously, of all the out-islanders, the Ngatik are the least liked" (35), though I cannot confirm this from my experience. Damas's work on Pingelap suggests that this feeling may be part of the Pohnpei Island–outer island contrast. He writes that for Pingelapese, "there has always been a feeling that high islanders do not appreciate the special problems of atoll living and also that Ponapeans were condescending or exclusive in their dealings with the atoll dwellers" (Damas 1985:49).

Among families permanently resident on the high island, marriage with *mehn Pohnpei* (and in Sokehs with neighboring Mortlockese) is frequent, and there is a constant small movement of people who shift from Sapwuahfik to Pohnpei identity. I did no formal research among Sapwuahfik residents of Pohnpei, but my impression is that those who wish to do so have little difficulty in "becoming" *mehn Pohnpei* (at least from the Sapwuahfik point of view; I do not know the Pohnpeian opinion of them). They do this by obtaining land, establishing ties of adoption, employment, marriage, and service with Pohnpei people, and by participating in Pohnpei custom (for example, contributing to feasts in their section and chiefdom or accepting a local title). Other Sapwuahfik people living permanently on Pohnpei keep up relationships and behavior that maintain Sapwuahfik identity.

The history of population movement between the islands has produced a maze of genealogical pathways and social connections that allows people to shift their identity with relative ease. In 1980 I attended the funeral of an elderly woman in Kolonia, at which most of the crowd were strangers to me. I guessed that they were *mehn Pohnpei* or *mehn Sapwuahfik* who lived on Pohnpei, and I asked a woman near me if the deceased had been *uhdahn* of Pohnpei or Sapwuahfik. "We're truly Pohnpei people," she replied. *Nohno*, "mother" (a classificatory kin term), went to Sapwuahfik and had children there, but was truly *mehn Pohnpei*. I later asked a Sapwuahfik person the same question, and got the answer that the dead woman was truly *mehn Sapwuahfik*. Indeed, her ancestry connects her with both the ancient Sapwuahfik people, because her mother's mother was a massacre survivor, and a prominent Pohnpei line, because her father's mother was identified as sister to the Nahnmwarki of Madolenihmw. The woman's children, who all lived on Pohnpei at that time, had married both Sapwuahfik and Pohnpei spouses; her funeral was a mixture of both "styles" of public ceremonial. Members of such a family have identity options, which also widen their choices of social and economic action.

CONSTRUCTING SAMENESS AND DIFFERENCE

Because of the demographics of the postmassacre resettlement of the atoll, Sapwuahfik and Pohnpei are related by history and descent, and by shared language, tradition, and custom. *Kiht duwehte mehn Pohnpei*, atoll people say, "We are the same as the people of Pohnpei." At the same time, they are as likely to comment, *Mehn Pohnpei ehu soahngen*, "Pohnpei people are another thing altogether" (lit., "another kind").

Sapwuahfik people describe themselves as a unique, distinctive cultural group. They talk about Sapwuahfik custom and dialect, and there are songs, food specialties, and elements of material culture that are readily identified as *stylen Sapwuahfik*. But the facts of language, custom, and descent cannot be overlooked. Of all the Eastern Carolines outer islanders, Sapwuahfik people are most like—indeed, they are very like—the people of Pohnpei. They speak the same language, practice the same lifestyle, believe in the same concepts, and are organized in the same social units. To an objective outsider, the trait list of things distinctively Sapwuahfik is extremely limited; an ethnologist could classify Sapwuahfik culture as a simplified local variant of Pohnpei culture. Sapwuahfik people, of course, would disagree. In fact, it is Pohnpei that they consider themselves most distinct from. We might say, rather glibly, that it is the extensive similarity with Pohnpei that requires the cultural elaboration of difference.[4]

When an informant drew the layout of a Sapwuahfik feast (described in Chapter 6), I asked him if it was also valid for Pohnpei. He said it was, going on to say, "We are truly Pohnpei people"—adding that Sapwuahfik and Pohnpei have the same traditional stories and so on. When Sapwuahfik people say they are "the same as" Pohnpei, they list shared language, folktales, clan affiliations, title system, and physical descent from Pohnpei people—the perceived sameness is a recognition of material and historical ties, not an expression of identity.

It is in other Sapwuahfik ideas about Pohnpei that sharply distinguish the two populations that we see the primacy of a sociological definition of group identity. The Sapwuahfik distinction from Pohnpei is a good case for Barth's (1969) pathbreaking argument that it is not objective cultural differences that separate two self-defined populations; rather, their felt distinctiveness is marked by selected diacritics validating the dichotomy. Sapwuahfik people are Sapwuahfik, in a sense, because they are not Pohnpeian—whereas, given historical and geographic circumstance, they might have become so. Because of the great similarity, the minimal contrast pairs Sapwuahfik people select and express are critical to maintaining their separate identity. Thus Pohnpei is conceptually maintained as the "other" against which Sapwuahfik identity is constructed and measured. The material content of Sapwuahfik custom, the trait list, identifies "who the Sapwuahfik are" among all Eastern Caroline Islanders. It is comparative contrast in particular aspects of culture that answers the more difficult question of why *mehn Sapwuahfik* are not, culturally speaking, *mehn Pohnpei* (Poyer 1988a).

Choosing to be *mehn Sapwuahfik* entails appropriate social behavior, including where one lives, who one relates to as kin, what dialect one speaks, and what choices one makes about religious and rank-related behavior. It is in their egalitarian ethos and in religion that Sapwuahfik people most emphasize their distinctive cultural identity vis-à-vis Pohnpei and other nearby islands. These two domains are not the sole areas of contrast. Other less-elaborated differences occur in verbal comparisons but lack structural or complex ideological support. Similar casual contrasts are often made between Sapwuahfik and other Eastern Carolines communities. For example, Sapwuahfik people say they have "white blood" and that compared to themselves some groups of people are "lazy." Presumably, then, they could point to differences in biological descent or economic practice and emphasize political similarities. In fact, however, they choose to contrast egalitarianism and religion and emphasize similarities of language, history, and material custom. Both contrasts and similarities are most common and most elaborated in speaking of Sapwuahfik and Pohnpei. Instead of the plausible proposition "we are *mehn Pohnpei*," Sapwuahfik people assert, "we are not (or should not be) Pohnpei people," an alternative proposition that is made true by action. It is possible for individuals to create their identity—rather than have it imposed as superordinate—because of the character of local theories of sameness and difference. Someone who lives away from the atoll for any length of time must decide whether to maintain personal ties with Sapwuahfik or let them drop, to identify himself or herself as *mehn Sapwuahfik* or use some other identification. In every conversation, a choice is made between speaking Pohnpei or Sapwuahfik dialect; in addition, a man chooses whether or not to use pidgin. A man living on Pohnpei must also decide whether to use the respect form of the Pohnpei language when speaking to high-titled people, and whether to strive to advance in Pohnpei's traditional title system or to pay it little attention. When planning a feast, he must decide whether it will be held in the Sapwuahfik or Pohnpei style. The local organization of cultural difference permits choices of specific, symbolically weighted behaviors to be read as statements of identity. Thus one can *wiala*, "become," *mehn Pohnpei* or *mehn Sapwuahfik*.

Note the contrast between this and an "ethnic" identity, which is superordinate and based on a biological metaphor. One cannot "become" Irish in Boston, because "Irishness" is held to be an innate biological state; to attempt to change one's ethnic category is to attempt fraud (see Lieber 1990). A person of Sapwuahfik ancestry acting Pohnpeian is not trying to pass as *mehn Pohnpei*—rather, he or she is choosing an available option, because cultural categories are accessible through behavioral choices. An individual's choice of action is a choice of identity. To act in ways not commonly accepted as *tiahk en Sapwuahfik*,

148

"Sapwuahfik custom," or *stylen Sapwuahfik* is not taken to be acting as a bad or incompetent *mehn Sapwuahfik,* but rather to be acting as a member of another group. In this way, being *mehn Sapwuahfik* is actively constructed. As Sapwuahfik involvement in regional and national political activity increases, though, it is likely that identity is being shaped, constrained, and pushed in the direction of the tighter boundaries of Western ethnic categories.

ORGANIZING *Mehn Sapwuahfik*

Until the last decade, Sapwuahfik has lagged behind Pohnpei, and Mwoakilloa and Pingelap as well, in Western education and in the political lobbying activity that results in status, power, and authority on the supralocal level. As the concrete benefits of such political activity become evident—showing how participation in elections, legislatures, and the judiciary results in schools, new housing, health services, loans, and wage labor— outer islanders living on Pohnpei have begun to organize for action.

The Sapwuahfik community on Pohnpei has only recently begun to have a sense of itself as such, and only in the past decade initiated activities that may eventually create an ethnic group in the political and structural sense (Poyer 1990). In order for Sapwuahfik leaders to create a coherent constituency, which implies political loyalty and a unified front, from what is by no means a tightly knit community on Pohnpei, several rifts must be bridged: between Sapwuahfik on the home atoll and on Pohnpei, between people in Kolonia and those scattered across the high island, and between Sapwuahfik people who identify themselves as such and others who are beginning to drift (through marriage, adoption, or choice) into "becoming" something else. I witnessed one such effort at unity in 1980, when a group of Sapwuahfik women went on an overnight fishing expedition from Kolonia. Women visiting from the atoll and women from families permanently residing on Pohnpei took part in the trip, the appeal of which was partly based on the self-conscious ideal that Sapwuahfik women (unlike those of most neighboring populations) know how to fish and enjoy fishing. On their return, a large part of the Sapwuahfik community on Pohnpei met them for a celebration. A major purpose of the occasion, expressed only obliquely by the women, but openly by the influential man whose sister had organized the trip, was to draw together Sapwuahfik people on Pohnpei. The event was underwritten by several politically important Sapwuahfik men.

When I visited Pohnpei at the end of 1989, I found that several new undertakings were moving Sapwuahfik people on Pohnpei nearer to formal organization as a politically active community. The house of Luhkenkolwof (elected chief magistrate) in the larger Sapwuahfik neighborhood of Kolonia was a focus for visitors from the atoll. Protestant services were held there (Luhkenkolwof was also a church leader). The 1989 Christmas celebration held at his house was explicitly presented as just like what would have been done on Sapwuahfik—in contrast to Pohnpei-style Christmas activities, which Sapwuahfik people thought less enjoyable. Protestants have begun fund raising and planning for a church as a meeting place and focus for the Sapwuahfik community on Pohnpei. (I was told that *mehn Sapwuahfik* were the only group, besides the Nukuoro, without its own meeting place on Pohnpei.) There are now two organizations for Sapwuahfik women on Pohnpei: a branch of a Protestant church-women's association and a completely new, nondenominational group, *Lihpad* (Women of Olpad), named after the legendary figure. The women's groups raise funds, hold parties, and provide planning and labor for Sapwuahfik projects on Pohnpei.

Until now, Sapwuahfik people have become involved in statewide politics only to the extent that they are personally concerned. There has been great interest, for example, in the mayoral race in Kolonia, because the longtime incumbent, though a permanent resident of Pohnpei, is of Sapwuahfik descent and maintains strong ties with the atoll. People's opinions about Pohnpei's 1979 gubernatorial race depended on their social or genealogical relationships with those running. But in recent years, growing political sophistication has increased local leaders' awareness of a useful constituency of minority groups. Although it cannot yet be said that Sapwuahfik people on Pohnpei vote as a bloc or see themselves as a political-action unit, there are signs that such intentional activity lies ahead. The ideology of ethnicity, which also can be seen developing in other minority communities of Pohnpei, is a way of reaching that potential by drawing on Sapwuahfik awareness of shared history, descent, and custom, and on the Sapwuahfik sense of distinctiveness. *Mehn Sapwuahfik* have also occasionally joined with Kapingamarangi and Nukuoro people in the tentative beginnings of a southern outer-island solidarity, to express mutual political and economic concerns that set them in competition with Pohnpei and with the eastern outer islands of Mwoakilloa and Pingelap. In January 1990 Sapwuahfik's state legislator was actively campaigning to be the southern outer islands delegate to the state constitutional convention.

Sapwuahfik people today appear to be in the initial stages of a process of political mobilization. An obvious element of this process is the selective emphasis on certain aspects of Sapwuahfik culture (such as history, the Sapwuahfik dialect, egalitarian distribution of feast goods) which begin to be objectified as tradition, perhaps eventually to play the role of unifying symbols for a Sapwuahfik ethnic group.[5] Despite the development of the organizational characteristics of an ethnic group as a politically salient entity, I see no evidence that Sapwuahfik people are adopting the biological theory of personal identity implicit in the Western popular concept of ethnicity. To be "one of Sapwuahfik" is still very much to act as a Sapwuahfik person, and to be formed as a Sapwuahfik person in the matrix of atoll life or the life of the Sapwuahfik community on Pohnpei.

Externalizing History

In implicit and explicit comparisons of Pohnpei and Sapwuahfik ways, Sapwuahfik people reveal the connection between their modern identity and their history. Through cultural elaboration of the markers that distinguish them, they play their own identity against their representations of Pohnpei, and so constantly recreate themselves as a distinctive community. Sapwuahfik representations of Pohnpei are representations of contrast, derived from a complex play of the meanings of tradition/progress, Islander/foreigner, virtue/vice. *Mehn Sapwuahfik* "externalize" their history,[6] projecting key symbols of their story onto elements of Pohnpei culture.

In every multicultural region, groups create their own identity in part through contrast with other groups, yet each group constructs its neighbors as "others" in particular ways. Sapwuahfik people construct *mehn Pohnpei* as others by encoding aspects of social life shared by the two populations in the symbols of Sapwuahfik identity, which in large part depends on the Sapwuahfik vision of the past. People understand choices of social action as choices of identity, because the local vision of history makes these behaviors plausible as statements about identity. (In this sense, we might casually say that history validates identity.) Sapwuahfik people do not point to empirical differences, such as dialect or food specialties, as markers of their identity. Rather, they explicitly contrast their culture with that of Pohnpei in areas which, to the objective observer, are much less distinct, and which take their validity not from the empirical facts of difference but from cultural assertions of it. Specifically, visions of the past present an ideology in which certain arenas of behavior become key symbols in contemporary statements about identity. Modern Sapwuahfik people are egalitarian in feasting and rank behavior—like Americans, among their ancestors—in contrast with Pohnpei's hierarchy. Christianity took root on Sapwuahfik as a reward for discarding pagan ways, especially sorcery; forcibly pulled into "enlightenment," Sapwuahfik people see themselves as different from those with a less-dramatic entry into the Christian world.

The symbolic structure of the Sapwuahfik vision of the past and of modern community identity are in a sense isomorphic. What is distinctively Sapwuahfik today draws legitimacy and emotional impact from its affiliation with the ever-present knowledge of the powerful tale of the massacre and its aftermath. Yet the past in itself would not be remembered, and would have no role in social life today, were it not for its intimate involvement in the structure of meaning that connects and separates Sapwuahfik and Pohnpei. I suggest neither history nor the web of cultural identities as prior. Sapwuahfik people have never encountered *mehn Pohnpei* without the knowledge of the massacre; Sapwuahfik people's speech, their appearance, the way they are stereotyped on Pohnpei reveal the continuing saliency of the massacre's outcome. Similarly, massacre stories have never been told in an environment free of the contrasting comparative tension of Sapwuahfik's large and powerful neighbor. Historical knowledge and the social practice of identity have shaped each other since a new culture emerged from the chaos of 1837. To be a massacre descendant, and an interacting neighbor of Pohnpei, have been inseparable aspects of being *mehn Sapwuahfik* since that time.

CHAPTER SIX

The Egalitarian Ethos

S APWUAHFIK'S EGALITARIAN IDEAL is expressed verbally, in social action, and in the structures of atoll political economy. The source of this ideology is complex; it involves common Pacific low island–high island differences, Sapwuahfik history, and the politics of modern Micronesia. The egalitarian ideal is challenged at times, by political competition among atoll men, by those who frankly desire to emulate Pohnpei custom, and by Sapwuahfik involvement in regional affairs.

Sapwuahfik does not have a word or phrase that I am glossing as *egalitarianism*, and I use that English term in a particular way. I do not mean that every adult has absolute political autonomy, because Sapwuahfik's title system is a formal structure of status differentiation. I use the term to refer to a consistent pattern of behavior surrounding the public symbolism of rank and the economics of redistribution. People openly discuss behavioral choices in these domains, usually in terms of how Pohnpei and Sapwuahfik are alike and different and what it means that a person chooses one "style" rather than the other.

When people choose to act in the public political realm, they are also deciding on a message about cultural identity. A twofold theme, which I gloss as egalitarianism, recurs in their decisions: Sapwuahfik does not display the close attention to rank found on Pohnpei, and Sapwuahfik style is to call for equal shares for all at redistributive events, rather than to give economic privileges to those of high rank.

Creating Social Equality

The organization of economic and social life that effectively maintains egalitarian beliefs and behavior on Sapwuahfik is built on cultural concepts of social equality. As a practical matter, social equality depends on symmetrical interpersonal interactions and relatively equal access to material resources and decision making.[1]

Social equality on Sapwuahfik does not mean equality among all members of the community. Marginal people, such as the very young, the senile, and those suffering severe mental or physical handicaps, are not social equals with other adults, and age and sex categories constitute hierarchical power relations. In addition, the wealth and power of individuals differs because of access to land, the number of workers under kin obligations to them, cash income, formal education, traditional knowledge, political and church positions, and useful contacts with people on Pohnpei or beyond. Despite such differences, socioeconomic processes on the atoll maintain rough material equality among households and among extended families over time. Furthermore, despite individual differences, the interpersonal relations of all adult men and all adult women (separately) can be characterized as those of social equals.

ECONOMIC PROCESSES

Equality in the limited sense used here is made possible by wide access to the means of production. Every family head, and nearly every adult, has the use of productive land. Use rights are widely shared across kin ties, and land is rarely alienated from the family through sale. Control of a family's land is vested in the legally inscribed landowner, who may grant others permission to use it. Land inheritance is predominantly from parent to child, called *sahpw en sousou,* "land of the grave." Inheritance in the male line is emphasized, though women hold, inherit, and pass on land in their own right. Land is also inherited from other relatives, and people occasionally receive land as a gift or, very rarely, purchase it from nonrelatives.[2]

The oldest sibling (or, often, the oldest brother) has greatest control over the family's land after the parent's death, though the sibling group shares rights in it. Although the initial division of Ngatik Islet's land after the massacre followed Aisikaya's personal judgment, inheritance since then demonstrates the pattern of sibling groups sharing "land of the grave" that is still the rule. As a result, heads of household in a locale tend to be related by descent from a sibling set of one or two generations past.

Other productive resources are also widely accessible. Many households have sailing canoes made by men of the family or purchased boats with outboard motors; men without vessels borrow them or join others to fish. Some gardening and fishing tools are made, others purchased; all are borrowed across a network of kin, friends, and neighbors. Children learn gender-appropriate subsistence skills from older relatives. Specialized knowledge about canoe building, carpentry, and weaving mats or hats is solicited from a relative or taught in exchange for payment.

Opportunities for cash income are scarce but diverse, giving every household an occasional chance to make money. Regular salaries go to teachers and the community nurse or medical aide—jobs controlled by the state bureaucracy on Pohnpei and not necessarily given to Sapwuahfik people. Locally appointed or elected salaried positions are frequently contested, and several people may hold them in the course of a year. (Salaried positions other than teacher or nurse have been held only by men.) I never heard job assignments spoken of in terms of "taking turns" or "spreading the wealth" (which are American concepts), but that is a result of frequent personnel shifts. Cash also comes from occasional government or private wage work and small-scale entrepreneurship (operating a store or selling baked goods, fish, animals, or crafts). Salaried and hourly wage labor are much more readily available on Pohnpei; people go there to work and receive goods and cash from kin employed there.

Another way access to cash equalized is by explicitly invoking egalitarian redistribution, as in the case observed by a visitor on the government ship that brought supplies for construction of the Sapwuahfik school in 1966 (Thompson 1966:13). "Everyone" worked to build the school—men and women, old and young and disabled. Not only did men and women receive equal rates of pay, but "it was later decided that the total amount paid for labor would be equally divided among those who worked regardless of how much work each one did."

A good mix of ages and sexes in a household lets members combine all these resources—subsistence gardening and fishing, craft skills, trade or sale of skills and products to others, and wage labor. Most households consist of three or four generations: a parent or parents, some or all of their children and spouses, and some or all of the children of younger generations. In 1979–80, five households consisted of siblings living together, alone or with spouses and children, and there were five single-person households. Households cooperate in labor, socialize children, and are temporary productive estates as husbands, wives, and perhaps siblings pool the use of their land.

Though lineal relatives form the core of most households, people frequently move to live with other kin for visits that may last years. Residence, land inheritance, and kin relations all indicate individuals operating in terms of a bilateral kindred, making economic and social decisions based on multiple, crosscutting ties binding them to many different households. Ethnographers have demonstrated how the flexibility of social organization on small islands lets individuals maximize their options in planning economic and political strategies to benefit themselves and their families (Brady 1976; Lundsgaarde 1974; Silverman 1969). Sapwuahfik kinship, with bilateral reckoning, generational terminology, and a high incidence of adoption, supports such flexibility.[3] Wide reckoning of kinship is expressed in extensive exchanges of labor and material goods among individuals and households, and in the transfer of rights in children and land.

Most households are built around a couple whose partnership has proven to be long lasting. Young men and women generally choose spouses for themselves; marriages are constrained by clan exogamy, an ideal ban on parallel-cousin marriage, and a strong preference for parental approval. Affinal relationships are important and extend each household's connections. A newly married couple usually lives for a few years with the parents of either husband or wife, sharing subsistence work. Some couples continue to live in the parents' house, taking it over on their deaths. (If a couple establishes their own residence, it is more likely to be on the husband's family's land.) The need for more than a small nuclear family to carry out all the work of a household interferes with many couple's initial efforts to live separately. As parents grow old and die, children grow up, adoptions occur, and ties with other relatives strengthen, a maturing couple gradually becomes the center of its own productive household.

At any given time, some of the atoll's households will be wealthier than others. A household will be better off if its members have access to more and better land, more labor (especially that of hardworking young men and women), better tools, more equipment or money as capital, more pigs, dogs, and chickens, or more ready cash. The most important variable governing wealth is household size and composition. The poorest households either lack a young-to-mature adult of either sex or consist of a mature couple with many young children. These households lack wealth only because of their current position in the domestic cycle. Adoption or relatives moving in might well change the situation even before the natural generational shift. Young people, especially, including young married couples, are free to relocate at will, and such a move may literally change the economics of an elderly widow's household overnight.

The second important factor creating wealth differences between households is access to a regular cash income, either through a salaried position, entrepreneurship, work on Pohnpei, or remittances from relatives. Cash buys durable and consumable goods, including materials for a wood-frame or concrete house, motorboats, generators, sewing machines, and gas lanterns. Consumer goods supplement local production at family-sponsored feasts, and cash and consumer goods may be loaned or given away. Though sewing machines, outboard motors, and some food purchases can be used to produce items for sale, cash is usually expended on consumer purchases rather than invested in capital goods (as in the economy of Kosrae, Peoples 1985). This means households do not accumulate wealth from generation to generation.

The organization of community life puts households on an equal social footing, despite temporary economic inequities. Fairness is an explicit concern when the community distributes incoming resources and assigns contributions to community efforts such as large feasts. The ideal is that everyone (variously: every adult, every man or woman, every section, or every household) contributes an equal share to a group effort and receives an equal share at a distribution.

This way of planning community projects, based on assumed equality, also promotes equality. First, those who are physically or financially unable to do their share are usually excused from contributing, which helps even out household wealth inequities. For example, the municipal council might assign every household with an adult man to provide a chicken for a community feast, protectively excluding the few households consisting only of women and children, or high-titled persons and salaried workers might be assessed five dollars for a contribution whereas others give one dollar. Second, community projects are organized to allow options in how individuals and households participate. A household may contribute labor, leadership, knowledge, locally produced food or goods, purchased food or goods, or cash—or a combination of these. This gives households flexibility in achieving the community-set standard, which reduces the significance of inequities in cash income, labor, and land.

As in most Pacific communities, exchange is the material substance of social life on Sapwuahfik, producing a constant flow of food, labor, goods, and kin ties (through marriage and the fostering and adoption of children) through the community, from which no household or healthy adult is excluded. Within a household and among close kin, generalized exchange is the rule. Exchanges with more distant kin, neighbors, and friends are more closely tracked via immediate complementary exchange (e.g., cooked garden food for fish) or delayed exchange of gifts. Household work is allotted according to age and gender; beyond this, siblings, parents and children, affines, and friends share labor without bookkeeping. A large task, such as rethatching a roof, is either repaid with a party for workers at the conclusion of the job or hired out. (Young men and women and adult women often form work groups for such chores, their earnings going to church contributions, a feast, or Christmas gifts.)

Exchanges of labor and goods, which connect people in networks of social equality, also identify women as categorically unequal with men. Women are free to marry, divorce, and adopt children, and they exchange labor and food freely among themselves in a kin network, a voluntary work group, or a church group, and with male kin. In her household of residence, however, older men and women can command a woman's labor, whereas mature men's labor is not similarly under the control of older women. Most important, except as part of courtship, marriage, or romance, women do not share or exchange resources with men outside their kin network and, in fact, seldom interact with them except in a church organization or, occasionally, as employees. Public life is sex-segregated and close friendships are with members of one's own sex. (Of course, men and women

FIG. 8. *Sapwuahfik men prepare* sakau, *"kava" (*Piper methysticum*), imported from Pohnpei. The pounded root is mixed with water to prepare a mild narcotic drink. Kava does not grow on the atoll.*

know one another on a daily basis as neighbors, visitors, church members, and so on. Men cannot casually command the labor of nonkin women.) This means that women as a group are structurally subordinate to men, who control the public sphere of exchange.

Feast giving is the formal mode of exchange. Because feasts (*kamadipw*) are an important arena of public behavior, including contests over ideology and individual statements of identity, I will describe them in some detail. *Kamadipw* involving the entire community are held for traditional events or government purposes. Many special circumstances call for a public feast, such as first-fruit celebrations opening breadfruit season or feasts dedicating public construction projects. Churches sponsor feasts for religious holidays, to welcome church officials, or for special events such as visits by church members from other sections or islands. A major communitywide feast, to which every capable household contributes equally, would include the preparation of elaborate dishes such as baked bananas, *morior* (a taro dish for which Sapwuahfik is deservedly famous), and breadfruit with coconut cream, as well as fish, octopus, taro, rice, and drinking coconuts. As an example, the September 1979 visit of the governor of Pohnpei State and his staff meant a large output of goods and energy by every family on the atoll. The municipal council assigned food quotas to each section and family contributions within sections. People spent the days before the visit fishing, octopusing, digging taro, cooking, and cleaning public spaces. A levy was collected to buy pigs, and some family pigs were killed. Roughly half the food was given to the governor; the rest was redistributed after the formal *kamadipw*.

In addition to official feasts, private feasts occur almost every week. Private feasts mark a child's birthday, a death or its commemoration, a new canoe, motorboat, or house, a wedding, recovery from serious illness, homecoming, departure, or bestowal of a title. Host families have a great deal of leeway as to the size, elaborateness, and formality of private feasts. News of feasts travels swiftly and widely, and even those held with little advance warning draw a quick response as relatives, neighbors, and friends appear at the house with contributions of food and labor. People told me repeatedly that "anyone" could contribute to any family's special-occasion feast, and though participation is not random, most private feasts draw in a net of relationships well beyond close kin. A family's largest private feasts will be for a child's first birthday and for an adult's funeral. At a funeral, pig and taro are distributed in a family-organized but usually communitywide feast. The family is responsible for providing pigs, but the whole community sometimes contributes a dollar or two per adult to purchase one for the funeral feast. To demonstrate the extent of contributions, record keepers at three funerals recorded 209, 212, and 270 contributors. Those "helping"

FIG. 9. *Preparing a community feast in the elementary school building. Contributions from households, brought in baskets and bowls, are divided into equal shares for the distribution.*

with money or other gifts are noted on a list, to be consulted when the cooked food is divided for distribution (in some cases, it is not eaten on the spot but taken home immediately). At the food distribution, every helper, regardless of rank or ties of kinship with the family or size of household or amount of assistance rendered, receives the same amount.

The competitive aspect of hosting feasts on Sapwuahfik is deflected away from long-term accumulation of wealth or power. Individuals, families, churches, and sections often strive to outdo others in hosting a successful event, and feasts are signs of political strength in elections, but the effect is not cumulative. Unlike on Pohnpei, competitive feast giving on Sapwuahfik is not a major means of rising in the political system. A family may hold a large feast for a child's first birthday—but, if resources are scarce for the next event, say a commemoration feast for the anniversary of a death, it will accordingly be a small affair. Although every family's feast-giving behavior is discussed, it is not seen as historically linear or directed at a political aim.

We can summarize by saying that rough economic equality of households is maintained by wide access to essential resources and considerable household autonomy in resource management. Like men in acephalous societies, Sapwuahfik men decide the allocation of the resources and labor of their households. They are constrained by community expectations, but no social institution has the power to determine these personal transactions. Women's and children's autonomy in this regard is limited by age and gender-dominance relations. All, however, are subject to having their resources summoned to achieve the goals of the entire community and the household, section, and church to which they belong.

Hierarchical societies develop from egalitarian ones, so it is worth asking what might shift Sapwuahfik from egalitarianism toward more differential wealth accumulation. The most likely source of such a change is the growing store of cash in families with access to well-salaried government jobs on Pohnpei. Since the 1960s, it has been possible for a person with a high school or college education to hold a state or federal job, giving his family the means to accumulate capital in the form of houses, boats, and collateral for business loans. If Sapwuahfik people ever begin to sell land, these families are in the best position to buy it. And only families with cash can support children through high school and college, ensuring a second generation of well-paid government employees. Access to income through education of children might be the form of "capital investment" that will produce permanent inequities in the future.

SOCIAL AND POLITICAL PROCESSES

In decision making as in the economy, certain social mechanisms create symmetrical power relations among age and sex peers. However, community life is complicated by the presence of two alternative structures of putative authority. Like all Micronesians, Sapwuahfik people deal with a double set of political systems—the indigenous hierarchy and an imported electoral democracy. As on Pohnpei, the introduction of elective political offices has not replaced the traditional title system but has resulted in a complex interplay of the two (see Fischer 1974; Hughes 1969, 1970, 1972, 1974, 1982; Meller 1969; and Ward 1975 for the interaction of traditional and elective offices on Pohnpei).

As local, state, and national government continues to develop, power comes increasingly into the hands of those in elective positions. The power of the chief magistrate and the state legislator depends on money—their salaries and control of government projects or monies that come to Sapwuahfik. Both elected and appointed positions can be and are used for personal and family advantage as well as for service to the community. Rumor and backbiting hover about the work of state legislator, chief magistrate, municipal councilors, and co-op manager (the cooperative store, the largest on the island, is run by a manager and a board of five directors) regardless of who holds office. Each position except that of legislator, which has a set term, sees frequent turnover. Family disputes and interpersonal rivalries are played out in public politics, as well as in church, the title system, feast giving, and personal interaction.

Sapwuahfik people comment that traditional titleholders have lost power to the more recent set of officials, but ethnohistorical evidence suggests that since the origins of the modern population, power has never rested in the title system. Rather, men whose opinions were followed, such as Aisikaya, derived their influence from gender, age, personal abilities, family strength, and physical and economic power.

The modern title system began when the European "captain" conferred the first three A-line titles of Pohnpei's system onto the three aboriginal boys who survived the massacre. As an adult, Aisikaya instituted the B-1 (nahnken) title, conferring it on a Gilbertese immigrant. At some point, or over time, the atoll adopted additional elements of Pohnpei's system.

In 1979–80, I collected a list of fourteen A-line titles and thirteen B-line titles in current use on Sapwuahfik. Let me emphasize that this does not constitute an official list of Sapwuahfik's titles but presents titles used at the time of my visit. These represent portions of an ideal title-system structure and can be matched with Pohnpei's system. Here is the ranked list of Sapwuahfik titles, in the incomplete form in which I obtained it:

A-line Titles	B-line Titles
1. Nahnmwarki	1. Nahnken
2. Wasahi	2. Nahlaimw
3. Dauk	3. Nahnsau Ririn
4. Noahs	4. Nahnapas
5. Nahnawa	5. Nahmadaun Idehd
6. Nahnipei en Ngatik	6. Souwel Lapalap
7. Nahn Kiroun Pohn Dake	7. Lepen Ririn
8. Nahlik Lapalap	8. Ou Ririn
9. Nahnid Lapalap	9. Kiroun Ngatik
10. Lempwei Lapalap	10. Kaniki Ririn
11. Soudel	11. Sedin
12. Mwarekehtik	12. Sou Madau en Ngatik
13. Nahntu	13. Lempwei en Isipahu
14. Kulap	

Although I was told that a complete list of Sapwuahfik's island-wide titles (*mwaren wehi*) consists of fifteen in each line, I did not learn the other titles. Most people could not name more than five titles; very few could list more than ten in each line. Those who were interested or who needed to refer to them (such as the Nahnken) had the list written down. Others told me there are only twelve titles in each line. (On Pohnpei, the first twelve titles in each line are considered most important [Riesenberg 1968:8]).[4] Informants stated that every adult man has a *wehi* title and that there are *kousapw*-level titles for young men (with

women holding titles cognate to their husbands'), but beyond
the first few in each line, individual titles are not important in
everyday life and are used only at formal events such as feasts.

Sapwuahfik's Nahnmwarki and Nahnken offer pronounce-
ments on public matters, but these are clearly distinguished
from *kosonned*, "law," and are recognized as unsupported by
sanctions beyond the disapproval of some community members.
Nonetheless, they have acted to influence public life, in one instance appointing an interim chief magistrate when the incumbent resigned. The extent of their influence depends on personal
qualities and the shifting currents of local politics, rather than
on the inherent authority of their titles. Those high-titled men
with political influence also possess other qualities or roles important in conferring power (for example, position in a church
hierarchy, acknowledged wisdom, or traditional knowledge). No
doubt they received their titles partly because of ability, but
there are also men of high title who have little authority. Black
(1983) describes the subtlety with which traditional Micronesian
chiefs lead, and it may be that more was going on on Sapwuahfik
than met my eye, despite my attention to the topic. Certainly
Sapwuahfik people enjoyed discussing the qualifications and performance of the Nahnmwarki and Nahnken. A few older people
even spoke of supernatural aspects of the nahnmwarki title,
judging the incumbent's ability to promote the atoll's well-be-
ing: the reign of a good nahnmwarki causes crops and fish to
flourish, but an error on his part depresses prosperity.

There are only a few high traditional titles, but there are
many other high-status public positions that a man can hold, of
which Luhkenkolwof (chief magistrate) and state representative
are the most prominent. The atoll's municipal council includes
an elected member from each section, a secretary, judge, chief
magistrate's representative on Pohnpei, shortwave radio operator, and several policemen (number and title of council positions
vary). The school board and the co-op board offer other official
positions. Church congregations are complexly organized (described in Chapter 7), with an internal church hierarchy and an-
cillary organizations. Add up all these groups—bear in mind that

others spring up for special purposes (e.g., singing or traditional dance practice groups) and that most positions frequently change incumbents—and compare the result to a total adult population of 285. It is apparent that everyone who so desires, within somewhat flexible age and gender restraints, can play a role in official community decision making. Every adult belongs to several crosscutting social groups (church, section, and municipality, as a minimum), playing a role depending on gender, age, abilities, reputation, and inclination. Thus, although the atoll's social structure provides positions varying in status and role, it provides many such positions and plentiful opportunities for individuals to cycle through them. Furthermore, both informal private and formal public decision-making processes on Sapwuahfik reduce the authority of these positions.

Public decision-making groups for community, church, and school muster and allocate resources, plan public events, and deal with paper work. Membership in these groups overlaps widely, and every group conducts its meetings similarly, making it easy for people to enter and move between leadership positions. Groups charged with making decisions regularly return power to the wider community by dispersing responsibility, refusing to intrude on personal autonomy, and frequently changing personnel. All this means there is no mystery about the operation of decision-making groups, nor much authority given to those who serve on them. Community decision making is consensual rather than adversarial, indirect, and in a sense depersonalized or abstract (one interacts, just as one exchanges, even with individuals one dislikes). These formal qualities contribute to the public construal of adult males as social equals (Arno 1980).

The most obvious example is that all significant issues are decided at communitywide meetings; nothing of public importance can be decided by any individual. At a large meeting, discussion of a topic may go on for hours, with each aspect being fully explored. People come and go (and, later, complain about the length of the meeting). Lengthy public meetings that I attended concerned matters such as whether Catholics and Protestants should join in a large Christmas celebration and, a recurrent question, whether drinking alcohol should be permitted on Sapwuahfik. Public meetings on policy matters like these aim to establish consensus and allow dissonant voices to express themselves, but they are by no means the forum for settling issues. Informal discussion will have been underway beforehand, and any decision will be reconsidered at length (and by the wider populace) outside the public forum. If consensus seems unlikely to crystallize, the meeting may be concluded either by secret ballot or by deciding to reconvene at a later date, allowing informal discussion to continue. Even in small decision-making groups, indirectness, formal politeness, and abstractness prevent tension, avoid personalizing blame or praise, create and present decisions as consensual, and, in all, prevent status distinctions in decision making.

The communicative styles that signal and maintain social equality are most visible when decision-making groups must deal with problems. Officials are obliged to act when individuals or social units use public resources in what some people, or the law, consider inappropriate ways. The municipal council had to respond when a man appropriated wood and sheet metal left over from public construction, or when another argued that the existence of fishing licenses meant that government money could be used to buy fish only from those who, like himself, held licenses. I attended the council meeting on one such problem concerning a council member—who was present, but silent, during the meeting. The discussion was conducted with extreme indirectness (a pattern followed also in private talk about personal problems). Abstract referents such as *lahpo* (that fellow) in place of names, *apeo* (those things), *wasao* (that place), neutral phraseology such as things being "lost," "errors" being made, or "poor behavior" having occurred, indicated the problem but did not accuse. Hints and allusions—to circumstances well known in the small community—characterize public mention of problems at a profound level of abstraction. "Let's not let anything ruin Christmas" was the only public reference to a contentious tangle of difficulties surrounding plans for one year's festivities (see Brenneis and Myers 1984 on indirect speech in Pacific communities).

The council did not concretely settle any cases of misuse of public resources that I knew about. The problem was officially discussed, information spread through the community, everyone deplored it, no one (as far as I know) confronted those held responsible, and in time it faded from public view. Such things fall into the realm of personal autonomy and are not under the legitimate coercive authority of Sapwuahfik's elected or traditional leaders. If they are resolved, it is in the private domain—either by affecting the subject's reputation or (in cases seen as a dispute between individuals) by methods of interpersonal conflict resolution. Because there is no central authority with legitimate rights to punish contraventions of municipal policy, the community faces a continual series of such difficulties. Fines or jailing are imposed only for a few specific violations of the written code, usually for drinking and fighting among young men. The difficulty of dealing with other violations was revealed when the municipal council consulted about a visitor from another island who was using firearms to shoot birds on Sapwuahfik. People felt this was not acceptable, though they did not know whether it was actually illegal. The council was unsure how to handle the situation, and the secretary ended the inconclusive discussion with the joking suggestion, "Why don't we just kill him?"

As his quip shows, Sapwuahfik people recognize the difficulty of settling problems in which interpersonal equality conflicts with the desire to protect the public, and the community makes attempts to deal with them. In some cases, rules can be added to the legal code, providing an impersonal referent for authority. This does not solve the problem of enforcement but relies on widespread knowledge of the law and social pressure to conform. Another recourse, though rare, is to authorities in the state or federal systems. Preventative action in the form of propaganda or practical measures may also be taken to forestall repetition of a specific problem. These choices indicate the lack of any acceptable way to express differential authority within the community of equals (cf. Silverman 1971).

Women are excluded from speaking in communitywide meetings and serving in most official positions, a fact critical to their unequal status. Women vote in municipal, state, and federal elections (though they do not pay taxes), but they automatically assume their exclusion from many decision-making groups and events and do not ask for an increased public voice. In my observation, in fact, women often are not sure whether they are supposed to come to a particular meeting or at which meetings they are to vote; men sometimes have to call them to attend. Women sit at the fringes of community meetings (youth and children orbit beyond them), come and go more than men, and never make formal speeches, although some may audibly comment on the proceedings. They speak publicly only at all-female meetings. Men represent households at feasts and other distributive events (except for the few households with no mature males), although women's labor and food contributions are informally, and sometimes publicly, acknowledged. Men perform most public acts at formal occasions. Lederman (1984) has argued persuasively, for the Mendi of New Guinea, that formal occasions are "men's" occasions because they allow performance of public, social identities, not private, personal ones. A man's personal identity is not appropriately expressed at a public occasion. But women have only personal identities and so cannot perform public acts. As a social category, women stand in a publicly subordinate relationship to the cognate social category "men," despite a certain symbolic equivalence, making gender relations a hierarchy of power. Lederman's analysis suits Sapwuahfik, where women possess considerable personal autonomy but are not men's social equals.

Sapwuahfik, Pohnpei, and the Ideology of Egalitarianism

It is an accepted generalization that in the Pacific, atolls display less social stratification than high islands (Sahlins 1958). If we were comparing aboriginal Sapwuahfik social organization with that of Pohnpei, the difference in sociopolitical complexity would be quite predictable. But we are concerned not so much with the ethnology of Pohnpei and Sapwuahfik as with how Sapwuahfik people use their perception of the differences between the two to construct a distinctive identity.

Like Sahlins, Caroline Islanders distinguish low and high islands and correlate the distinction with political and economic differences. Because Pohnpei is large, it is thought to possess more natural wealth than the "small islands," the neighboring atolls. Although in its precontact history Sapwuahfik was not part of any Pohnpei polity, canoes voyaged to the high island, and there is a perceived tradition of Pohnpei as giver, and Sapwuahfik and other atolls as receivers, of cultural and natural goods. Recall the Sapwuahfik elder who remarked that it was inappropriate for a Sapwuahfik plant variety to have been taken up on Pohnpei, saying, "Things should come from the big land to the small one." It does not seem odd, then, that Sapwuahfik's social organization should be imported from Pohnpei. At the same time, although current federal politics makes the outer islanders a political minority, Sapwuahfik people assert their traditional political independence from any other island.

A vital aspect of the perceived contrast is the proposition "Pohnpei is hierarchical; Sapwuahfik is egalitarian," stated explicitly in conversation and public rhetoric and explained by reference to the atoll's history. Because *mehn Sapwuahfik* adhere to an ideology of social equality among age and sex peers, they consciously frame choices of social action in those terms. Public acts symbolically indicate adherence to Sapwuahfik or Pohnpei culture. In many situations on both Pohnpei and the atoll, a person must decide whether to speak Sapwuahfik dialect or Pohnpeian; one's choice of vocabulary, pronunciation, and grammar is at the same time a public statement of identity as *mehn Pohnpei* or *mehn Sapwuahfik*. People make deliberate choices about using—or avoiding—titles and the complex etiquette surrounding them, and about collecting and distributing feast goods. They can follow Sapwuahfik custom, de-emphasizing rank and emphasizing equal portions, or they can follow Pohnpei custom, using elaborate rank etiquette and respect language and giving high-titled men a larger share of feast goods. *Mehn Sapwuahfik* understand both cultural codes, and they evaluate choices between them. Because local ideology presumes that "being *mehn Sapwuahfik*" means "acting egalitarian," people who choose to act otherwise make identity an issue. Those who follow Pohnpei "style" by using honorific "high" language or distributing feast goods unequally, for example, must then deal with the entailment of "being *mehn Pohnpei*." Sapwuahfik's egalitarian social order is reproduced as a condition of its community identity.

I did not conduct research on Pohnpei and cannot describe Pohnpeian social organization and attitudes toward the title system firsthand. Though the ethnographic literature in general presents Pohnpei as a set of centralized chiefdoms, and its people as vitally concerned with the traditional system, Glenn Petersen (1977, 1982a) has argued that there are also strong forces in Pohnpei society operating against chiefly authority and for personal autonomy. Petersen describes Pohnpei people as determinedly egalitarian, employing traditional hierarchy as a device to maintain the locus of government in the local community. He describes the holders of the highest titles as political leaders who rather than wielding authority and collecting tribute, govern by redistributing power, speak of themselves in the humiliative linguistic form, and contribute more to feasts than they receive. He also describes feast organization as egalitarian. This revisionist argument suggests that sociopolitical organization on the high island may share attributes of the atoll social system (though we should not disregard use of a humble attitude as a sign of power on Pohnpei [Falgout 1984a:106–8; Petersen 1982a: 122–3]). The contest of personal autonomy and culturally valued hierarchy may be part of a wider Micronesian pattern. Certainly Pohnpei ideas about custom have changed and continue to change. Remarking that Kiti people are considered "traditional," "noted for the care they take in proper custom and formality," Suzanne Falgout (1984a:39) writes, "This adherence to tradition is seen by more progressive Ponapeans as being backward, ignorant, or at least finicky."

Whatever the actual situation on the high island, the people of Sapwuahfik do not see Pohnpei as Petersen does—or, rather, they emphasize the apparent hierarchy of Pohnpei sociopolitical organization, visible to them in honorific language and etiquette, gifts to chiefs, unequal feast goods distribution, and individual men's efforts to rise in the title system. These are clearly enough described by local informants, and ethnographic reports, to make Pohnpei sociopolitical life a potent symbol of hierarchical organization, despite its internal complexities.

In contrasting Pohnpei thinking with that of his own community, one man said (using the English words in quotation marks):

> Pohnpeians like "high rank," "high culture" . . . They think it good that one man is nahnmwarki, and one nahnken, and so on down, for twenty-four numbers of "high rank." But *mehn Ngatik*, if they say, "You, will you be nahnmwarki?" I will say no. They [Ngatik people] don't like [or "want"] it. But if a Pohnpei man were asked, he'd say—"Oh, sure, sure, sure!" They want [those titles]: nahnmwarki, nahnken, wasahi, dauk.

TITLES AND THE ETIQUETTE OF RANK

Most Sapwuahfik men do not consider attaining a high title to be an important personal goal. In contrast, Daniel Hughes (1982:17) wrote, "It is difficult to exaggerate, even today, the importance of titles to the Ponapean people. Certainly acquiring a high state title remains one of the greatest goals of most Ponapeans." (Ward 1989 conveys a vivid sense of the felt importance of the rank system on Pohnpei in the 1970s). Although every adult Sapwuahfik man has a section or *wehi* title, only the few highest titles are normally used. Holders of low-ranking titles are very much "in name only." (In one story I heard, men attending a funeral feast at which titles were called for the food distribution—rather than names—remained seated, not recognizing their titles.)

The Pohnpei ideal of receiving titles is that one rises step-by-step through the title sequence in either the A or B line. A title is achieved through genealogical ties and seniority, and, more practically—and increasingly in recent times (see Hughes 1982:11)—community activity, especially feast giving and service to chiefs. Pohnpei titles are associated with matrilineal clans, more precisely with matrilineages (not the same ones in each chiefdom), but the system is somewhat flexible. To be eligible to be honored with a title, a man needs a genealogical "path" to the title, but beyond that he demonstrates his worth by giving formal feasts at the section and chiefdom levels, which reveal his skills and capacity, and in other service to men of higher title and to the community. An ambitious man can increase his visibility and make himself a plausible candidate for a title by hard work. This means not only agricultural work—producing the pigs, impressively large yams, and *sakau* (kava) that are the centerpieces of formal Pohnpei feasts—but also learning history and mythology, becoming an excellent orator, being skilled at respect language, knowing the details of etiquette, and acting as a loyal and useful member of the section and chiefdom. Succeeding financially and holding elected or appointed political office can also help, if the fruits of success are used to assist other people and the section and chiefdom in general. Besides contributing to feasts and receiving feast goods, and being honored by traditional ceremonial etiquette and honorific language, high-titled persons also organize much of the social and political life of their section and chiefdom.

As Riesenberg and Petersen have demonstrated, a Pohnpei man's political rise is not in fact automatic, step-by-step, or largely determined by genealogy, and changes in the title system in the last few decades have further altered the pattern of title inheritance (Hughes 1969, 1970, 1982; Ward 1975:7–8). However, the idea on Sapwuahfik is that this orderly promotion is the Pohnpei way, and that the atoll's title inheritance history does not approach this ideal. Sapwuahfik titles, they say, are inherited inconsistently with genealogical rules and clan affiliation, nor are acts of service or generosity clearly correlated with advance-

ment (because men do not actively compete for promotion).
"Ngatik," one atoll man said to me, "is somewhat *tiahk en wai*
[foreign/American custom], not entirely *tiahk en Pohnpei*, who
really know customary respect [*wahu*]." Patrilineal bias has also
played a role in Sapwuahfik title inheritance. Today a general
lack of interest in titles, especially among younger men, leaves
leeway for those who are concerned with titles to arrange the
system more freely than would be the case on Pohnpei, where title assignments are made in the midst of public scrutiny and discussion.

On both Sapwuahfik and Pohnpei, nonlocalized, exogamous
matrilineal clans[5] are an element of the title system. Each of
Sapwuahfik's clans can be traced (by the ethnographer, though
not by most local people) three or four generations to a woman
who introduced the clan to the atoll. The two aboriginal clans
can be traced to Ngatik women who survived the massacre. The
clans are: Dipwilap (descendants of an aboriginal Sapwuahfik
woman, though there is also a clan Dipwilap on Pohnpei), Dipakwa (imported from the Gilbert Islands), Diapik (Gilbert Islands), two clans Dipwinpahnmei (apparently unrelated; one descended from a Sapwuahfik woman, one from an immigrant
Pohnpei woman), Dipwinwai (Pohnpei), Dipwinpehpe (Pohnpei),
Sounpwok (Pohnpei), Dipwinmen pwetpwet (Pohnpei), and
Dipwinmen toantoal (consisting of two lines that cannot be related matrilineally but seem to be descendants of the brother-
sister pair Noah and Likur; one Dipwinmen toantoal includes
Likur's descendants in the female line; the other consists of descendants of Noah's Gilbertese wife. A Dipwinmen toantoal also
exists on Pohnpei).

Any description of Sapwuahfik's clans cannot help but exaggerate their local importance. Many people do not know or are
uncertain of their clan affiliation; in general only a few older
people are knowledgeable about their family's genealogy. Clans
regulate marriage (few intraclan marriages occur) and play at
least an ideological role in title inheritance, but they do not possess estates or otherwise act as corporate groups.[6]

The relative unimportance of matrilineal clans in title inheritance is evident in the list of current titleholders. Of fourteen A-line titles in 1979, nine belonged to the Dipwinmen clans (either toantoal or pwetpwet); but in the thirteen B-line titles, the greatest clustering is three each of Dipwilap and Dipwinpehpe. Of twenty-seven titleholders in 1979–80, however, only four are "out of place" in terms of clan. With these four exceptions, A-line titles are held by Dipwinmen toantoal, Dipwinmen pwetpwet, Diapik, and Dipwinwai; B-line titles by Dipwlap, Dipwinpehpe, Sounpwok, and Dipakwa (Dipwinpahnmei clansmen hold one title in each line). No pattern of kinship relates holders of A- and B-line titles to one another. On Pohnpei, there is a tradition of intermarriage between A and B clans (Riesenberg 1968:16), today a tendency rather than an obligation.

The history of Sapwuahfik's highest titles from the immediate postmassacre period to the present demonstrates the lack of fidelity in assigning titles according to a consistent genealogical scheme (Table 3). (I could not gather enough information to assemble lists of previous holders of lesser titles.) Some variability is due to postmassacre conditions; clan considerations were offset by the scarcity of capable men. Other factors affecting who received these titles are the same as those operating on Pohnpei: personal and family ambition, and individual character and health.[7]

When I inquired about the history of succession to the nahnmwarki title, I was told that "Ngatikese haven't strictly applied the law of clan," which they think Pohnpei people consider most important in title succession. Some called the appointment of the fifth nahnmwarki a "return to the path"—that is, to traditional Pohnpei practice, because he was of the appropriate clan. Others, though, provided explanations that made alternatives to matrilineal succession acceptable in terms of a distinctive Sapwuahfik culture, described as "a bit *wai.*" People generally agree that Dipwinmen toantoal is the proper clan of the nahnmwarki of Sapwuahfik, and I was told clan affiliation was the reason for the appointment of the current incumbent (who belongs to a different lineage of Dipwinmen toantoal than that of the former nahnmwarki). This is recognized as a tie to Kiti,

TABLE 3

Holders of Highest Titles from Postmassacre Era to Present

Nahnmwarki	Nahnken	Washai
Aisikaya (Dipwinmen toantoal)*	none	Noah (Dipwinmen toantoal)
Nahior (Dipwinmen toantoal)	David (Diapik)	Alek (Dipwinmen pwetpwet)
Werek (Dipwinpahnmei)	Timothy (Dipwilap)	Benjamin (Dipwinmen pwetpwet)
Ahti (Dipwinpahnmei)	Mr. Are Panuel (Dipwilap)	Mr. Walte Inek (Dipwinmen pwetpwet)
Mr. Seneris Nason (Dipwinmen toantoal)	Incumbent	Incumbent
Mr. Winden Salmon (Dipwinmen toantoal)		

*Presumed; his genealogy is unknown

which is ruled by a nahnmwarki of that clan, but I was not able to clarify a genealogical link between the aboriginal massacre survivors of Dipwinmen toantoal and the Pohnpei clan.

Aisikaya's clan is not definitively stated in oral history and cannot be deduced from genealogical information; his wife was the daughter of a Gilbertese woman, and he had no biological children. Nahior was the son of Likur, an aboriginal woman who was Noah's sister or classificatory sister. The first transfer of power could be read as consistent with the Pohnpei ideal of inheritance by a genealogically senior male of the ruling matrilineage. One person said that Nahior had been Wasahi in the later years of Aisikaya's reign, which is also consistent with the step-by-step ideal. Yet the next nahnmwarki, Werek, was Nahior's biological son, a member of the Dipwinpahnmei clan. One local explanation for disregarding matrilineal succession in this case is that Werek's mother laid careful plans for his promotion. Another is that Japanese authorities intervened in favor of patrilineal ties. Werek appointed his biological brother Ahti to succeed him as nahnmwarki. (In fact, when Fischer visited Ngatik in 1951 he described Ahti [then chief magistrate] and Welsin [municipal secretary, a son of Timothy] as "sons and heirs of Nanmwarki and Nahnken respectively" [Fischer n.d.]; it is not clear from his notes whether they were explicitly identified as such by local people.) When Ahti died in the 1970s, the high-titled men decided to give the title to Mr. Seneres Nason (Likur's daughter's son), who was then Wasahi; thus the title returned to Dipwinmen toantoal.[8]

Sapwuahfik people often cited this famous Nahior-Werek case of father-to-son inheritance to me to demonstrate the irregularity of title succession on the atoll. As suggested in the brief discussion of aboriginal Sapwuahfik, the pattern may have had premassacre precedents, though postmassacre influence by patrilineally biased Westerners is also likely.[9] In one version of the story of the last aboriginal leader, Sirinpahn succeeded his father as nahnmwarki, but the account does not indicate whether this was the normal pattern of succession.

Irregularity also appears in the early history of the nahnken title. David, a Gilbertese man (Diapik clan) was assigned the title by Aisikaya, who had adopted him (this recalls the Pohnpei tradition of the B line as "children" of the A line). David was succeeded by Timothy (Dipwilap clan), whose father was also Gilbertese. Contrary to Fischer's prediction, Welsin did not succeed his father as nahnken; the current nahnken is a man of Timothy's clan.

Sapwuahfik's system of title inheritance, then, is viewed both as a deviation from the known and respected Pohnpei pattern and as a distinctive form validated by the atoll's unique history. I was not on Sapwuahfik at a time when title succession had to be discussed in order to fill a high position, but conversations about hypothetical futures indicated the system's ideological flexibility. In an extreme example, a shrewd older man predicted to me that the nahnmwarki following the 1979–80 incumbent would be elected, not chosen according to traditional rules (in the event, this did not occur; the sixth nahnmwarki was decided on by Sapwuahfik's prominent public men). I found this idea widespread on Sapwuahfik, and generally viewed with approval. One person said of the previous Nahnmwarki, "If this man still wants to be Nahnmwarki, let him stand for an election." The idea of electing a nahnmwarki diverges so far from notions of the traditional polity as to be shocking (at least to the ethnographer), but it well expresses Sapwuahfik's distance from this traditional system and its adherence to a strongly developed egalitarianism and sense of being affiliated with American ways.

Along with what they see as a lack of rigor in assigning titles, Sapwuahfik people describe the lack of *wahu* (honor, respect, the customary ways) given high-titled persons on Sapwuahfik, compared to Pohnpei. *Wahu* is expressed to persons of higher status through personal etiquette (such as handing items right hand crossed over left and keeping one's head on a lower level), deference in decision making, proper attention to rank in ceremonial contexts (for example, in seating and in distributing feast goods), and the use of honorific language (*meing*, "high" or "respect" language) when speaking of or to them (Garvin and Riesenberg 1952; Riesenberg 1968). According to Sapwuahfik people, *mehn Pohnpei* "show *wahu* to" their traditional leaders; Sapwuahfik people do not show forth much *wahu*. In fact, they joke about their lack of respect behavior, and some give their ignorance of proper etiquette as a reason for disliking visits to Pohnpei. One informant encapsulated the difference: "Pohnpei people will bow and say *Kasele-ehlie, meing* [a formal greeting, with the central vowel elongated to show respect]. We will say, *Kaselel, Nahnmwarki!* [the equivalent of `Hi there!']."

The prevailing informality regarding rank is a consequence of continual social choices about *wahu* made according to situation and individual preference. Because *mehn Sapwuahfik* have not only a continuum of formality to choose from (which Pohnpei people also have) but also the option of almost completely disregarding rank, there is plentiful scope for individual choice. Take, for example, someone who consistently uses Pohnpei dialect, conducts family feasts according to Pohnpei custom, and shows *wahu* and speaks *meing* to high-titled persons in everyday social interaction. Such a person would be off the scale of appropriate Sapwuahfik behavior, and my guess would be that he intends to move to Pohnpei and shift allegiance to that cultural community. On the other hand, to be completely ignorant of high language, to always speak Sapwuahfik dialect, never use titles, and ignore the status of even Nahnmwarki and Nahnken would be equally unacceptable, and suggests someone not fully competent as a socially mature adult. But each Sapwuahfik person chooses specific actions, shifting with circumstances, to take his or her stand on matters of rank. Most people speak Pohnpei dialect with outsiders, and it is used for religious sermons and prayers on the atoll, but few women and not all men know respect language well enough to speak properly to, say, a high-titled visitor from Pohnpei.[10] People refer to Nahnken and Nahnmwarki alternatively by name or title in conversation, and there is little "role distance" between personal identity and title (Marcus 1984), but except for close relatives and friends do not joke with them casually, and they (along with others of high title and secular officials) always receive respect etiquette in formal contexts.

What determines an individual's choice of showing more or less *wahu*? Women and the young are implicitly excused from knowing the details of etiquette. Women who choose to use it are usually older women whose philosophy leans toward preferring tradition and formality in social relations, who have personal ties with Pohnpei or are involved in their family's efforts to shape their position in the community through a strategy of traditional status. These are also men's reasons for using *wahu*, but because men are public actors as well as private ones (see Lederman 1984), all adult men, consciously or not, make a public statement of their philosophy and intentions with their choice of action in the domain of rank.

Whether based on historical precedents or explanation of Sapwuahfik's distinctiveness as "somewhat *tiahk en wai*," the title system is open to symbolic and political manipulation. This is generally true of complex political organizations; on Pohnpei, titles are assigned with attention to immediate and long-term goals of individuals, lineages, and subclans. On Sapwuahfik, in addition to individual and family interests, the working of the system also provides the opportunity to make a public statement about Sapwuahfik culture.

FEASTS AND OTHER PUBLIC DISTRIBUTIONS

Feasts are critical forums for indicating participation and non-participation in the ideology of rank, where people make deliberate choices about language, etiquette, and the collection and distribution of food and goods.

The physical organization of a public feasting event is governed by the ideology of the traditional polity as a structure of rank. The accompanying diagram was drawn by a Sapwuahfik man who explained it as a scheme of the arrangement of a *nahs*, a traditional feast house. It simultaneously represents the social structure of the polity (*wehi*), with the highest titleholders seated along the top bar of the raised platform of the U-shaped building. *Serihn*, it was explained to me, is "God on earth"; like God, there is but a single title here—nahnmwarki. Ninlahng (lit. "the sky") are *soupeidi*, "those who face downward," both figuratively and literally from their central, superior status (Riesenberg 1968:16–17). These are the highest title holders and others given places of honor at the feast. *Ninsei* are the middle rank—they are like a canoe on which the *soupeidi* travel; and *raronpwel* are those who do the work of the feast.

This layout is also that of a Pohnpei feast, and could be elaborated with much more detail for the high island (as it is in Shimizu 1982, 1987). After explaining the diagram, my informant went on to say that today on Sapwuahfik this structure is lost, the precise relationship of the nahnmwarki to the other titles and the interrelationships of the stations is no longer

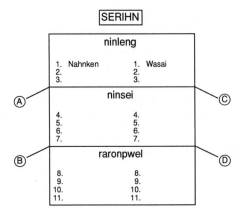

DIAGRAM. *Representation of a* nahs *(feast house) and of the "work of the feast" by titleholders. The numbers represent titles. A–D are the places (both physically and metaphorically) of those called up at a feast, e.g., to pray.*

known. The loss of this ideal structure could be said to parallel the loss of the "structure"—this man's house, recently built when I spoke with him, was the only one on the atoll built in the *nahs* shape. The usual site of communitywide feasts is the rectangular cement municipal official building (also called the *nahs*). Like the school, church outbuilding, or any room or open area, the office space is organized in a *U* shape when a feast is arranged. The ideal *nahs* organization of this diagram is then formally reflected in the physical arrangements for feasts.

The formality of a Sapwuahfik feast is determined in part by its type. A public feast planned by the municipal government to welcome the governor of Pohnpei State is noticeably more formal in its adherence to traditional (that is, Pohnpeian) etiquette than a family feast celebrating a child's first birthday. The degree of formality displayed in a feast depends on physical arrangements, seating, food distribution, and language. Nahnmwarki and Nahnken, and sometimes other high-titled men (usually any or all of Wasahi, Dauk, and Noahs), church leaders, and government officials are seated in places of honor (these are the *aramas lapalap*, lit. "big people"). In the municipality office, this is along a slightly raised dais built into the eastern edge of the concrete floor; in a house or yard, they sit next to each other on mats, against a wall or simply in a line. This line of honored guests is the equivalent of the top bar of the *U* of a *nahs*, as shown in the diagram. The others sit facing "those who face downward." Visiting government officials or community guests, such as the medical worker assigned to the atoll or the ethnographer in residence, might be requested to join the honored guests. These people are served first, in the respectful style, right hand holding food or cup, presented over bent left arm, with a slight bow. Others at the feast, of lesser *wahu*, sit (in the office) at two rows of banana leaves on which food has been set out, or (in a house or yard) in no particular arrangement but grouped informally by family or friendship.

Prayers and speeches always accompany a feast of any size. The Nahnmwarki, true to Pohnpei tradition, does not often speak in public. The Nahnken, if he is present, invariably speaks. Other leaders or guests may be called on for a speech or a prayer. The head of the household giving the feast may speak, or may call on someone else to speak. At a more formal feast, the speeches will be entirely in honorific language, as prayers always are. There is much more attention to etiquette directed at the high-titled persons at a feast than there is in daily life, including bowing, keeping the head low, food-presenting etiquette, and consistent use of titles and respect language.

Food, prepared and amassed during the several days preceding the feast and divided into equal portions during the formalities, is distributed following the speeches. A man of moderately high title calls names from a list of honored guests and contributing families and individuals. Someone from each household collects the share. At communitywide feasts, individual portions may be set out on tables in the school or rows on the floor of the municipal office and eaten during the speeches. The kind and amount of food depends on the type and size of the feast. Pig and taro are served at funeral feasts; hosts of weddings and house blessings usually serve baked bread or doughnuts and hot coffee or tea; a child's first birthday might mean chicken, pig, dog, or fish, with taro dishes and rice; a feast for a new canoe calls for a group fishing expedition to be met on shore with taro dishes and other agricultural foods. Although women do much of the everyday food preparation, men take a large part of the responsibility for organizing feast foods, including killing and cooking pigs and dogs in earth ovens, whereas women take charge of foreign foods such as rice and bread.

As an example, people who own land on the islet of Wad held a large feast on Ngatik Islet in July of 1979 as a dedication and thank-you for help in building a protective wall against pigs around Wad's taro garden. Throughout the morning people brought palm-frond baskets and large plastic or metal bowls filled with drinking coconuts, taro, breadfruit dishes, and rice into the municipal office. A young man wrote down the contributing household as each container arrived. In early afternoon the men and boys who had left to go fishing before dawn returned, bringing boats and canoes to rest on the lagoon shore next to the office, where the feast was laid out and guests were seated. In single file, five older men walked up from the shore to the office, each carrying one or two raw fish, cut in a particular way, each wrapped in a leaf. Behind them came the young men and boys, in pairs, carrying between them poles looped with strings of fish. Each of the seven high-titled persons or honored guests (seated in a line across the top of the *U* formed by three sides of the open office building) was presented with a leaf-wrapped fish. Later, taro dishes and drinking coconuts were distributed to them. A server seated before each honored person opened the coconuts, cut the fish, and shared the food of the honored one. Prayers and speeches began. Outside the office, the division of the catch into piles got underway as the speeches continued. The recipient of each pile was called out, starting with the men of highest title. A list of sixteen titles (with my name added at the end) was called out; the announcer went on to distribute the rest by calling out the names of heads of households. After the speeches, the crowd dispersed casually and the food inside the office was distributed.

I have described feasts in detail, because it is on the stage of feasts and other public events that Sapwuahfik people reveal and re-create their identity as members of a distinctive Sapwuahfik cultural community, again by way of comparison with Pohnpei. Bascom (1948, 1965), Petersen (1977), Riesenberg (1968), Shimizu (1982), and Ward (1989) have described Pohnpei feasts in detail; I focus on what Sapwuahfik people see as distinctive in their *kamadipw* (feast). An important difference is that on Pohnpei feasting is integral to the political system: a man participates actively in it by a conscientious display of service when he contributes labor, yams, kava, pigs, purchased goods, and cash to feasts in the section and chiefdom in which he holds a title. Because a Sapwuahfik man is not likely to hold a high title as a goal in life, and because the correlation of feast work and promotion in the system is not consistent, feasts on Sapwuahfik lack this close integration with the title system.

Sapwuahfik people are aware of the importance *mehn Pohnpei* attribute to feasting behavior, and they also perceive feasts as, in a sense, a path to status. Generosity, diligence, and productivity in family and community feasts are important in establishing a man as an adult and a fully functioning member of the atoll community. Like people on Pohnpei, those on Sapwuahfik may speak of a community feast as "a time of men" that is, time for a man to fulfill his obligation and present a pig. The context is not that of title-seeking competition but of every adult male, and every household, maintaining its place in the social order and doing its part to ensure the success of a community event. Also, Sapwuahfik egalitarian ideology does not reject the etiquette of formal occasions, though feast ceremonial is less rigorous than on Pohnpei. Whether a large community event or a small house blessing, a feast is always organized with the formal elements described above. At a small private feast as at a major event, it is still necessary to have a set of honored people at the focal end of the space in which the feast is being held. Men of midlevel titles, elder men, or secular officeholders may be asked (even badgered) into seating themselves in places of honor. Some older people (but not everyone) will bow when approaching them; an effort will be made to go behind instead of disrespectfully crossing in front of them, and the person of highest rank will always be served first and mentioned before a speech is begun. Sapwuahfik ideas about rank etiquette do not inhibit them from carrying out this sort of ceremony with aplomb. Interactions between servers and high-titled persons, for example, are neither constrained nor self-consciously formal ("nonchalance" is Petersen's very good description of the similar casualness of much greater ritual politeness on Pohnpei). After prayers and speeches, when the food distribution takes place, the highest titles are called out first, using respect language. Below the first several titles and nontitle calls (e.g., "Legislator of Sapwuahfik;" there is no set form for how many titles are called), the rest of the contributors are called by name or by household to receive their portions.

On Pohnpei "not a week passes without some form of feast, often two or three, with two or three a day occurring within a single community during yam season" (Petersen 1977:141). Honor feasts for section chief and nahnmwarki, title validation feasts, and mortuary feasts are the most formal events; special occasion feasts, funeral feasts of several sorts, and community and family feasts vary in formality and size. I was told that elaborate honor feasts for Sapwuahfik's nahnmwarki are no longer held, though informants in 1979–80 said they had occurred as recently as fifteen years earlier. A small honor feast is said to be held for the nahnmwarki in January. People also said that title validation feasts are held when a man accepts a high title, though none occurred while I was on Sapwuahfik. The only full four-day mortuary feast I heard of was held for a Sapwuahfik man by Sapwuahfik people on Pohnpei; funeral feasts I attended on the atoll were simpler, one-day feasts. On Sapwuahfik, then, feasts are also held for many different reasons, but the great majority of Sapwuahfik feasts fall into the category of less-formal affairs. They are also on the whole much smaller than Pohnpei feasts, in terms of food distributed and people involved.

Above all, it is the general, often-mentioned, and firmly held idea on Sapwuahfik that Pohnpei feasting benefits those holding high titles at the expense of the common folk (*aramas tikitik*, lit. "little people"). This is explicitly contrasted with the Sapwuahfik style of feasting, in which all contributors share equally in the redistribution. The titles of the highest ranking Sapwuahfik men are called out first, but their shares are only slightly larger or better than those of everyone else. Sapwuahfik people speak openly of the difference, describing how, in the *nehn en Pohnpei*, "Pohnpeian division," the feast goods are shared by nahnmwarki, nahnken, and high-titled persons only. That is why, one Sapwuahfik man said, Pohnpei people "fight for titles," in order to get food. But *nehn en Sapwuahfik* is among "all men and women, down to children who are old enough to eat." Another man used quantitative terms, saying that on Pohnpei perhaps 5 percent of the people share in the distribution, though all work and bring food. On Sapwuahfik, all who bring food receive an equal share of the total (the exception is the *kamadipw en wahu*, "honor feast," for the nahnmwarki and nahnken, at which the nahnmwarki's family is said to receive a quarter of the feast goods. Unfortunately, I was not present on Sapwuahfik for a January honor feast).

That relative informality and egalitarian distribution at Sapwuahfik feasts has existed for decades is demonstrated by the field notes of John Fischer (n.d.), then Pohnpei (Ponape) district anthropologist, who attended a 1951 feast marking the arrival of the U.S. flag on Sapwuahfik after the war. The elaborate affair included a procession centered on a large, decorated, food-laden platform carried on men's shoulders. Yet the Nahnken's speech centered on the theme "give everyone food," Christian names (rather than titles) were called for distribution, and the Nahnken told Fischer, "Everyone gets the same. The Nahnmwarki and the children get the same." Though the Nahnken later amended his statement, saying that those holding the highest titles receive "a little more," Fisher noted, "Actually they do not appear to get much more." Fischer also noticed the "sons and heirs of Nahnken and Nahnmwarki respectively" sitting on the mat properly reserved for chiefly women. He comments, "Ngatik appears to be an informal place." The rhetoric and public display of egalitarianism appeared in much the same form thirty years later.

In feasts as in other economic processes, procedures to allot work, food, and cash contributions to community efforts constitute an explicit attempt to share islandwide obligations equally. Equal effort is expressly invoked and implemented in community feasts or feasts sponsored by a voluntary association, and other projects, such as work on the municipal office building or school, similarly demand equal contributions from every social unit. Households (in this context called *um*, "earth oven"—those who regularly produce and eat food together) are a common economic counter used to plan community work or feasts. Speeches and conversation during and after large feasts frequently invoke the virtue of everyone (every adult or every household or section) contributing to and sharing equally in the event.

Plans for community or group-sponsored feasts are made in small group meetings of the municipal council, school board, or church association. Because most feasts follow a standard plan, the meeting agenda is easily set. Nonetheless, each point is explicitly agreed on by all, even details that seemed to me, after several similar events, to be "givens." This lengthy discussion is the place for subtle decisions about symbolic expressions of Sapwuahfik style. Planners decide on the level of formality by choosing a location, setting the physical layout, deciding on the scale of contributions, and choosing guests of honor. (Some of these decisions are made less formally outside the meeting, and even while the event is being set up.) At the planning meeting, food, cash, or labor assignments are listed on a blackboard or on paper, so that the fair division is evident. Contributions to every feast, from a child's birthday feast to an islandwide celebration, are carefully written down when feast goods are brought in. Neither the amount nor the kind of contribution is noted, only the name of the individual or the head of the household providing it. The list is referred to when feast goods are distributed.

FIG. 10.   *Contents of boxes donated by U.S. military in the 1980 Christmas airdrop were sorted out on the schoolhouse floor into equivalent numbered piles, one for each person on Sapwuahfik. Individuals then chose lots for the piles.*

Care in distribution is also seen on occasions other than feasts. The annual U.S. Air Force Christmas airdrop of food, toys, and miscellany splashed into the atoll's lagoon in 1980. The huge boxes were taken to the school, where the contents were sorted into hundreds of small piles, each assigned a number. The miscellaneous nature of the goods made the creation of "equal" piles problematic, but at last it was satisfactorily achieved, and the piles were distributed by lot, with every adult and non-infant child receiving one (see fig. 10). (When it was later discovered that one of the airdropped boxes had gone astray and been found by two men fishing at the other end of the lagoon, a great deal of rumor and bad feeling enhanced lively discussion of the rights of finders-keepers versus the obligation to share received goods equally among all members of the community. The finders had acted quickly to disperse the goods among their kin, presenting the community with a fait accompli.)

In another case, Ewenedi *kousapw,* "section," invited the entire atoll to a religious service in preparation for the Christmas season (this was October 24; that year, Christmas celebrations were maximized). Each section, in turn, had been holding a brief weekly prayer service for several weeks, but Ewenedi planned a special event. My field notes convey some of the ambience. After prayers, sermons, and refreshments,

> a man spread a mat in front of the emcee's table. The people of Ewenedi began singing a well-known hymn. Several people started to clap, and others joined in; the clapping continued throughout.
>
> A few bars of bathing and laundry soap fell onto the mat. Slowly at first, then faster, other items were tossed on by the people of Ewenedi. Three or more women holding huge bowls filled with goods moved through the crowd and tossed them onto the growing pile on the mat: soap, shirts, dresses, cloth. The clapping and cries of delight and encouragement from the crowd continued, especially from the children crowded close to the mat. All was ecstasy and confusion (intentional)—singing, clapping, yelling, tossing, and also women squirting everyone with American spray cologne [a version of the traditional anointing with scented coconut oil as a mark of favor or festivity].
>
> At the climax, the big bowls themselves were tossed onto the pile. The three women converged there, and with a swirl (somehow) four or five live chickens suddenly appeared on the pile.
>
> The noise died down. The man who had spread the mat called on an elderly church teacher known for his humor, who stood up and gave a short, funny speech, starting with (in English): "Ladies and gentlemen, boys and girls! I'm happy you are all here!" Then, he named four people as dividers. These four started dividing the pile, handing things out apparently at random, mostly (it seemed to me) to the children near them. I looked around, and most of the crowd had gone (someone had estimated two hundred to me earlier, and maybe so, if we include children). So who got the goods?

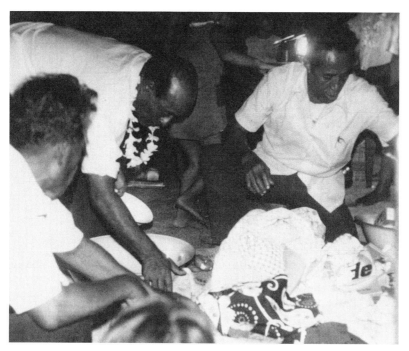

FIG. 11. *After the climax of the giveaway at Ewenedi's special event, those assigned to redistribute the pile of goods begin to sort through it.*

I found out a few days later, when I came into the municipal office just as the official division of items from the Ewenedi event was finishing. As on all such occasions, the gifts were sorted into roughly equivalent shares for everyone on the island. The marked contrast between the enjoyably hectic confusion of the giveaway and the deliberate care in attending to the details of the division displays the seriousness Sapwuahfik people feel about proper sharing of publicly distributed goods.

As in most small Pacific communities, the flow of goods among siblings, household members, wider kin networks, peers, and neighbors is constant on Sapwuahfik; as elsewhere, it tends

FIG. 12. *Gifts piled high for a public gift exchange, Christmas 1979. The community divided into two groups for a series of cooperative/competitive celebrations. Here, one group's members prepare to distribute gifts to their opposite numbers. Gifts include handmade sleeping mats, woven hats, and patchwork skirts, as well as purchased goods.*

to even out the accumulation of property. These examples of distributive and redistributive behavior (at feasts, at a windfall, at a giveaway, at the Christmas festivities shown in figs. 12 and 13) are redistributive at a higher level, and it is at this level that Sapwuahfik people's rhetoric distinguishes their custom from that of Pohnpei, most explicitly, but also from that of Americans and other Islanders. The ideal of egalitarianism is expressed verbally when people talk about feasting behavior; it is expressed actively in any situation involving quantities of goods that belong to the community as a whole. This is not to say that individuals do not act or try to act counter to the ideal: remember the finders of the stray airdropped box. But on the level of the community, the ideal, and the social rule, is equal shares to all.

Sapwuahfik people say Pohnpeians realize that Sapwuahfik

FIG. 13. *Public distribution at Christmas gift exchange, 1979. Men hold up a gift and call "Merry Christmas from X to Y!" The gift from the Nahnmwarki was handed out first.*

feasts are more egalitarian and thus an advantage for the "little people." They say Pohnpeians enjoy coming to Sapwuahfik feasts held on Pohnpei because they receive equal shares of the feast goods. Similarly, the Nahnken of Sapwuahfik expressed to me his discomfort at being the recipient of large quantities of food at a feast on Pohnpei at which he was an honored guest. Despite this, Pohnpei customs do affect Sapwuahfik feasts. The greatest impact is on feasts held by *mehn Sapwuahfik* living on Pohnpei. But Pohnpei ideals of feasting behavior also affect feasts on the atoll itself, through the influence of those of Sapwuahfik living on Pohnpei who participate in both Sapwuahfik and Pohnpei social systems. These people on the margins, though few in number, introduce an element of tension when they visit the atoll, in that they suggest the preferability of Pohnpei custom over that of Sapwuahfik.

Challenges to Egalitarian Ideology:
Stylen Pohnpei *on Sapwuahfik*

The assertion that Sapwuahfik is and should be egalitarian does not go unchallenged. In describing how a community's boundaries are symbolically constructed and maintained, Anthony Cohen (1985:74) comments, "The boundary as the community's public face is symbolically simple; but, as the object of internal discourse it is symbolically complex." Counteracting individual action and more diffuse social forces operate to keep the question of the role of rank in Sapwuahfik's community life an open one. Some Sapwuahfik people switch into Pohnpei's system, moving to the high island, seeking Pohnpei titles, and operating in accordance with Pohnpei notions of social relations. People of Sapwuahfik descent who reside permanently on the high island are especially likely to become involved with Pohnpei titles. Sapwuahfik people's response to those who enter Pohnpei's rank system depends on the extent of their continuing ties with Sapwuahfik. Some "become *mehn Pohnpei*" and enter completely into the section and chiefdom system of their Pohnpei homes, gradually losing kin ties and communication with the atoll. Some men retain their atoll identity but also compete with pigs, yams, and kava in Pohnpei feasting practices. These Pohnpei residents provide information and assistance on Pohnpei matters for other Sapwuahfik people. A few individuals become focal points for public discussion of differences between Sapwuahfik and Pohnpei custom. For example, the death of a Sokehs man of Sapwuahfik descent and high Pohnpei title precipitated much comparative discussion of Sapwuahfik and Pohnpei styles of funeral feasts (Eve Pinsker, pers. comm. 1979). Feasts sponsored by Sapwuahfik people on Pohnpei are characterized by an explicit mixture of the two traditions. Such constant interaction keeps Sapwuahfik ideology on the subject of their style consciously to the fore.

In feasts given by *mehn Sapwuahfik,* as in nearly every aspect of their lives on Pohnpei, Pohnpei customs have entered into the usual way of doing things. When *sakau* (kava) is found at a Sapwuahfik feast on Pohnpei, Pohnpei customs of preparation and presentation accompany it. On Pohnpei a Sapwuahfik family may hold a very large death commemoration feast; on the atoll such feasts are as a rule small, confined to near relatives. Sapwuahfik people recognize that things are done differently on Pohnpei and on the atoll, and they comment on the prevalence of Pohnpei-style behavior among Sapwuahfik people on the high island.

A brief description of one large feast will demonstrate the mix of Sapwuahfik and Pohnpei ways in the lives of Sapwuahfik people on Pohnpei. The feast marked the commemoration of the death of the daughter of a Sapwuahfik man and a Pohnpei woman from a high-ranking family. Some five hundred people attended the event, held in the feast house belonging to the mayor of Kolonia (a Sapwuahfik man permanently residing on Pohnpei), in a Sapwuahfik area of the city. Representing the girl's Pohnpei relatives, a Nahnmwarki and other Pohnpei titleholders sat in the place of honor in the feast house; most Sapwuahfik people were outside. Quantities of cloth and tables piled high with food were prominently displayed. I was told that more than a thousand dollars had been spent on purchased food.

Compared with most Sapwuahfik feasts, especially those on the atoll, this one was very large, but it was not remarkably so by Pohnpei's standards. Sapwuahfik people explained the size of the feast by saying that many Pohnpeians joined in because of the deceased's ties to the family of the Nahnmwarki. Both *mehn Pohnpei* and *mehn Sapwuahfik* brought the gifts of food and purchased goods, which, following the high island's custom, would go to the Pohnpei family of the deceased. Some who attended the feast brought food, but others came and ate without contributing, which would not normally happen on Sapwuahfik. A pig was brought to be killed in a rush because of the Nahnmwarki—atoll men explained that it is Pohnpei custom that an earth oven must be made if a nahnmwarki is present; the pig was owned by a Sapwuahfik person. Pohnpei custom was followed for the distribution of the feast goods: the Nahnmwarki was to receive half of the pig, and the group of high-titled Pohnpei men received much of the food.

This feast, then, essentially followed Pohnpei practice. In addition, on the morning of the feast a Pohnpei ceremony was held at the grave of the dead girl, which involved prayers and a give-away of cloth goods at the grave site. Sapwuahfik people expressed dislike of this giveaway and in general commented negatively on the Pohnpei style of the commemoration. Referring to the high-titled men receiving a large share of the food, one Sapwuahfik man who had helped said, "Why should I do it? I do the work and the Nahnmwarki gets it all. I'm like a slave, eh?"

The reasons Sapwuahfik people gave for being involved in this costly and elaborate feast centered on their ties with the mayor. The mayor in turn was "helping" the dead girl's father, a relative of his. The father of the dead girl was pleased with the show of support from his family; it was perhaps more than he expected, because he is not a person of high status and his ties with the Sapwuahfik community are not particularly strong (his mother is a Marshall Islander, and he was adopted by *mehn Pohnpei*).

The details of this feast indicate both *mehn Sapwuahfik* willingness to conform to Pohnpei customs of feast giving in order to make a point (in this case, to underscore the cohesiveness, wealth, and pride of the Sapwuahfik community, with political undertones related to the mayor's role and the Sapwuahfik community's support of it) and how they nevertheless retain ideological distance from those customs and assert the uniqueness and preferred status of their own ways.

On the atoll, a few Sapwuahfik men use notions of traditional title and status as weapons in ongoing political competition.

Because every public event is accomplished through extensive consultation, matters of rank can be used to negotiate for power. Some men of high traditional title make much of it in public life; others are all but invisible. An extreme form of this, which could be motivated by either personal ambition or sincere traditionalism (I don't know which), is the occasional effort toward a social-moral reform that would remake Sapwuahfik's system after the Pohnpei model. This has been done or attempted several times in the past; John Fischer (1957:180) notes a 1950s request from Sapwuahfik (then Ngatik) for "an authoritative list of titles in Madolenihmw District, which is considered the arbiter of such matters, so that Ngatik could make the necessary adjustments in their titles."

Reform movements may be encouraged by some high-titled *mehn Pohnpei*, who consider Pohnpei the "elder sibling" of Sapwuahfik and act in a way that suggests a sense of obligation to educate their atoll "kin." Men of Sapwuahfik descent who hold Pohnpei titles also have an interest in increasing atoll conformity with Pohnpei custom. Sometime in the 1970s, what sounds to me much like an official delegation from Pohnpei came to Sapwuahfik expressly for this purpose. Including the Nahnmwarki and Wasahi of Sokehs and the Nahnmwarki of Uh, the group held a meeting in the municipal office to instruct Sapwuahfik people in *meing* and *wahu*, the proper etiquette of rank. It appears that none of these efforts has succeeded. Of the delegation of noble instructors, an elderly Sapwuahfik woman said,

> No one told them to come. They came to say that we should do what the Pohnpei people do . . . none of us went to listen! They said we should bow to the Nahnmwarki, in giving anything to the Nahnmwarki, even a cigarette, to put it on a banana leaf. *Mehn Ngatik* refuse, because we are truly not going to do that, for we are going to follow our own ways, not those of Pohnpei. We don't like their customs.

The recurrence of "reform" efforts indicates constant pressure on Sapwuahfik's egalitarian ethic as a source of community identity. They demonstrate the continuing viability of alternatives to an egalitarian social order.

In the two domains where an ideology of social equality is explicitly elaborated (respect behavior and feast organization), individual choices of social action either maintain the validity of the ideology or, more rarely, intentionally contravene it to state the preferability of the alternative (i.e., hierarchy, the perceived Pohnpei style, tradition—but not Sapwuahfik's tradition). When this happens, the entire community becomes involved in discussion of which style they prefer. This arises frequently on Sapwuahfik, sparked by decisions about organization of an official feast, visits to or from Pohnpei, the death of a high-titled person, or other events involving matters of rank and feasting. The most heated discussion of this sort that took place during my residence concerned a family's choices about how to organize the funeral feast of an elderly woman. The controversy indicates the deliberateness with which Sapwuahfik people consider their adherence to an egalitarian ethos.

In 1979 an elderly woman died on Sapwuahfik. A feast marking her death was held a few days later under the direction of her brother's son, Thomas (a pseudonym), a sixty-eight-year-old man who has lived for many years on Pohnpei, where he holds a title. Perhaps because of his desire to make the funeral feast of his father's sister an example of the right way to do things, he planned it differently from the usual Sapwuahfik way, and considerable tension surrounded the event.

The family of the dead woman passed the word that they didn't want other people to "help," that is, to contribute to the feast. For several days the island was filled with gossip and rumor about this unfriendly notion (in talking about it, people spoke of it as a clan matter, as the dead woman's clan vs. the rest of Sapwuahfik). During the funeral feast itself, Thomas spoke in Pohnpei dialect and in high language (a man sitting next to me commented on how well he spoke Pohnpeian and knew Pohnpei custom). He compared Pohnpei and Sapwuahfik ways of dividing feast food, and urged the dividers to make the shares equal, as Sapwuahfik people do. Word came from where the Nahnmwarki and Nahnken were sitting that two pigs were to go to the family (the only time I knew this to happen on Sapwuahfik). Large feasts call for many speeches, and this more than most. In the course of a long speech, the Nahnmwarki of Sapwuahfik discussed the danger of a clan setting itself apart, "destroying its name," and interfering with the usual process of collecting and distributing feast foods (a lengthy public speech by the Nahnmwarki is uncommon in itself). After this commentary, Thomas stood up again, to say briefly (again in high language) that "we didn't mean to do anything wrong" and to thank the Nahnmwarki's clan (that of the dead woman's father) for their help sitting with her while she was ill. Finally the Nahnken spoke, beginning what was to be a conciliatory speech by saying twice, "*Kitail sohte duwehte mehn Pohnpei*" (We are not the same as Pohnpei people). Asserting that how a feast is run is the business of the family, he said the work of the high-titled men was simply to come and assist—though he didn't like the arrangements, he would go along anyway. This conciliatory attitude held throughout the distribution.

The focus of public concern was not the aggrandizement of high-titled persons, which apparently was not in the family's plan (food shares were equal), but the closing off of patterns of contribution that usually draw a wide net around all the atoll's households. Holding to an ideal of "equal shares" means maintaining the right to contribute, as well as to receive.

The pressure of community complaint brought to bear on the organization of that funeral feast suggests how powerful social forces common to small communities operate to keep public behavior true to local ideology. Gossip, private discussion with the individuals involved, public speeches, and economic transactions all affected Thomas and his family as the community rejected their choices of action as invalid. Yet the fact that they had Pohnpei custom available to them as an alternative indicates that implementing it is a valid "readable" cultural message on Sapwuahfik. Community members correctly interpreted the statement of difference as a political act, perhaps to be read in light of other choices by members of that family, which seemed to some to add up to an effort to act inappropriately. Even those who are most legitimately "big people" (in terms of title, personal ability, and church standing) are dethroned by negative gossip and the refusal of others to participate in their efforts to gain for themselves what is regarded as illegitimate status, acts that are regarded as *aklapalap*, "acting pridefully."

On Sapwuahfik a man can gain a traditional title or a position in public office through careful politicking and the right kin and allies. But achieving any sort of widely sanctioned authority would require the cooperation of the entire community. Because such authority can only be created and expressed through signals of status (rank etiquette) and economic processes (public contribution and distribution), it is susceptible to control by community members. Those who don't think it right that a particular man should receive formal tokens of respect or a larger share of feast goods are free to act against his accumulation of status. Similarly, anyone is free to attempt to garner status by trying out aspects of Pohnpei custom—which trials, if not accepted by others, at best will have no impact, at worst will backfire in charges of "wrong talk" and "acting pridefully."

This curious situation—to seek status is to use Pohnpei style, which probably will not increase one's status—persists because of the shared understanding of Pohnpei custom as the legitimate, traditional, proper way to do things associated with rank. As long as Sapwuahfik continues to maintain a title system, Pohnpei custom as the source of that system will continue to be admired as correct, and men who speak high language and know the intricacies of *wahu* will be respected for their knowledge. At the same time, that style is felt to be inappropriate for the atoll community.

The existence of radical suggestions such as electing the nahnmwarki by popular vote indicates that it is possible the traditional system could become entirely transformed on the atoll. The ideological lever for such transformation exists. Yet the continual and increasingly multifaceted relationship with Pohnpei, and the strong sentiment invested in traditional rank (to which is attached much of myth, regional and clan history, and geographical knowledge), contribute to the traditional system's strong emotional appeal. It is this delicate balance between rejection of and attraction to the system that gives it enormous semiotic "play" and provides actions in the domain of rank and feasting with the power to convey locally meaningful social messages.

CHAPTER SEVEN

Christian Commitment and Community Identity

MODERN SAPWUAHFIK interpretation of the massacre is phrased in a religious discourse that owes much to introduced and local Christian philosophy. In reflecting on their history, *mehn Sapwuahfik* today see their ancestors as having been punished for aboriginal paganism, and then as having discarded traditional beliefs to accept Christian teachings. In line with this, Sapwuahfik people consciously reject and separate themselves from the modern use of sorcery, the clearest example of pre-Christian paganism extant. They also see themselves as a mix of immigrant peoples given Christianity under special circumstances and so set on the road to increasing "enlightenment." Similarly, today, they feel themselves to be continuing the progressive movement in decisions about atoll sociopolitical life.

The Acceptance of Christianity

Modern knowledge of aboriginal religious belief and practice is scanty, nor is there much ethnographic or historical information about this aspect of eastern Micronesian atoll culture before major mid-nineteenth century changes. Today, people on Sapwuahfik regard the most important characteristics of aboriginal culture as the absolute power of chiefs, the worship of spirits, and the practice of powerful sorcery. Judging from oral traditions and a few missionary documents, between 1837 and Christian conversion in 1889–90 atoll people held both aboriginal and imported (Micronesian and perhaps Christian) beliefs. Modern accounts of preconversion religious practice, then, could refer to pre- or postmassacre times. Oral history describes the immigrant and native population interacting with *eni*, "spirits" or "ghosts," many of them attached to particular locales marked by shrines for worship. Some *eni* appear in traditions as helpful and protective, others as dangerous to humans—the pattern is similar to spirit beliefs throughout Micronesia. Spiritual sanctions upheld the nahnmwarki's reign, indicating a second dimension of the supernatural: *manaman*, an intangible power invested in legitimate authority.

"At the time of Aisikaya," one man told me, "they simply no longer knew anything. There were only *soai* [tales] of long ago." By destroying and dispersing the population, the attackers ensured the near-destruction of aboriginal religion, though nineteenth-century missionaries' reports suggest that the postmassacre population did have religious practices. We know from Frazer's 1855 letter that at least some people were learning about the Bible from him, and 1874 visitors reported a "stone idol" on a large platform, where religious offerings were made. Whether religious beliefs and practice as a whole in the postmassacre decades were individually various, syncretistically integrated, or freely mixed is impossible to determine.

Local tradition indicates the great value Sapwuahfik people today give to their ancestors' acceptance of Christianity and emphasizes the positive emotions that surrounded the reception of the "good news." The gospel's arrival is celebrated annually on February 2. Oral histories contain numerous references to the use of indigenous magical practices until the establishment of a Christian community and their abandonment thereafter, so marking the transition strongly. Aisikaya and his people are said to have used offerings to *eni*, leaf divination, and other magical techniques to locate turtles or predict a ship's arrival. The tale of religious change begins with Aisikaya's rejection of the first offer of Christian teachings. Later, however, he requested that mission teachers return with their message. We have already explored the historical facts of the introduction of Christianity; oral traditions suggest its cultural meaning. Here is one account of the island's conversion:

> In the time of Nahnmwarki Aisikaya, people came on a boat bringing "the good news," bringing to Ngatik what we call the church or religious belief. This belief was the belief in Christ, or Jesus, which had appeared on Pohnpei and then came down to Ngatik. They came and told Aisikaya that the belief had been carried here to Ngatik. Aisikaya replied: You take away your stuff; he was not going to accept it. And so they took back the belief, took it back to Pohnpei.
>
> Time passed, and months later, or almost a year later, Aisikaya decided that about that belief, he was going to take it. He asked them to bring it back again. And so they brought back the good news of Christ, the good news spread on the small island of Ngatik, that: "Nahn! [interj.] Jesus has redeemed the people of the world, and we on the island of Ngatik are included. He has redeemed all of us sinners."
>
> They then decided that "everyone is going to meet Christ because He redeemed all the people of the world." But at that time, also, the people of Ngatik often danced traditional dances. They then decided, because they were very happy that the people of Ngatik or (that is to say) all of us are going to God, to heaven because Jesus had taken away their sins. And so they composed a song, so they could dance to it . . . It was made in such a way that they could apply it to a kind of dancing called *kepir* [a paddle dance], an old dance. . . . This song made the Ngatik people very happy, because we realized, or they realized,

"After all, I am going to be able to meet Jesus because He redeemed us." The joy of redemption is what made the people of Ngatik compose this song for us on the island of Ngatik.

In this account, Islanders greet the new religion in the forms of the old, with traditional dances and songs. A song written about a later phase of conversion shows that although the value of the Christian message is unequivocally celebrated, the reputation of mission teacher John Francis suffers somewhat in oral tradition. This song and the occasionally renewed debate about the propriety of holding traditional dances are surviving indications that the transition to Christianity involved tension and conflict as well as joy. Luten Pohl, who narrated the song, also explained it to me. According to Mr. Pohl, Ngatik's leaders used to sit with John Francis at the altar when he preached. Following the rules of the Protestant mission churches, when he discovered that Nahniau was a smoker, Francis removed this high-titled man from his usual place of honor and put him among the common people, to sit facing "up," toward the altar. This move triggers images: recall that in a Pohnpei feast, *soupeidi*, "those who face downward," sit on a raised U-shaped platform; commoners sit at a lower level in the middle of the *U*.

Some time after the dramatic humbling of Nahniau, the people learned that John Francis had committed adultery with a local woman. At first, the story goes, people wanted to shoot him. Instead, they composed this song (footnotes are Mr. Pohl's explanations):

> The news came up and went around
>
> That they want to make another church.
>
> Then they demoted Nahniau—
>
> He went down to sit in the servants' place.
>
> And they raised up the bad Christian
>
> To go and kneel at the altar.
>
> Don't do anything you'll regret later, Nahniau[*]

Because he[†] hands it out that we are sinners,

As if he is Gabriel, come down among us,

To come and preach that we smokers will die in sin.

Where are the Pohnleng people?

    For they didn't prepare the way.[‡]

The altar is breaking apart.

We want to be close to Madolenihmw,[§]

Because we want to journey, to move around.

[We] want to reform as soon as [we] can.

    [*]That is to say, don't shoot John Francis, because we know you haven't sinned.
    [†]John Francis.
    [‡]Pohnleng is an old name for Ohwa in Madolenihmw (Pohnpei), said to be John Francis' home. Ngatik heard that people there were converted and were good Christians. This line asks the people of Pohnleng to come prepare the way.[1]
    [§]That is, we want to know the true Christian way.

The song, like Francis's incendiary action, reverberates with traditional motifs. "The altar is breaking apart" could refer both to the fragility of the new religion and to a Pohnpei prophesy connecting the physical destruction of a stone altar at Nan Madau (a sacred area on Pohnpei) with the dissolution of Pohnpei's chiefdoms. Pohnpei itself can be translated as "upon [*pohn*] a stone altar [*pei*]" (see Hanlon 1988). The several references to Pohnpei as a source of example and assistance could refer to the simple chronological priority of Pohnpei's conversion. Yet it also echoes postmassacre Sapwuahfik people's ancestry and the feeling that "big islands" lead "small islands" in traditional matters.

Modern Sapwuahfik Religious Life

Religious organizations and events organize much of the social life of this small community, and provide a forum for reflection and action for the genuinely devout. Most adults spend several hours each week in religiously inspired activity—Sunday and weekday services, hymn practice, prayer meetings with the sick, prayerful wakes with families of the dead, feasts for visits from church officials or delegations. Many of these events collect a crowd: the children taken with adults or drawn by the excitement; adolescents generally at the edge of the action, seizing the opportunity to contact lovers and have fun with friends; younger adults attending perfunctorily as a statement of solid citizenship; older adults with increasing commitment of time and energy as they take on responsible positions in church organizations.

The Protestant and Catholic churches remain the largest and most socially complex and influential religious groups. The Protestant church operates without a resident missionary or ordained minister. The church leaders are *wahnpoaron,* "apostles," or lay ministers, men elected by the congregation to serve until they retire to even greater eminence at the age of seventy. There were four *wahnpoaron,* two retired, in 1979–80; in 1990, two men in their forties had been appointed. *Wahnpoaron* officiate at services and are called on to bless weddings, baptisms, funerals, and the sick. They are men of secular, as well as religious, social status and political power. One 1979–80 lay minister was Nahnken; a 1990 *wahnpoaron* was Luhkenkolwof (chief magistrate). At the next level of Protestant church hierarchy are *sounpadahk* (teachers), younger men of serious disposition chosen by the lay ministers. These men give sermons and do much of the administrative work of the church. Under them are *sounkowe* (deacons), who assist the others and are not obliged to be as upright under public scrutiny as teachers and lay ministers. The wives only of *wahnpoaron* comprise a named group; they are steadfast attenders of church services, assist with Sunday school, and work at organizing feasts and special activities.

In addition to the church's internal hierarchy, Christian Endeavor, also called Jugenbund—originally a German Methodist church group—exists throughout the Micronesian Protestant church. Christian Endeavor began on Sapwuahfik in the early part of the twentieth century, when Germans took over the Micronesian mission from the American Board. Membership is open to anyone (there were about thirty members in 1979–80, mostly older people). Members swear to a simple declaration of Christian belief that includes abstinence from alcohol, tobacco, and adultery; those caught indulging in any of these are dismissed with a fanfare of gossip and reinstated after making a public apology in church. Another Protestant church group is *Lihen Alem*, "Friday women," who hold their own Friday afternoon services.

Catholic church organization is simpler. Sapwuahfik's Roman Catholic community is served by visits from a priest from the mission on Pohnpei. Catholic *sounpadahk* on Sapwuahfik are empowered to run Sunday services, preach sermons, baptize, distribute consecrated hosts sent from Pohnpei, and perform weddings, which may be formally consecrated during a priest's visit. Catholic church business is handled by a group of men elected from among the Catholics of each section. Another group cares for the altar furnishings and physical arrangements of the church. Social, work, and worship groups for young men and women respectively and older people of both sexes are introduced and abandoned according to need. There are also religiously oriented work groups, St. Ignatius (for men) and Mercedes (for women). For example, one year Mercedes women worked together to make thatch and to weed in exchange for cash, which they put into a Christmas fund for themselves.

The importance of the various church groups shifts over the years, depending on religious commitment, off-island church and missionary input, and the personalities involved. The fact that so many groups exist, and that several are quite active, attests to the importance of church-sponsored activities in the atoll's social life. In addition to regular worship services (two on Sunday in the Protestant church, one in the Catholic, and several evening services every week), there are special events—Easter and Christmas vigils, holy days for Catholics and historical commemorative days for Protestants, weddings, and funerals. The church also stimulates more purely social events. Coreligionists in a section may hold a public service, with food, hymns, sermons, prayers, reading from the Bible, and more innovative celebrations such as Ewenedi's potlatch-style giveaway. Churchgoers from Pohnpei annually come to Sapwuahfik for a progressive visit from church to church, an occasion for socializing, feasting, and singing, and a Sapwuahfik group will also travel on Pohnpei as guests of a municipality or section. Churches sponsor feasts for events such as religious holidays and visits; feast preparations generate ad hoc planning and work committees. Most church events feature hymn singing, and practice sessions before a competitive singing event (either among sections or between Catholics and Protestants) can take place nightly for weeks—occasions for socializing, rowdying, and romance as well as for singing practice.

Protestant (United Church of Christ, inheriting the missions of the American Board) and Roman Catholic churches are the dominant affiliations on Sapwuahfik, on Pohnpei, and throughout Micronesia. Other denominations have increased missionary efforts since the 1960s, when the U.S. Trust Territory became easily accessible to civilian travel. On Sapwuahfik in 1979–80, members of five local families had converted to become Seventh-Day Adventists, Calvary Baptists, and Jehovah's Witnesses. By 1990, only Seventh-Day Adventists had significantly increased membership on the atoll.

On some Micronesian islands, and on parts of Pohnpei, there were prohibitions on the introduction of new denominations until religious freedom was enforced by the government. People object to the perceived factionalism, especially the creation of splits within families, introduced by conversions. Introduction of a Seventh-Day Adventist mission to Pingelap, for example, generated strong local opposition in 1978–80 (Damas 1985) and Nukuoro's refusal to allow missionaries to teach there generated controversy about the local applicability of the American legal concept of freedom of religion. Sapwuahfik people, though they did not respond with enthusiasm to conversion efforts in the late 1970s/early 1980s, did not prohibit such activities. *"Kaidihn kiht Koht,"* a *wahnpoaron* replied when I commented on Sapwuahfik's openness to different religions—"we are not God," to decide what people should believe. "A person can believe whatever he wants."

When a couple marries, the wife most often changes her religion to match that of her husband's family, though she is not obliged to do so. People seem to feel that it is more convenient for the entire family to belong to the same religion. The Baptists, Seventh-Day Adventists, and Jehovah's Witnesses on Ngatik in 1979–80 were not single individuals but families.

When I visited Pohnpei at the end of 1989, I found that many more people had become Seventh-Day Adventists, including a former state legislator and his father, a former *wahnpoaron* of Sapwuahfik's Protestant church. Nonconverts estimated about thirty Adventists on Sapwuahfik; the congregation met in a church (the foundations of which had been laid by the few Adventists on Sapwuahfik in 1980) and had an American pastor in residence. Since I did not collect conversion accounts I cannot explain what moved more individuals to join this relatively new church. Denominationalism may be growing as an expression of political factionalism. Religion has always been a route to community power for men; to hold a high church position reflects high community status, and political fortunes are in part played out in the arena of church business. Sapwuahfik's Protestant *wahnpoaron* have included men of high title and holders of elective office. Denominationalism itself as a political force is new on Sapwuahfik; it is more familiar on Pohnpei, where foreign missionaries have concentrated their activities.

Sapwuahfik people today are practicing and thoughtful Christians. Most attend church regularly, children attend Sunday school, and many older people express their devotion by joining in additional practices such as holding church office, Jugenbund, Bible study, hymn practice, church-sponsored trips to Pohnpei, and personal and family prayer sessions and Bible reading. Several have explicitly intellectual interests in religious topics, for example, attempting to relate traditional history to biblical origin accounts or examining differences among denominational beliefs.

It is in this dominant context of Christian belief that we

should see the concern with magical practice and with *eni*. I have already noted widespread agreement that *eni* were plentiful and much involved with ancient Sapwuahfik life. One man explained that some *eni* left when the missionaries came, "for they were afraid to hear the voices of the Christians." But others remained, and continue active, occasionally accessible to human experience.

The category *eni* is a broad one and includes several sorts of beings. Named *eni* inhabit particular places on land, reef, or sea; the sites of ancient or massacre-era shrines where some of these were worshiped are known. Other *eni* either have no names or their names are unknown. Some are helpful, guarding the atoll from typhoons, sorcery, and unwelcome visitors. Others are dangerous, preying on human beings, luring people to their deaths. Children are urged to obedience by frightening threats of *eni*; sometimes they have nightmares about them. Children and some adults are fearful at night, disliking to walk alone or without a light. The forest, the ocean, and a few places on Ngatik Islet known to be inhabited by particular *eni* are especially fearsome at night. Fear of *eni* is particularly evident after a death, for some deceased people become *eni*, at least temporarily, after they die. The presence of such *eni* is revealed by odd occurrences, for example, glimpsing a preternaturally large pig, hearing music when one is at sea without a radio, or hearing noises without seeing anyone. I was on Sapwuahfik at the time of several deaths, and for weeks after each one, rumors of sightings flew around the island, clustering ominously whenever one had to go outside at night or cross the island after an evening church service. Whether the *eni* is a dead relative or a "spirit of the land" or sea, encountering one is a terrifying experience, made more so because a person is most likely to see *eni* when he or she is ill or unhappy.

Although there are treatments for the illness brought on by seeing *eni*, Sapwuahfik people do not deliberately interact directly with them, and there are no trances, shrines, prayers, or divination to contact them. Christian services are not explicitly used as protection against *eni*, though the practice of watching with the family for several nights after a death, singing hymns and keeping company with the bereaved, certainly helps people through the critical period when the deceased is most likely to appear as a spirit.

Eni are directly connected with the native soil and water of Sapwuahfik. Their connection with the atoll extends into mythical time, and most are associated with a particular locale. For example, the islets of Sirop and Pikenkelung are the lands of one family, half-spirit, half-human. The spirit Enihnohna owned Wad, and Lematra ruled Wataluhk. A spirit named Dingenpwel owned Ngatik Islet long ago. He and the other *eni* of Ngatik fought with the *eni* who ruled over the other islets. There was a war of spirits over the possession of Ngatik; in the fighting Dingenpwel was speared, and when he fell, he created a plot of taro garden. The most important of the atoll's *eni* remained even after the introduction of Christianity. The winners of an epic spirit battle for the islet of Ngatik still live there: "It is in a sense they who take care of Ngatik"; thus, identified spirits continue to "work" on Sapwuahfik as protectors.

Christian practice, by contrast, is mobile. An imported faith, recognized and celebrated as such, it is practiced in the home, at church, when one is traveling, unconnected to locale (see Silverman 1971). *Eni* are often spoken of as explicitly "of Ngatik," whereas Christian belief unites Sapwuahfik people with other Micronesians and with foreigners. What binds people together as Christians are shared beliefs and values, and social ties in the form of church organization. Despite this universalism, the Sapwuahfik vision of history constructs Christian belief as a distinctive component of local identity.

Sorcery and Identity

The aboriginal Sapwuahfik people were punished for being pagans, and their successors on the atoll turned willingly to embrace Christianity, making the atoll's history a sort of morality play. Oral tradition abounds with mentions of the pagan beliefs and practices of the aboriginal Sapwuahfik people, such as malevolent spirits, clan totems, and magic, and ancient sorcery continues to be a topic of speculation on Sapwuahfik. Although no one knows details, people are convinced that their aboriginal ancestors were extremely effective magicians, feared throughout the Eastern Carolines. The ancients knew magic for foretelling events (which they used to predict the *Lambton*'s fatal second trip to Ngatik), catching turtles and fish, speaking directly with spirits (for example, as a way to learn new songs), gaining protection from typhoons, turning back enemy canoes, warfare, superfast sailing, and flying. They were also expert in forms of magic still used elsewhere in Micronesia: sorcery for magical healing and to cause illness, crop failure, and death.

Mehn Sapwuahfik today express confidence in their widespread reputation as sorcerers even as they disavow all modern practice. Other Islanders, they say, have continued to fear them long after the reason for fear has disappeared. They repeatedly emphasized to me that all such knowledge was discarded as a result of the massacre and in response to the Christian message, "because God doesn't think it good." Of the numerous cases of sorcery of which I learned, none was, even speculatively, attributed to aboriginal Sapwuahfik magic.

Although the other Eastern Caroline Islands received Christian teachings well before their atoll, and Pohnpei and Kosrae were the centers of Christian influence in these islands, Sapwuahfik people today see themselves as more "truly Christian," as they say, than some of their neighbors. Again, the focus is on comparison with Pohnpei, and on two specific points. One is a widespread opinion that Pohnpei people have "two sides"—their interior state and external behavior do not coincide, whereas Sapwuahfik people feel they themselves are consistent and forthright in their thought, speech, and actions.[2] The second point is that Sapwuahfik people believe that some *mehn Pohnpei,* although attending church and showing the signs of Christian belief, actively practice sorcery.

It is not that Sapwuahfik people see themselves as more perfect than their neighbors—as one would expect, their view of their own community is complex. They are not at all reluctant to speak of what they see as negative attributes of *mehn Sapwuahfik*, from complaints about boys drinking and women smoking to castigations of the community's unwillingness to cooperate. My emphasis on one element of their self-concept should not be mistaken for the complex whole of Sapwuahfik cultural identity. But their vision of the massacre as a tale with moral meaning enters closely into their perception of themselves vis-à-vis their neighbors and supports the idea of Sapwuahfik today as a cleansed and protected place, an island made distinct by its unique past.

Those on the atoll after the massacre voluntarily abandoned sorcery and other pagan practices to embrace Christianity. As a reward, God provided them special protection, which today reassures Sapwuahfik people in the face of typhoons, war, and sorcery by outsiders. Especially in regard to the legendarily powerful sorcery of Sapwuahfik's aborigines, the notion of them voluntarily "throwing away" (*kesehla*) pagan ways is important. In a strict sense there was little "throwing away" to be done; surely the greater part of traditional magical-religious skills had been lost as a consequence of the massacre, though immigrants brought their own knowledge. But Islanders today do not regard this as an inevitable result of the disruption. One narrative recounts a conflict that divided the Spanish-era population into two groups when the "Nahnwmarki's son" was killed, and describes an *ohl en sarawi* (holy man) of the ancient beliefs standing on a rock and declaring that he was throwing away the atoll's magical knowledge. *Mehn Sapwuahfik* today always speak of their ancestors as having discarded the old ways of their own will, in return for which they have been rewarded with divine protection.[3]

People on Pohnpei, by contrast, are often described as using magic maliciously and freely. It is again important to emphasize that I did not conduct research on Pohnpei, and I do not know the extent or nature of modern Pohnpei sorcery belief or practice. People on Pohnpei are practicing Christians, along with a small number of Bahá'ís. Sorcery is a common topic of conversation on Pohnpei and, as Falgout says, "a common explanation for sickness and death" (Falgout 1984a:112), but its contemporary use is generally denied. (See Fischer 1957; Riesenberg 1948; Ward 1977 on illness, curing, and sorcery on Pohnpei.) Sapwuahfik people talk a great deal about the dangers of Pohnpei sorcery, however, and they emphasized to me their own lack of evil magic.

Magical practice in the Eastern Carolines includes both useful and harmful acts. Good magic (*wini mwahu: wini,* "medicine," *mwahu,* "good") is curing magic, working with spells, plants, or both to cure diseases. (Some diseases can be cured by scientific medicine, by Western-trained doctors or hospital techniques; others require local medicine or magical spells. Not all local medicine involves magic.) Evil magic or sorcery, *wini suwed* (*suwed,* "evil" or "bad") causes sickness, death, sexual infatuation, destruction of property, or other misfortunes. Other tasks can be, or have been in the past, performed by means of magic: foretelling the future, moving objects, attracting ships or keeping them away, flying, and so on. People speak of these magical practices in morally neutral terms.

Sapwuahfik people say the practice of sorcery is widespread in the Eastern Caroline Islands, and that outer-island sorcery has always been more powerful than that of Pohnpei. In modern times, however, they describe only Pingelap people as retaining sorcery stronger than that of Pohnpei. Sapwuahfik people consider that their own aboriginal ancestors were once the most powerful and feared sorcerers in the region, and I heard stories indicating that Pohnpeians and others may still think of Sapwuahfik *wini* as dangerous. But Sapwuahfik people emphasize that all knowledge of sorcery and magic was discarded as a result of the massacre and in response to the Christian message. Most of the expressed concern about *wini suwed* among Sapwuahfik people today is with magic that originates on Pohnpei.

The cases of sorcery that I observed or heard about, and the level of rumor and discussion of magic, indicate that *mehn Sapwuahfik* certainly take sorcery seriously as a mode of social action. They believe Sapwuahfik people use imported sorcery when they envy someone's good fortune or economic resources, such as good taro gardens, or because of anger, arguments over children of a Pohnpei-Sapwuahfik marriage, or romantic jealousy. When I asked why *mehn Pohnpei* (in general or in a specific instance) performed sorcery, I received some of the same answers: envy over economic, political, or romantic circumstances is a common precipitator of sorcery actions or allegations. One victim of Pohnpei sorcery, for example, said he was attacked because he was one of very few Sapwuahfik men to have attained success on Pohnpei's terms. By amassing pigs and yams and contributing generously to feasts on Pohnpei, he had shown himself to be a "real man" (*ohl mehlel*) in the Pohnpei style; the sorcery attack was thus motivated by jealousy. Yet my inquiries about instances of Pohnpei sorcery also produced responses that attribute it to obscure, even casual, motives.

Mehn Sapwuahfik deal with Pohnpei sorcery when they are on Pohnpei, when Pohnpei people come to the atoll, or when a Sapwuahfik person obtains and uses Pohnpei magic. Concern with sorcery is verbalized in the context of visits to Pohnpei, interaction with Pohnpei affines or associates, and participation in Pohnpei social events and political activities. Practitioners are said to put *wini suwed* in food, cigarettes, or kava, or to implement magic by touching a person with lotion or oil or by sending it through the air. Pohnpei men, women, and even children are said to know magic that can cause illness and misfortune, and people can readily point to Sapwuahfik individuals who have been attacked by Pohnpei sorcery.

Individual Sapwuahfik people have many business, marriage, and friendship ties with individual Pohnpeians. Older men who were sheltered by Pohnpei families during the hard times of World War II, people who attended school with *mehn Pohnpei* or worked with them and, more recently, joined them in business or political enterprises, consider themselves friends and, in many cases, relatives. The permanent Sapwuahfik community on Pohnpei constantly creates more friends and relatives among *mehn Pohnpei.* Sapwuahfik people travel freely to the high island, often staying months at a time. Sapwuahfik and Pohnpei churches cooperate for special celebrations. Yet despite the large number of positive personal ties of affection and respect, there is a common rhetoric of caution among Sapwuahfik about Pohnpei people in general.

Despite frequent mention of *wini suwed,* and though Sapwuahfik people follow commonsense guidelines of self-protection (for example, being wary of food given to them on Pohnpei), they feel a certain amount of reassurance about their personal safety. Whereas they speak of Pohnpei as a "dangerous" place (referring not only to sorcery but also to crimes in the urban area), they say they feel safe on their home atoll. Sapwuahfik's protector-spirits forbid the operation of foreign sorcery and will physically attack anyone who performs it. Yet people have been, and are, ensorcelled on Sapwuahfik by *mehn Sapwuahfik.* The few instances I recorded were cases of physical affliction—headaches, vomiting, or a general sense of illness. The attacks were said to have been motivated by jealousy. According to rumor, the magic used in each case was originally from Pohnpei, inherited from, bought, or given by *mehn Pohnpei,* which Sapwuahfik people brought back to use on Sapwuahfik. The assertion that *mehn Sapwuahfik* have no magic is retained; all magic used on the atoll is imported. Sapwuahfik people even reject learning sorcery from others in self-defense; they would, they say, be "ashamed" to do that, because as believing Christians they do not credit the power of magic. Besides, as one man told me, if one dies of a sorcery attack, the Christian will go to the Lord, so one should not be too disturbed about it.

At first I suspected that my questions about Sapwuahfik sorcery were simply being blandly turned aside with polite negatives, but I became convinced that no Sapwuahfik people possess aboriginal *wini suwed.* That does not mean that there is no magical practice on Sapwuahfik; there is certainly much talk about the use of imported magic or visits to Pohnpei practitioners among *mehn Sapwuahfik.* There are also rumors of old men knowing aboriginal magic, and eyewitness accounts of one man using supernatural forces in harmless ways—to help a canoe win a race or cause someone to forget a story he has just heard. Some people pointed to a recently deceased man of knowledge as one who had known and used evil magic (his death, in fact, is said to have been magically caused). A few are willing to suggest, but not assert, that one older man noted for his knowledge of tradition might have learned something of magic. It is said there are Sapwuahfik and Pohnpei people afraid of this man's knowledge, but most agree he is not likely to use sorcery even if he knows any because of his kindness and high church position. That man is aware that people think he knows magic, but dismisses the rumors almost wistfully: "*Mehn Sapwuahfik* have thrown away all that." He explained to me that even the famous Sapwuahfik sorcerer who died by magic got his knowledge from Pohnpei.[4]

The construction of a Sapwuahfik cultural identity by contrast with that of Pohnpei is less distinct in the area of religion than it is in the sociopolitics of egalitarianism. When attacked by sorcery, or when provided with the opportunity to obtain *wini suwed,* the choice of action is in part a statement of identity.

As in feasting and public political behavior, then, Sapwuahfik identity is also created by negative contrast in the realm of religion: Sapwuahfik people do not use sorcery. Yet there is a positive element as well: Sapwuahfik enjoys the reward of divine protection from both natural disaster and deliberate attack.

Sahpw Paiamwahu, *the Fortunate Land*

In the 1960s, it is said, a group of high-ranking *mehn Pohnpei* visited Sapwuahfik. In the course of this visit, a nahnmwarki of one of Pohnpei's *wehi* made comments about certain aspects of legendary Sapwuahfik history. His comments angered *mehn Sapwuahfik,* and they held a meeting after the visitors left on the interisland ship (which was to go south to Nukuoro and Kapingamarangi for five days). After discussing how best to react, they decided to hold a feast when the ship returned and force some sort of resolution. People prepared large amounts of food in anticipation of the feast. Several elderly men, wearing traditional head garlands, chanted old chants. It is said that the man most knowledgeable about traditional history planned a sort of intellectual showdown with the nahnmwarki in question, each of them telling history until the one unable to respond to a question or tale lost, and died.

All these preparations proved unnecessary. Despite perfectly clear weather until that day, when the ship again approached Sapwuahfik, the atoll was hidden by clouds, waves, rain, and wind. The ship was unable to find the entrance to the channel. After sailing around in vain, short on gas and oil, it went on to Pohnpei. *Mehn Sapwuahfik* are unanimous in attributing this protection (not only of the atoll, but also of the life of the visiting nahnmwarki) not to any magical act by the Sapwuahfik people themselves but to the protection of the atoll's *eni*, especially those female spirits that guard the lagoon channel and control the wind and waves there.

Sapwuahfik people speak of Pohnpei as a "dangerous" place and extol the virtues of Sapwuahfik as a *sahpw mwahu* (a "good land," a "virtuous land"). "You don't need to be afraid here on Sapwuahfik," people reassured me. They referred to the absence of crime, the lack of indigenous magic, and the protective spirits of the atoll. Several stories of events in the last two decades demonstrate the willingness of these protective *eni* to attack outsiders who try to use magic on Sapwuahfik. During one sports event, for example, visitors used magic, as was their habit, to help them win. One of them was badly frightened and nearly strangled by the atoll's *eni*.

In addition to the protection of *eni*, Sapwuahfik people see evidence of the reward for their acceptance of Christianity, compensation for the suffering of 1837, and God's special protection of the atoll in events of the present and recent past. Sapwuahfik has not experienced a typhoon since 1905; in contrast, Pingelap experienced typhoons in 1957 and 1972 (Damas 1985:46). During a 1979 typhoon warning, people expressed to me their confidence in God's protection of the atoll from storms. In addition, the atoll's large taro gardens provide abundant food, whereas nearby atolls suffer occasional scarcity. As a result, Sapwuahfik people sometimes call their home *sahpw paiamwahu,* a "fortunate land." As a local person said, "God preserves Ngatik; the people of Pingelap, Kapingamarangi, and Pohnpei use *wini.*"

During World War II, not only was Sapwuahfik spared destruction from the fighting—the people actually benefited from gifts of tinned beef, cigarettes, and chocolate dropped by American planes. Though two people were wounded on Sapwuahfik, and many others suffered in Japanese work groups on Pohnpei during the U.S. bombings, the last years of the war are now regarded with something near glee as far as life on the atoll was concerned. Pohnpei suffered shortages of everything; Sapwuahfik benefitted materially from the American invasion. One man told me he sometimes blames foreigners for the 1837 massacre, but then he recalls World War II and how Sapwuahfik was not bombed and thinks, Maybe it comes out even. His comment expresses very well how Sapwuahfik people weigh their history in moral scales.

"From Darkness to Light": Local Visions of History

Like many Pacific Islanders, Sapwuahfik people conceptualize history in terms of colonial regimes: the aboriginal era; periods of control by Spain, Germany, Japan, and the United States; independence. The 1837 massacre marks the watershed of change from aboriginal life to the colonial era, from the aboriginal population to the ancestors of today's Sapwuahfik people. As *mehn Sapwuahfik* see the first era, that of aboriginal Sapwuahfik, as the physical source of their modern population, so they conceive of the events and circumstances of that time as the wellspring of significance for their modern identity.

As they see it, the history of the massacre is a story of sin, punishment, and reward—which, as my choice of words suggests, partakes of Christian theology. Nineteenth-century missionary emphasis in Micronesia, consonant with the dominant vision of contemporary American evangelical Protestantism, was on the sinfulness of pagan ways and the need to exchange them for civilized ways. (On the content of this specific sort of Christian teaching in the Pacific, see Boutelier, Hughes, and Tiffany 1978; Gunson 1978; and contemporary missionary writings.) Hanlon 1988 describes the close ties between Christian teachings and American culture in the efforts of Protestant missionaries on Pohnpei (see especially pp. 142–43; also Hezel 1978). Sapwuahfik absorbed from this theology a way of looking at the world that merges Christianization, adoption of Western material culture, and Americanization (Poyer 1988b).

The key symbolic element of this scheme is the metaphor of darkness and light, briefly introduced in Chapter 2. The most common description of the aboriginal Sapwuahfik people is that they were *rotorot*. This word is from *roht*, literally, "darkness"; the *Ponapean-English Dictionary* defines *rotorot* as "pagan, uncivilized, uneducated, uncultured" (Rehg and Sohl 1979). The introduction of Christian teachings is the key to the metaphorical distinction of *rotorot* and its antonym, *marain*, "light" or "enlightened." Nothing before conversion can be called *marain*, though even after conversion, and in reference to Christian peoples (such as Americans), "unenlightened" can apply to persons or actions that are evil, stupid, or un-Christian. Because Christianity is identified with American/European civilization, technology, democracy, a peaceable nature, literacy, schooling, a specific sexual morality, good works, and puritanism (i.e., rejection of alcohol, traditional dances, and smoking), uses of "enlightened" and "unenlightened" may refer to any of these.

The metaphor is found also on Pohnpei, where, according to Falgout, people "often refer to the past as *ansouen rotorot*, a 'time of darkness' before they became enlightened (*marain*) and guided by the principles of Christian love and cooperation" (Falgout 1984a:110). It appears in one of the few lengthy, locally produced Pacific histories, *The Book of Luelen* (Bernart 1977; see also Fischer, Riesenberg, and Whiting 1977; Hanlon 1992), written in the 1930s and 1940s. Luelen Bernart, a Pohnpei man very knowledgeable about his culture's traditional history, modeled his narrative in some respects after the Bible. Like Sapwuahfik attitudes about their past, though less explicitly, Bernart's manuscript contains references to the darkness and sinfulness of certain ancestors, the progressive advance of technology, morals, and knowledge, and Christianity's transforming effects in moving people toward civilization.

This evolutionary view of history, with darkness/light as its key metaphor, is by no means unique to central Micronesia. It is described, with close attention to its complexity, by Shore (1982) for Samoa and by Silverman (1967, 1971) for Banaba; many Pacific Islanders have adopted the evangelical metaphor to contrast pre- and post-Christian times (Thomas 1989), and it is common as well to other evangelized areas of the world.[5] Furthermore, although Sapwuahfik historiography is strongly influenced by Western thought, elements of Sapwuahfik understanding contradict my simple model of a one-way arrow of "enlightenment." *Mehn Sapwuahfik* admire much about their aboriginal ancestors, such as their ability in magic, navigation, and subsistence tasks. But the small sample of premassacre traditional history that has survived, and discontinuity in the transmission not only of lore but also of attitudes about history, make it impossible to segregate the aboriginal Sapwuahfik vision of the past from imported and recently proposed ideas. What people now express is their own creation, built on Islander and foreign intellectual influences of the nineteenth and twentieth centuries.

In discourse about the 1837 massacre, the light/dark opposition serves to label ancestors of the present population. Modern *mehn Sapwuahfik* have three sorts of ancestors: aboriginal Sapwuahfik people, Islander immigrants (from Pohnpei and other Micronesian islands), and American/European immigrants. Although ideas about all these ancestral groups express ambivalent evaluations of them, Western and aboriginal ancestors are in general represented as opposites, in the Sapwuahfik view, along that critical axis of "light" and "darkness." Although the aboriginal Sapwuahfik people are admired for certain skills, such as sorcery, they are condemned as pagan for worshiping spirits, for actively using that famed sorcery, and for their displays of sexual promiscuity. The feeling that they were *rotorot* is expressed strongly in oral tradition, culminating in the graphic tales of heathen activities during the reign of Sirinpahn, the last aboriginal ruler of Sapwuahfik.

Americans and Europeans, on the other hand, are described as *marain*. This refers to their being, by nature as it were, Christian (Sapwuahfik people have little acquaintance with non-Christian Americans or Europeans). In context the word is often used to explain foreign technology, and why Americans are politically and economically dominant in Micronesia today. The word describing their technological superiority is *loalekeng*, "intelligent" or "smart." *Loalekeng* is acquired by way of formal education, which is a function of increasing "enlightenment." (On Sapwuahfik one says "he is intelligent because he went to school," not "he is intelligent, therefore he does well in school.") This broad use of "enlightenment" conflates religious belief and material culture—much as the early missionaries did.

The position of Americans/Europeans and of aboriginal Islanders in the massacre story is necessarily, in the outsider's view, paradoxical (see Chapter 2). The Americans/Europeans are the attackers, the murderers; yet some are also cultural and biological ancestors. The people of Sapwuahfik today are very aware of the biologically mixed nature of their population, and of the tenuous cultural ties binding the present to the aboriginal past. Rather than present this as a paradox or simplify their ancestral background into a unity, they express ambivalent perceptions of both groups of ancestors. Though the aboriginal Islanders were unenlightened, they were clearly innocent of any crime against their murderers. Though Hart and his crew are, by their nature as Americans/Europeans, classed as enlightened, they were also guilty of murder.

There is, in addition, a second level on which these moral values are reversed. Here, the aboriginal Sapwuahfik people are seen as "guilty" and the attackers as "innocent." The aboriginal Sapwuahfik people were in darkness and were becoming progressively more pagan and evil; this sinful darkness called for divine punishment. And so Hart's crew, although immediately guilty of

226

murder, were operating under higher orders, as it were, and so in a sense were innocent. Referring to sinful pagan ways, one informant said directly, "That's the reason foreigners came and killed, for God permitted them to cause such [behavior] to be punished." This explains why the traditional protective spirits of the atoll, normally even today quick to keep Sapwuahfik safe from outside threat, failed to help on that critical occasion.

If the massacre was a punishment, a sign of the wrath of God, it was followed by God revealing another of His attributes, mercy. Angry at Sirinpahn and the people of Sapwuahfik, God punished them with the massacre. After this, He had mercy on them, sending them Christian teachings and protection from, for example, sorcery and typhoons. Today the people of Sapwuahfik continue to rely on God's special protection, for which one group of their ancestors paid so high a price.

Conclusion

THE LAST SEVERAL DECADES of ethnohistorical research have immeasurably enhanced the study of histories as culturally informed texts. We are now able to use oral traditions for recent generations, with care, to inform ourselves about past events and circumstances. We now recognize oral traditions as history—not the raw material of history—and so acknowledge indigenous historiographies, culturally distinctive representations of the past. We have used these insights to recognize that people have various uses for history, interpretations of past events, and modes of relating past to present. Understanding historical discourse as a cultural product (rather than an unproblematic dissertation on past events) has opened a new set of questions to ethnohistorical inquiry.[1] We now need to understand more clearly how perceptions of the past come to be taken as prescriptions for practical action (e.g., Feinberg 1980; Sahlins 1981a, 1981b), and, conversely, how historical knowledge is altered in response to changing circumstances (for example, Black 1978; Borofsky 1987; Maude 1968; and Petersen 1982a on the alteration of tradition in small-scale Pacific societies; Appadurai 1981 on cultural rules about debating the past). In this examination of the Sapwuahfik case, I have approached the question of how history operates as ideology through a cultural analysis of historical knowledge, or, more accurately, of the local meaning of history. The goal of such analysis is to identify the symbols and concepts, and their interrelationships, in terms of which a community understands its past, and to locate these in the entire set of shared symbols and meanings that constitutes local culture (in David Schneider's sense; Schneider 1968, 1976; Dolgin 1977).

Western contact precipitated radical alterations in Sapwuahfik's population, society, and culture. Through the massacre, resettlement of the atoll, and conversion to Christianity, survivors and immigrants created a new society. The modern Sapwuahfik community's sense of identity is based on both an awareness of the atoll's unique history and contemporary comparisons of Sapwuahfik customs with those of other cultural groups.

The vision of the past presented here, which sees the modern population of Sapwuahfik as a sort of chosen people, punished by God but also saved, sets in context the present-day maintenance of that identity through a constant comparative tension between Sapwuahfik people and others. We might think of Sapwuahfik identity as woven from the influences of three models in terms of which they evaluate their own "style." The most powerful model is Pohnpei, characterized by Sapwuahfik people as correctly following etiquette and rank rules of a local Great Tradition of which Sapwuahfik is part. A second model is Sapwuahfik's own past, *mehn mahs*, "people of long ago," the aboriginal atoll dwellers. A third is the United States, identified as economically powerful and characterized by democratic political and interpersonal practices. Each of these "models" is also an ancestral population for modern Sapwuahfik—they are not external abstractions but are represented, in local history, as inherent in being *mehn Sapwuahfik*. Statements about modern identity are simultaneously representations of history.

Sources and Directions of Sapwuahfik "Style"

The darkness/light metaphor is used frequently on Sapwuahfik and Pohnpei, as elsewhere, to contrast the old ways of paganism and the despotic powers of ancient chiefs with new beliefs and behaviors.[2] More than forty years of American involvement in Micronesia has led Islanders to perceive the United States as a source of "enlightenment" in the region. (Micronesians are not naïve, however; they recognize that many Americans are not particularly enlightened.) Christianity, education, democracy, and industrial technology are all perceived as part of the movement from "darkness" to "light." The existence of American/ European ancestors validates a self-conscious distinction of Sapwuahfik as less hierarchical, less tradition-bound, and more egalitarian than Pohnpei. *Mehn Sapwuahfik* compare themselves to Americans in several respects: the atoll has blended imported democratic voting and bureaucratic practices with indigenous decision making forms; Sapwuahfik is a land rich in food, like the United States; both populations speak English (Sapwuahfik's pidgin); and, importantly, both devalue rank and emphasize the equality of individuals. (One Sapwuahfik woman compared Japanese to *mehn Pohnpei* in valuing respect behavior, whereas Americans are more like *mehn Sapwuahfik*.)

Mehn Sapwuahfik also criticize Americans, and laud what they themselves have and what they share with Pohnpei. The persistent interest in rank etiquette and its deliberate and careful use in formal situations, the use of Pohnpeian and high language for formal speeches and sermons, and the sturdy continuation of the title system testify to the strength of the ideology of rank. But it is rank with little authority, and it is in the careful negotiation of this social form that we can see how the social order is reproduced by individual choices of public action. Though the Pohnpei title system was imported to Sapwuahfik, today things central to Pohnpei life are attenuated and inconsistently observed on Sapwuahfik: respect behavior, honorific language, deference to high-titled persons in decision making, and attention to rank in ceremonial. Although Sapwuahfik feasts are conducted formally and men of high title sit at the front and are served first, everyone receives the same amount of food, in dramatic contrast with the Pohnpei custom of apportioning feast goods by rank.

In examining community identity, what is important is not an argument about the objective facts of a Sapwuahfik-Pohnpei contrast (indeed, we have seen that the two are very similar) but an understanding of the local perception of difference, and the social process that maintains and alters it. It is not that "Pohnpei is hierarchical; Sapwuahfik is egalitarian" in a scientific-ethnological sense, but that that statement is true as a cultural proposition for Sapwuahfik people.

The introduction of the Pohnpei title system on the atoll is represented in oral tradition not as a direct import from the high island but as the idea of an American/European officer; the three surviving aboriginal boys who first held the highest titles established their rank by literally pulling names out of a hat—a less than awe-inspiring historical charter. Although *mehn Pohnpei* of high title appear in oral histories, they are not explicitly credited with a role in establishing the title system. The nahnmwarki title remains attached to the "truly *mehn Sapwuahfik*" clan of Dipwinmen toantoal, and the new Constitution also reserves the highest elected position to a particular definition of *mehn Sapwuahfik*. Though Pohnpei men of rank have provided opportunities for Sapwuahfik people to conform more closely to the high island's system, their offers have been rejected. Though some Sapwuahfik men are active in the Pohnpei system, they are not free to introduce its usages into public events on the atoll. The difference in attitude toward traditional systems of rank and status is the single most important distinctive feature, readily pointed out by people of both Pohnpei and Sapwuahfik as what sets them apart.

Sapwuahfik people explicitly compare their perceived egalitarianism to American ways, and *mehn Pohnpei* share the recognition of American style as egalitarian. Describing an equal distribution of food on Pohnpei during a meal intended as a demonstration of feast ceremonial, Paul Dahlquist (1972:225) writes that "no distinctions were made on the basis of rank since this was a school in the American tradition, not a feast in the Ponapean tradition." Similarly, Suzanne Falgout presents the Pohnpei view of the open access to knowledge in American schooling:

> Ponapeans regard the American educational system as the outcome of our democratic socio-political ideals. They equate our ideal of equal status of individuals with our educational system that grants equal rights to knowledge. They explicitly contrast this educational system with their own ideals for education. In accordance with their notions of status hierarchy and privilege, Ponapean epistemological assumptions stress the management of knowledge—its control and manipulation—instead of mere possession and replication. (Falgout 1984a:141)

Sapwuahfik's sense of having special ties with Americans is founded on a number of historical incidents, beginning with uncertainty about Hart's nationality, which for some people has become the determination that he was American (from the documents, he appears to have been a British citizen; the *Lambton* was registered in Sydney, Australia). (One man joked to me about filing a claim for damages against the United States on account of the massacre.) Sapwuahfik's history of affiliation with Americans can be traced through stories about the immediate postmassacre period (when several memorable Anglophones, some American, lived there), the American missionary era, World War II (when the U.S. military visited and bestowed gifts on the atoll), and the post-1960 era of U.S. economic generosity. Anecdotes of World War II include personal encounters with flyers and soldiers that emphasize the bravery, friendliness, and generosity of the Americans. Because they alone spoke English, Sapwuahfik men on Pohnpei acted as interpreters and assistants to incoming U.S. troops.[3]

Today it is the people of Pohnpei, and to an extent other Micronesians in the Eastern Carolines, who have greatest access to and familiarity with American ways. Yet Sapwuahfik people retain a sense of identification with Americans. In their view of the past, they moved from a state of darkness through the trial of the massacre onto a path of increasing enlightenment, which today is consonant with the general shift in Micronesia toward political democracy and decreasing emphasis on traditional rank as a source of power. The construction of history is thus strengthened by American ideals of democracy and social equality, in which *mehn Sapwuahfik* see themselves as more like Americans than are their Eastern Carolines neighbors.

A second symbolic elaboration of Sapwuahfik identity is as sincere Christians, in distinction from neighbors who are thought to use sorcery. Concern about possible magical harm pervades discussions about illness or misfortune, and caution about sorcery dangers accompanies Sapwuahfik visitors to Pohnpei. Throughout much of the Pacific and elsewhere, it is "others" who employ magic, and "we" who are true Christians. The Sapwuahfik claim partakes of this general phenomenon. Yet beyond this, the notion of Sapwuahfik virtue (like the assertion of egalitarian socioeconomic relations) is supported by a historical argument: atoll people rejected pagan ways as a result of the massacre and are now firmly committed to increasing "enlightenment" in both religious and political terms. God's mercy on the island after the terrible punishment of the massacre is a reward for their faithfulness to his religion. Sapwuahfik's claim of special divine protection rests on uniquely local indicators—people point out that Sapwuahfik does not suffer from typhoons or food scarcity, as other islands do, and that it was preserved from bombing in World War II.

Egalitarian and religious considerations are thus potent markers, affirming the forward-looking, allied-with-power, "enlightened" qualities of Sapwuahfik culture. Disagreements about choices of personal action in these domains focus public attention on them as important symbols of identity. Such disagreements arise frequently because of constant contact with *mehn Pohnpei*, other Islanders, and other foreigners—and because of differences among *mehn Sapwuahfik* themselves. Despite the evolutionary metaphor, Sapwuahfik people do not see traditional Pohnpei sociopolitics as backward. In fact, there is much about

Pohnpei's culture that Sapwuahfik people find attractive and admirable, and in which they participate; some Sapwuahfik men actively seek Pohnpei titles. Attitudes about sorcery are similarly ambivalent: disvalued by Christian belief, sorcery is nonetheless seen as real and dangerous. The persistence of tension in these matters maintains the assertion of a distinct Sapwuahfik identity as a community concern, rather than something taken for granted. Individual choices about sorcery, the title system, and respect behavior are acted out on the public stage, and so provide continual opportunity for affirming and contesting the ideology of Sapwuahfik identity.[4]

Social Practice and Indigenous Representations of History

Sapwuahfik's philosophy, then, has its roots in three different traditions, both objectively and subjectively. If Sapwuahfik people are *duwehte mehn Pohnpei,* "the same as Pohnpei people," and *uhdahn mehn Ngatik,* "truly Ngatik/Sapwuahfik people," they are also *ekis mehn wai,* "a bit foreign (American/European),"—all phrases they frequently apply in self-description. The result is a balanced tension among alternative styles of action, kept in check by social processes. Many of these processes are widely characteristic of Micronesia, others of small community life everywhere. The ideology that justifies and guides choices of social action is a unique product of Sapwuahfik's own creating.

The relative recency of cultural destruction and rebuilding on Sapwuahfik, and the relative accessibility of documentary and oral history, lets us see quite well in this case what is now taken to be universally true of culture: that it is creative, constituted, invented. Insistence on studying culture as dynamic represents a continuing effort to move ahead on theoretical issues of structure and practice, cogently outlined by Sherry Ortner (1984), to reveal culture "in the making" (Fox 1985:196–211) rather than as a timeless entity. Trends of work in political economy, ethnographic writing, and problems of meaning coalesce in the current interest in the interrelationships of history and culture, and historiography and anthropology. (The problematics and potential of the intersection of history and culture studies can be pursued through the citations in the useful review of ethnohistory by Krech 1991; also Biersack 1989, 1991; Comaroff and Comaroff 1992; O'Brien and Roseberry 1991; Rebel 1989; Roseberry 1989; Sahlins 1985; and Sider 1986.)

History has been called on as an explanation for social action (especially, I might note, in the field of ethnicity) so often that it might be, and too often is, taken to go without saying. Why does a consciousness of the past often play an important part in decisions about social action? In part this is an artifact of analysis, because Western social science and common sense rely on history as an important form of explanation. (Cohn [1987:51], writes, "Everything for Europeans has a history, and to discover the history of something is to explain it.") Although we may assume precedence in time as a possible causal factor, we are still left with questions about the symbolic role of historical representation in indigenous explanations of social action. Another way to understand the custom of calling on history to validate present behavior can be found by reading Ortner's questions of system and process ("How does the system shape practice?" "How does practice shape the system?" [1984:152–57]) in part as a matter of how individuals act within an inherited order of meanings and values, and how their actions react on that order to maintain and alter it—then how that system (kept or changed as it is) is transmitted to the following generation. History is a common symbolic element of cultural systems because patterns of social relations and physical environment combine to weave the weft of the past around each new generation's experience of life.

MODES OF REMEMBERING

In understanding the symbolic potential of history, we need to look at the universe of means through which a sense of the past is developed in each generation. Although I would argue that

Sapwuahfik people value history and consciously hand on oral traditions, the transmission of history from one generation to the next involves much more than telling tales. By restricting our definition of history to written or spoken texts, we limit our view of how notions of the past take on persuasive and even coercive roles in shaping contemporary social action.

Analyses of "structures" or systems of meaning (e.g., Geertz 1973, 1983; Sahlins 1981b; Schneider 1968, 1976) have been criticized as static, as not fully accepting lived experience, human agency, or the entailments of power. This criticism is unfair to the implications of symbolic and interpretive approaches. It is the very concreteness, potency, and immediacy of lived experience that makes culture (in the symbolists' sense) effective, convincing, and powerful. Bourdieu's *habitus* confirms the hard reality of culture for us every day. Far from being removed from the realm of action, study of the order of meanings and values encoded in symbols (i.e., culture) is an essential analytical element of recognizing—and, much more, of understanding, interpreting, and explaining—social action.

Investigations of indigenous representations of the past concentrate, often exclusively, on oral tradition, which has been well studied as text, as myth, as history, as ideology, and as politics. Just as for written accounts, understanding oral history requires attention to all these facets of its creation, alteration, transmission, and use. Although there is much more to the process of remembering (Shils 1981), as we shall see, even oral tradition is a broad term, encompassing many forms of expression: genealogy, narrative, sermon, song, even nicknames and jokes. Each of these has its own characteristics in terms of the material it encodes and transmits (both information and ethos), the explication it requires, the circumstances in which it is taught and learned, and its capacity for social differentiation and integration (as oral knowledge is variably shared by kinship, gender, age, and other affiliations). These forms also partake in the general characteristics of discourse and theories of knowledge in the society at hand (e.g., Lindstrom 1990).

Chapter 1 described how oral accounts of the massacre are

transmitted, and indicated that knowledge of premassacre Sapw-uahfik is learned under more restricted conditions suitable to se-cret-sacred knowledge. Other oral forms that, on Sapwuahfik, have clear historical referents include teasing and nicknames re-ferring to ancestry, songs (such as that in Chapter 7), and the use of pidgin. One speaks self-consciously of clans and genealogies when connections are traced for land disputes, when the nahn-mwarki title (at least) is discussed, when a couple decides to marry, when people recall from whom they learned something or tell stories of those now dead. All these speech events invoke history. In other places, where diversity of ancestry is not marked, the history invoked by everyday talk might be of indi-viduals or families. On Sapwuahfik, although it is that, it is also a history of affiliations among the groups comprising Sapwuah-fik ancestry—simultaneously connecting present generations with the past, *mehn Sapwuahfik* with other populations.

Mehn Sapwuahfik also meet history, as we all do, in locale, in material goods, in social activity, and in intellectual explana-tion. I have already introduced the idea that explanations of ele-ments of modern life refer to the ancient Sapwuahfik people, the massacre, and postmassacre events. This includes physical ob-jects, personal appearances, and also, more generally, why *mehn Sapwuahfik* are the way they are (e.g., why they speak pidgin). History's explanatory role connects abstractions of personal and community identity with sensible reality. The church's impor-tant part in social life empowers an additional voice, appealing to history in judging desirable and undesirable ideas and acts in a continuing refrain of "darkness" and "light" that despite the wide distribution of the metaphor resonates uniquely with his-tory on Sapwuahfik.

Beyond the oral dimension, we can turn to the localization of historical memory. There are no deliberate memorials to the massacre (although Micronesia has many memorials erected by Germans, Japanese, and Americans, it is not a local habit), but physical remains—rounded stones (said to be the weapons of the immigrant Gilbertese), shell adzes (said to be those of the an-cient Sapwuahfik people), and coral-rock walls (said to be remnants of earlier dwellings)—are stimulants to oral history. Architecture plays a role as well: the one house built in a *U* shape, and the echo of the *nahs* every time a *U* arrangement is set up for a feast or special event make history concrete in the production of social activity. Not only do many locales retain names assigned by the aboriginal people, but many also host spirit presences and are known as sites of particular historical or ancient events. On Sapwuahfik, *eni,* "spirits," cannot be brought to mind without an echo of the massacre and Christian conversion, which is in part what gives *eni* their particular meaning on Sapwuahfik; and to call this to mind is also to recognize what that line of thought suggests about the meaning of being *mehn Sapwuahfik.* Sapwuahfik canoes have a distinctive *fedlatch* shaped at the prow and are painted with a pattern of dark and light, narrow and wide bands of color. The canoes are tied with knots known only to a few men and glued with purchased glue (but when that is not available, or costs too much, with boiled breadfruit sap). Building a canoe is a self-consciously traditional act, as well as a practical one, because those with cash may and usually do choose to buy a motorboat instead. So the act of making a canoe resonates with historical consciousness. Beyond that, a Sapwuahfik canoe requires the two elements—*fedlatch* and paint design—that mark the canoe as Sapwuahfik. All these everyday things and acts contribute to form in a new generation what Françoise Zonabend calls "the enduring memory" (1984).[5]

Paul Connerton (1989) points out that historical memory is transmitted as well through ceremony and "bodily practices." Sapwuahfik does not ceremonialize the memory of the massacre, but it does commemorate days marking the establishment of Christianity and changes in political status. Yet we could speak of "bodily practices" of etiquette and the ceremonial of feasts, *meing,* and *wahu* as "embodying" history in that an understanding of Sapwuahfik etiquette entails comparison with Pohnpei and reference to history. To perform a physical or verbal act of rank etiquette, however unselfconsciously, is to remind oneself of the reality of the historical and contemporary relationship of high island and atoll.

These are all modes of remembrance. Some form structures, either material (land boundaries, walls, canoes, a *nahs*) or conceptual (clans, genealogies, the title system). But beyond that, we can say that collective memory is "structured" and embodied, sedimented and encoded and inscribed—all different forms of being lived in the everyday and ceremonial social process. As Shils (1981:34) writes, we "live in the present of things from the past." History is built into the structure in the sense that what we have, do, and experience is in large part inherited. And also, "history" (perceived history, *ethno*history) is built into the present as well: nothing that is recognized comes without an ideological spin.

Paul Connerton reminds us of Marcel Proust's demonstration of the profundity and complexity of recollection, how one thing triggers another in personal memory. Something like that happens in a community, so that where the past is a significant component of the community's modern existence, consciousness of it is reproduced through a lifelong enculturation. Children are raised surrounded by signs of the past. They participate in a habitus that shapes everyday life in certain forms that will—because they are experienced concretely in material objects and routine, and because of the sense of attachment that children form to how things are—become the dowry, the cultural capital, the inheritance of the next generation. Richard Fox (1985:138–39) speaks of each generation as "apprentices" who "labor to constitute society" and "work to create cultural meanings" from what they inherit.

European examples, such as Behar 1986 and Zonabend 1984, have been especially prominent in exploring the depth of history embedded in ordinary life (the new social historians are important here, and Foucault [1972, 1978] is essential). We have many examples of specific encodings of the past in ritual, landscape, and ruins, as well as in verbal art. But as in those European villages, on Sapwuahfik (and elsewhere) it is best to widen our gaze to see historical potential in many things and acts of daily and ceremonial life. Our surroundings, imbued with memory, are phosphorescent: when the right conditions are present, the past becomes visible.

For members of a society as well as for historians and anthropologists, then, history is a form of discourse about culture—as well as, more directly, about certain elements of culture (it may be about ethnicity in one place or context, religion or politics or gender in another). Its role is not unselfconscious: to the contrary, talk about the past is a heightened form of talk about ourselves, of negotiation about community, identity, politics, power, and morality. Discourse about the past is made convincing and persuasive by appeal to visible signs in the local world: these gardens our ancestors cultivated, these values our forebears died for at this site, these children our grandparents buried beneath these gravestones.

For analytical purposes, however, such rhetorical appeal to the reality of the structures inherited from the past needs to be untangled from the social, economic, political, and material structures themselves. Persistence in form over time is a separate issue, for social scientists, from discourse about persistence in form over time—for example, about whether a custom or artifact is "traditional." Simple as this may seem, it is very hard to do in any particular case. But it is an important key to the difference between history and anthropology, as well as a clue to why the two are inseparable. Just as kinship studies need to—and hardly can manage to—separate genetics from kinship (Schneider 1984), so we must study to separate history from discourse about history, and collective social processes from concepts of ethnicity.

POWER AND THE PAST

Arguing that the past is present in material culture, locale, sentiment, personal relations, and codified knowledge, as well as in oral tradition, leads us next to ask how this body of knowledge and oratory about the past becomes instrumental for individuals as they make decisions about the course of their lives and their community.

On Sapwuahfik there is a recognition of historical expertise
that identifies people knowledgeable about the past. What they
know, or don't know, are historical facts: names, places, narrative details, songs. Local experts work toward a fuller understanding of "what happened" in the historians' sense: identifying characters in oral traditions, ships that came to Sapwuahfik,
the sequence of events preceding and following the massacre.
What everyone shares is the general outline of events and a
broad grasp of the significance of these to the present. Everyone,
expert or not, has a stake in the wider meaning of the past,
which sets the context for contemporary action: current social
behaviors are understood to be a result of past events. This does
not sanctify them (as it might in some epistemologies) but explains them. Yet "explains" is too passive a word. In addition to
providing a story that tells how things came to be, Sapwuahfik
historical representation also maintains the viability of a set of
symbols that are (can be, and in fact must be) used in the expression of community identity. To live one's life one must speak a
language, engage in exchanges such as feasts, and deal with political authority. On Sapwuahfik, as described in Chapters 5 to 7,
choices about such everyday acts are simultaneously claims
about cultural affiliation.

The argument that historiography is politically motivated is
anticipated in the islands: everyone uses history, consciously
and deliberately. In order to claim rights to land, knowledge, respect, or a title, one must know history (genealogies and the secret and important history of *poadoapoad*), and one must be
willing to use one's knowledge as a weapon. The "using" begins
in the immediate present, in the form of gossip, as different versions of an event are swiftly generated to suit the interpretations
of current factions; it includes ancient history as well.

The change to the name *Sapwuahfik* is a good example. The
constitutional committees consisted of a wide range of men on
the atoll, but that did not neutralize competing political interests. I never heard the name *Sapwuahfik* in 1979–80, and the
Sapwuahfik people I asked when I visited Pohnpei at the end of

1989 agreed that they had not heard it before the constitution was written. What does *Sapwuahfik* mean? I guessed that *sahpw* means land, as it does in Pohnpeian, but no one I spoke with knew the rest. On the other hand, perhaps they were not telling. Knowledge of the meaning of ancient words would, on Pohnpei, be secret-sacred knowledge, and I wouldn't be surprised if this was felt to be a powerful bit of information. During my brief visit at the end of 1989, *mehn Sapwuahfik* on Pohnpei used *Ngatik* and *Sapwuahfik* interchangeably and told me that no one had trouble with the change. One of the minority faction members (as I read it) discounted the significance of the name, saying it was "made up," merely a phonetic variant of *sahpw tik* (small land). But then, he also said that he and others thought such secret information shouldn't be made public—suggesting that knowledge of ancient Sapwuahfik has power in the same sense as Pohnpei's *poadoapoad*. This seems to me quite reasonable, and as ethnicization proceeds, we might expect that fragments of knowledge and speculation about ancient Sapwuahfik will become more valued and more attended to—and, at the same time, more secret.

The play of politics around the name change indicates the increasing salience of self-conscious tradition in constructing a political identity in a regional context, encouraged by the rewards of money and political power that accrue to men who succeed in the state political arena. Historical knowledge connects a man to his land, to his relatives, to his claim to be *mehn Sapwuahfik* (which might be called into question at any time, especially considering the new constitution), even, for some, to a title. All these connections imply an understanding that to be Sapwuahfik is something that must be argued and manifested in choices of emblematic public action.

We are not here talking about a claim of autochthony. No one claims to be indigenously Sapwuahfik. To claim to be *mehn Sapwuahfik* at all, then, is to know the story, at least in its outline, of the massacre, the Christian transformation, and the modern entailments of these, egalitarianism and faith. Therefore one's private knowledge is embedded in a broader context of collective knowledge, a general story of the past (and so, of the present) within which one's own claims are to be understood.[6]

HISTORY AS IDEOLOGY

Numerous cases in the ethnohistorical and ethnographic literature have described the uses of history to validate contemporary ethnicity. I do not, therefore, simply argue that Sapwuahfik people apply history to matters of identity. I have been more interested in the question of how historical representations are plausible in the role of supporting or guiding social action. There is nothing unique or acultural about historical representation. Accounts of the past (including my account of Sapwuahfik's past in this book) are subject to the same social processes and cultural phrasings as every other aspect of human life. Certain characteristics of historical representations, however, make them particularly effective as bearers of value and guides to action. In a masterly study of Yaqui history and identity, Edward H. Spicer develops the concept of "enduring peoples" whose sense of community persists despite incorporation into nation-states. In generalizing about the persistence of "a sense of common identity," Spicer writes,

> We find in every case of an enduring people common understandings concerning the meaning of a set of symbols. It is awareness of, or common understanding concerning, these meanings on which a sense of common identity depends. The kind of symbols involved are those which have associations with the unique experience of a people through their history. (1980:347)

On Sapwuahfik, historical representations articulate powerfully with concepts of local identity such that past events are conceived of as creating contemporary categories of cultural identity. An evolutionary vision of the past and the comparative-contrastive view of contemporary neighbors (including Americans) constitute a set of conceptual tools or images that recur in Sapwuahfik thought. My presentation has identified sets of symbols that I grouped together in discussions of egalitarianism and religious belief; these comprise a cultural order that explains who *mehn Sapwuahfik* are, how they act, and how they came to be as they are. History and identity are "isomorphic" in terms of certain key concepts; "enlightenment" is a sort of summarizing symbol (Ortner 1973) for my analysis of these.

This does not explain what gives history its power to validate identity (rather than vice-versa). Why is history seen as the privileged domain, against which choices of action (here, in the realm of identity) are evaluated? Let me suggest that the flow of control from history to actions that affirm identity results from a difference in the level of generalization in the two domains.

Sapwuahfik identity is self-consciously asserted by informants, explicitly formulated, and acted out in choices of personal and community behavior. When a Sapwuahfik person makes a decision about how to act toward a person of high title, or what sort of a feast to give, or how to deal with an illness that might have been caused by sorcery, he or she acts in terms of a particular understanding of what it means to be *mehn Sapwuahfik* (particularly, recalling Chapter 5, in contrast with what it means to be *mehn Pohnpei*). The cultural concepts underlying Sapwuahfik identity are accessible to members of the culture, are constantly evaluated against the background of daily life, and can readily be verbalized as descriptions of custom or regularities of behavior. These propositions are specific to a certain range of behavior, that which involves relationships between cultural communities.

The propositions implicit in the Sapwuahfik vision of history, in contrast, are neither specific nor readily accessible to the social actor. The summary of local historiography presented in this book is an abstraction based on my analysis of field data, especially oral traditions and records of informal conversations about the atoll's past. It does not exist in the given form as an intellectual construct on the part of any Sapwuahfik individual. For Sapwuahfik people, this vision of history is relatively implicit and unselfconscious.

Because the two domains are related through a core of shared concepts but exist at different levels of specificity, cultural ideas about the meaning of history can act effectively to shape propositions about identity. Historical discourse can be described as an objectified representation of the past. Although such representation changes over time, it often appears synchronically as factual truth. Because a local vision of the past is—or rather, appears to be—static, immutable, and true, it stands above and beyond the patently transitory, expedient, and ambiguous exigencies of everyday activity—even while individuals manage and alter it in the course of that activity. Where historical knowledge is culturally valued, individuals draw conclusions from the realm of historical discourse (the "lessons of the past") that they see to be metaphorically applicable to related domains of contemporary life. Sapwuahfik is one of many cultures in which historical concepts play a role in validating or explicating some aspect of contemporary life. Thus for *mehn Sapwuahfik*, problematic questions of community identity are resolved by recourse to well-established historical truths. The past judges the present by evaluating the acts of individuals as appropriate or inappropriate to *mehn Sapwuahfik*. History and biography are intertwined; individual actions and sociopolitics form a dialectic with history.

What is striking about the process is that it appears natural and obvious to the social actor. The application of historical referents to contemporary situations does not seem to call for explication. There is a sort of transparency of historical validation: the domain of history is taken to be a source of truth, authenticity, and validity, and the dependent domain (identity) is assumed to benefit from reference to it. The difference in levels of authority of cultural concepts suggests how internal relations among meanings and values, expressed in symbols, generate choices of action. In recognizing culture as constantly created by purposeful social actors, we must also recognize the configuration of the conceptual world within which they choose their actions. Culture is an ordered set of elements—not static, not neatly coherent, not immune to the contingencies of material relations—but nonetheless possessing characteristics that require us to investigate its form, as well as its content.

Sapwuahfik was built, after 1837, through the material and social action, the physical and symbolic work of indigenous survivors and immigrants. They had conflicting interests, formed by their cultural presuppositions and personal desires. Woman, man, father, sister, farmer, fisherman, weaver, fighter, beachcomber, trader, indigenous survivor, *mehn Pohnpei*, Gilbertese, Irishman, Englishman, African American—as they built a new society in the landscape of the old, they negotiated their conflicting interests, varying presuppositions, and individual motives. Each person, with some sharing among those of similar background, used systems of meaning and bodies of knowledge at his or her command; all were acting in a physical environment built by the preexisting indigenous Sapwuahfik systems of meaning and body of knowledge. The outcome depended very much on what was at hand both materially and conceptually. But it also depended on the context of constant interaction with regional and global forces. We know this to be true for all societies—none can be considered in isolation. But how obvious it is for Sapwuahfik: immediately after 1837 there was immigration from Pohnpei and elsewhere, economic domination by European and American traders, the requirements of production for market, drift voyages, and ships' visits that required the use of English and exposed local developments to the editorial eye of men such as Blake and the title-bestowing captain.

At first, "boundary" was not an issue. Boundaries are complex social mechanisms; it took time to build the patterns of interaction that produced them. For decades a good number of people shifted on and off the atoll—to and from Pohnpei, and farther afield as well. There was internal differentiation, "American town" and enough boundary sensibility to destroy arriving Mortlockese. But there was no "Ngatikese" community until two creative processes intersected: the internal (intermarriage, a stabilized population core, and increased community of interest) converged with the external (the treatment of people living on the island at any one time as a community, for example, by missionaries). As late as 1910 most of the people "perceive[d] themselves as Ponapeans" (Eilers 1934). But processes were already in motion that would increasingly bind them to symbols and social interactions that would become the raw material of a distinctive identity and define them in the colonial context as a distinct population. So internal and external contingencies came together to form a new identity, crystallized in symbolic forms whose content combined the local, the regional, and (in places) the global—what both "we" and "they" focused on as markers. Having a new identity, they began to tell themselves and others about it, in a way that made sense of current situations—a discourse that inevitably entails history. The fast-growing structure of political and economic interaction between outer islands and Pohnpei Island, and of all these populations within colonial orders, and now the Federated States of Micronesia, constantly increases attention to boundary, probably in the direction of increasing ethnicization.

For Sapwuahfik, identity is debated in public evaluations of individual actions, although interpretations of history are rarely explicitly debated as such. Nonetheless, both are subject to change through individual choices of action. In Sapwuahfik, the symbolic significance of the American affiliation, the identification of Hart as an American, and American political influence are all probably (but not, in the case of the first two, provably) recent, related to the postwar dominance of the United States in the region. Political innovations, such as the establishment of new Sapwuahfik associations on Pohnpei, and larger-scale alterations as the new nation develops will certainly produce changes in both the social action and the symbolic representation of identity. These, in turn, are likely at some point to change the Sapwuahfik vision of history.

Notes

Introduction

1. The new Sapwuahfik Constitution was written in 1985; 1986 marked the implementation of the compact under which the Federated States of Micronesia became a sovereign state in "free association" with the United States. I should add that documentary sources can neither confirm nor deny *Sapwuahfik* as the atoll's aboriginal name (see Conclusion).

2. See Bascom 1965; Hughes 1970, 1982; Petersen 1977, 1979, 1982a; and Riesenberg 1968 for descriptions of Pohnpei sociopolitical organization.

3. Ngatik Islet consists of twenty-four named areas not bounded by landownership or obvious geographical markers but nonetheless used in oral traditions and referred to when giving directions or identifying locales. These may have been aboriginal names of small political units or otherwise significant places. Although people identify their household locations by using these traditional place-names, the old locales are not

part of the structure of modern political or social organization. The geographic component of modern sociopolitics is the *kousapw,* commonly used to mean "section" or "neighborhood," though the term is also applied to the smaller, traditional named areas. Although I translate *kousapw* as "section," here as on Pohnpei, there is some difference between Pohnpei and Sapwuahfik *kousapw;* compare Riesenberg 1968; Petersen 1977, 1982a.

4. Perhaps most surprising to a visiting American, sections—despite their tiny size and population—are characterized by stereotypical traits, and some have localized legends explaining the origin of these. Identifying character with small-scale locale occurs elsewhere in the Pacific, for example on Rotuma (Howard and Howard 1977), and A. Cohen (1982:41–45) gives a strikingly similar European case. On Sapwuahfik it suggests that sections draw on sentiment affiliated with older named locales. For example, here is one person's explanation of the meaning of the phrase *mwekid en mehn Ewenedi,* "movement or activity of an Ewenedi person," a comment on tardiness:

> If you were to check at feasts, if one group brings their food contribution late people will say, *mwekid en mehn Ewenedi.* I don't know why they call the people of Ewenedi slow-moving, but it's apparently true. All the time, it's Ewenedi people who are always late. It's also how they move in terms of fishing and so on. If you were to say, "We're leaving before dawn"—it is said that long ago the Ewenedi people would wait until day had broken, and then go. The other *kousapw* would have gone while it was dark, they would have left before daybreak. That's why, if something is done late or slow, if the person is not of Ewenedi, people say, "Ah, *mwekid en mehn Ewenedi.*" But if you are of Ewenedi, they'll say, "That's how the movement of that *kousapw* is."

5. Spelling of place-names and Pohnpeian words follows Rehg and Sohl's *Ponapean-English Dictionary* (1979), with the exception of the names of polities that have officially changed since 1979 (including "Pohnpei").

6. Of course this is not necessarily true of other "progressive" theories of history, but it requires careful effort to sort indigenous from introduced philosophies of history. Possibly this can be explored by way of a sensitive analysis of oral traditions and myth; however, on Sapw-

uahfik the devastation of the massacre and the transformation of Christian conversion make it unlikely that any sense of the aboriginal historiography can be recovered. Without claiming to identify the source of Sapwuahfik historiography, then, we can nonetheless discern its outline.

7. My discussion of cultural ethnicity and identity here and throughout the book, particularly as it relates to the Pacific Islands, owes much to the Association for Social Anthropology in Oceania symposium "Cultural Identity in Oceania," and to its participants. I especially acknowledge the value of collaborating with Jocelyn Linnekin in writing the Introduction to the volume produced from that symposium (Linnekin and Poyer 1990a, 1990b); working with her helped clarify the ideas here. She also indicated the importance of Boas's insistent argument in its cultural context. Ethnicity studies today are in a stage of ferment similar to that of the 1960s, though characterized by less-heated exchanges. Rather, scholars are casting about for new ways to understand a phenomenon that is as undefinable as it is persistent (see reviews of ethnicity research by R. Cohen 1978; Muga 1984; Reminick 1983; and Yinger 1985). Efforts such as Hobsbawm 1983 and Bentley 1987 indicate how much this perennial field of study can benefit from adventuresome approaches. Recent general critiques of ethnicity as an analytic rather than a folk category include Chapman et al. 1989; Comaroff and Comaroff 1992; Handler 1988; and Linnekin and Poyer 1990a.

8. Useful examples of studies of the intersection of history and identity in this sense include Blu 1980; Braroe 1975; Fox 1985; Friedman 1992; Peel 1989; Tonkinson 1990; Warren 1978; and White 1991.

9. Case studies on the cultural bases of group identity include Dominguez 1986; Watanabe 1990; and articles in Carroll 1975; Lieber 1977b; Linnekin and Poyer 1990b; Tonkin, McDonald, and Chapman 1989; and White and Kirkpatrick 1985.

CHAPTER ONE: *Preludes and Contexts*

1. European activity in the Pacific has been well explored by historians of the region; recent general histories covering the relevant era include Campbell 1989; Howe 1984; Oliver 1989; and Spate 1983, 1988. Some of these more recent histories include discussion of indigenous,

as well as European, society and activity. Bach 1968 describes the efforts of the British Navy to control Europeans and Americans in the Pacific. Hezel 1983 is a general history of Micronesia to 1885.

2. Riesenberg 1968 summarizes early European voyagers near Pohnpei. Hezel 1979 summarizes information about these European sightings of Ngatik: Tompson in the *Nuestra Seniora de la Consolacion* (in 1773), *Brittania* (1793), *Sugar Cane* (1793), Page in the *Ann & Hope* (1798), Lafita's vessel (1802), *Patterson* (1803), *Henry Porcher* (1826), Lütke's *Senyavin* (1828), *Peru* (1832), and *Pallas* (1835). On various names for the atoll, Hezel 1979 and Bryan 1971. Dr. Saul Riesenberg generously shared information he gathered from several ship's logs and other sources. On Tompson and the *Sugar Cane*, see also Sharp 1960; on the *Brittania*, Riesenberg 1974.

3. On the 1835 *Pallas* visit, Henry Archer's *Journal*, seen in microfilm copy of the Pacific Manuscript Bureau collection at the Hamilton Library, University of Hawaii, Honolulu; on the report of wreckage at Ngatik, L. H. Gulick's letter in the *Friend*, 17 December 1852, reprinted in Ward 1967, vol. 6:167–68; also Gulick 1932:90; Blake 1924 [1839]. On the *Waverly* and associated incidents, see Ward 1967, vol. 3:558–59; Hezel 1983:113–14; Krämer and Nevermann 1938. Hezel 1979 summarizes information on these events.

4. David Hanlon's 1988 work is the most complete history of Pohnpei; Hanlon 1984, Hezel 1983, O'Brien 1971, and Riesenberg 1968 also discuss this era in the Eastern Caroline Islands, and Cheyne 1977 [1855] provides an eyewitness view of traders' activities. Zelenietz and Kravitz (1974) review Pohnpei's "beachcomber" population in detail. See Chapter 3 for other sources for nineteenth-century Islander-European relations in the Pohnpei area.

5. Thanks to Robert Borofsky for suggesting this perspective on Hart's actions.

6. An anonymous reader of this MS reminded me of the less sentimental possibility that this story could be a postmassacre introduction, presumably by Pohnpeians familiar with Isokelekel narratives.

7. Damas 1979, 1981 and Schneider 1980 debate unilineality in the social organization of the Eastern Carolines before European contact. Weckler concluded that "Mokil has been, even anciently, a patrilineal

stronghold completely surrounded by matrilineally organized societies" (1949:66–67). See also Chapter 6.

8. The notion that Micronesian paramount chiefs controlled all land, as Fischer (1958) describes Pohnpeian characterizations of pre-German conditions on Pohnpei, is contested by suggestions that they actually may have had little direct local control (Petersen 1977). Sapwuahfik informants presented the ancient nahnmwarki as the controllers of land. Note also that my broad presentation of "premassacre" Sapwuahfik fails to indicate adequately the atoll's history before European contact. Sapwuahfik oral traditions, though more scarce and harder to work with than in many other areas, include stories of dynasties, internal conflicts, external contacts, and transformative events preceding European arrival in the area—including, for example, suggestions that Sapwuahfik was at times governed by two nahnmwarki.

9. Isoah's story and accounts of Sirinpahn's reign are summarized from tape-recorded accounts, with quotations indicated. The version describing Sirinpahn as an enemy, rather than a son, of the previous Nahnmwarki was told to me in English in 1990 but not tape recorded. The tale of how Sirinpahn became Nahnmwarki well illustrates the diversity of accounts that the outsider, and to a lesser extent even the insider, can collect. Traditional history has no "official" version, and the many variations of a well-known story serve important political and personal purposes (see Falgout 1984a and Petersen 1982a for detailed discussions of the uses of oral history on Pohnpei).

A variant on the account of Isoah's deposition given here is that Isoah's wife knew of the people's agreement to kill him and went home and told the Nahnmwarki and his son Sirinpahn about it. Sirinpahn was very angry. After the gathering met the next day, he stood up and (though he was not nahnmwarki) gave a speech: "You all know this!: That today, Father is finished with being nahnmwarki. It is I who will be nahnmwarki." Sirinpahn refused to let them kill his father. This account is interesting for its implicit acceptance of patrilineal title inheritance.

10. Jan Vansina (1961, 1985) remains a key source for thinking about and investigating oral history. On issues of history, ethnohistory, and oral history in the Pacific, see Biersack 1991; Dening 1966, 1980, 1988, 1989; Hanlon 1988:xiii–xxii; Mercer 1979; Mitchell 1970; Spear 1981; and Thomas 1990.

11. These interviews were translated into English by Mr. Sinio Nahior and myself. Mr. Nahior also assisted by investigating questions I had after I left Sapwuahfik.

CHAPTER TWO: *The Massacre and Its Meaning*

1. Information and quotations in this chapter about the events of 1836 and 1837 are from Blake 1924 [1839] unless otherwise noted. This citation includes not only Blake's report but also sworn testimonies, including those taken in Macao, and administrative letters included in two packets of documents on Hart's activities sent to the governor of New South Wales in 1839 and 1840. Blake's original report is entitled "Report from the Officer commanding H.M.S. Larne, on the Occasion of her Visit to the Bonin and Caroline Islands, in regard to Acts of Violence Committed on the Natives by British Subjects and Particularly by the Master and Crew of the Cutter Lambton of Sydney." References to these documents in this and the next chapter are not cited separately. The events of the massacre are summarized in Dunbabin 1926 and Hezel 1983:120–21, and with careful detail in Riesenberg 1966. See also Poyer 1983, 1985.

2. Blake collected testimony about the *Falcon* affair; the source again is documents in Blake 1924 [1839]. The events are summarized in Fischer, Riesenberg, and Whiting 1977:105, 138–39; Hanlon 1988:49–58 examines them with detailed attention to Pohnpei sociopolitical history. A Pohnpei song about the tragedy is in Bernart 1977. In my summary, quotations not otherwise attributed are from Blake.

3. Although I have found no evidence that Hart was ever punished or brought to trial for the *Falcon* and Ngatik crimes, Sapwuahfik informants asserted, and even described, his punishment by a government or naval official. One lengthy story of Hart's capture and brutal punishment is so rich in detail that I think the incident must actually have occurred—perhaps to Captain Lass (whose activities are described in Chapter 3; in this narrative, the *Wailua* or *Waialua* is named as "Hart's" ship). I could not determine whether the notion of Hart's punishment was a local invention or Islanders were at some time falsely assured by foreigners that justice had been done.

4. It is more difficult to discern the categorical significance of immigrant islanders, those who came to Sapwuahfik after the massacre from the Gilbert Islands and Mortlock Islands and who mediated (we might say) between American/European and aboriginal. In fact, in oral traditions of the postmassacre period described in the next chapter, these immigrants, always identified by island of origin, do act as links or take intermediate positions between the separate settlements of Pohnpeians-Sapwuahfik people and Europeans-Americans. David, a Gilbertese man, is made nahnken, the title that mediates between the man of highest title (nahnmwarki) and the people.

CHAPTER THREE: *Reconstructing Society*

1. To reduce the burden of citations in this chapter, only quotations are attributed their sources in the text. Written sources are given in notes for each section of the chapter.

2. MacVie appears erroneously as the major perpetrator of the massacre in Eilers 1934. Thanks to Jane Underwood for drawing my attention to this.

3. Sources for information about the earliest postmassacre years on Ngatik: on Gorman's initial resettlement, Blake 1924 [1839] (the comment on foreign men "with their Girls" is from William Marshall's testimony); on Westerners in the region, his mid-1840s visits to Ngatik, and unfulfilled plans for bêche-de-mer establishments on Pohnpei and Ngatik, Cheyne 1852, 1977 [1855]; on the *Frances Charlotte*'s 1839 visit, an 1840 letter to the *Polynesian* reprinted in Ward 1967, vol. 5:145; on Godby's 1841 visit on the *Clarinda*, Godby 1845; "sole proprietors" is from the *Chandler Price*'s 1846 visit reported in the *Boston Daily Advertiser*, 26 June 1847, in Ward 1967:147–48. Assorted notes on early Euro-Americans, including reference to Rodwright, are in "Notes on Raven's Island," an anonymous and undated handwritten MS at the Hawaiian Mission Children's Society in Honolulu. On the 1844 *William & Henry* visit, Hezel 1979:47; on the 1844 visit of HMS *Vestal*, *Nautical Magazine* 1845:337–38; on the *Genii*, Hezel 1979:55, and in Ward 1967, vol. 4:362, 616, the *Friend* 17 (1860):82–84; "John M'vea" reported on Ngatik some years earlier, letter in *Nautical Magazine* 1852:334; on a plan, later abandoned, to remove a troublemaker from

Mokil to Ngatik, an 1852 letter from J. T. Gulick in Gulick 1932; on the wreck of the *Sarah Mooers*, the *Friend* 17 (1860):82–83, and in Ward 1967, vol. 5:149–51. On the deaths of Williams, Steward, and MacVie, Cheyne 1977 [1855]:287; on George May's death, Cheyne 1977 [1855]:208 n. Dr. Saul Riesenberg generously provided me with notes from his research into the visits of the *Gideon Howland* (at Ngatik in 1841) and *Trident* (in 1842), both after hogs at Ngatik, and 1848 stops by the *Fortune*, *Adderline*, *Minerva*, and *Elizabeth*.

4. Information about trade with Ngatik in the 1840s to 1870s comes from ships' logs. Hezel 1979 and Ward 1967 are valuable summaries of information from logs and other maritime sources of this period. Hezel 1979 summarizes information for these visitors to Ngatik: the *Frances Charlotte* (at Ngatik in 1839), *Clarinda* (1841), *Gideon Howland* (1841), *London Packet* (1841), *Wilmington and Liverpool Packet* (1842), *William & Henry* (1844), Cheyne's *Naiad* (1844), HMS *Vestal* (1844), Pease's *Chandler Price* (1846), *Fortune* (1848), *Adeline* (1848), *Minerva* (1848), *Elizabeth* (1848), *Benjamin Tucker* (1850), *Massachusetts* (1850), *Menkar* (1850), *Maria Theresa* (1850), *Harvest* (1851), *George & Mary* (1851), *William Hamilton* (1852), *St. George* (1852), *Genii* (1853), *Sarah Mooers* (1853) and its 1854 rescuers *Delta*, *Thomas*, and *Sea King*, *Martha* (1855), *Norman* (1856), and *Mohawk* (1861).
Dr. Saul Riesenberg shared his research into the logs of these visitors to Ngatik in a personal communication (1979): *Gideon Howland* (1841), *Trident* (1842), *Elizabeth* (1848), *Fortune* (1848), *Benjamin Tucker* (1850), *Massachusetts* (1850), *Menkar* (1850), *Maria Theresa* (1850), *Harvest* (1851), *George & Mary* (1851), *Martha* (1855), *Hamlet* (1856), and *Norman* (1856). Ships' logs for the *William & Eliza, Massachusetts, Harvest, Mohawk,* and *Martha* were seen in microfilm of the Pacific Manuscript Bureau at the Hamilton Library, University of Hawaii.
Detailed descriptions of the Pohnpei area in this period, including discussion of the trading economy and relations between Islanders and Westerners, are Hanlon 1984, 1988; Hezel 1978, 1983. Marshall and Marshall 1976 detail the role of liquor in beachcomber and Islander life, and the missionary response to it, in nineteenth-century eastern Micronesia.

5. Dr. Saul Riesenberg kindly supplied me with the information that the log of the whaler *Peruvian* (of Nantucket, Captain Edward B. Hussey), in at Pohnpei in 1855, refers to a small schooner at Mudok Harbor that was built at Ngatik.

6. Although the narrator used the modern title Nahnmwarki, Aisikaya was probably invested as Isipahu, the title that appears next to his name on the 1890 list of founding members of the Ngatik Protestant church. Isipahu was the term used by Westerners as the paramount title for Madolenihmw; Riesenberg 1968:44 gives it as a term of address for the Nahnmwarki of Madolenihmw and, sometimes, of Uh. It was in use on Ngatik as late as 1910 (Eilers 1934). An anonymous reviewer drew my attention to the similarity between the story of the boys receiving titles and the widespread Pacific myth motif of the younger brother's success (Kirtley 1971).

7. The *Wailua* is mentioned in notes in the *Friend*, October and November 1862. My thanks to Agnes C. Conrad, State Archivist, Hawaii, for archival information about the *Wailua*. Spelled *Waialua*, the ship is mentioned in a note in the *Friend*, 2 September 1861, as at Tarawa; at Pohnpei, 2 April 1862, in Hezel 1979:70, from the log of the *Thomas Dickason*.

8. The letter from Frazer is summarized in the *Missionary Herald* 52, no. 8 (1855):227 and mentioned in the American Board of Commissioners for Foreign Missions' (hereafter cited as ABCFM) "Annual Report of Ascension Island" for 1855, seen on microfilm at the Hamilton Library, University of Hawaii, Honolulu. I have not located the original.

9. In a 1900 report, the German vice-governor at Pohnpei records an early account of the Mortlock conflict. Perhaps confusing immigrant men with aboriginal *mehn Sapwuahfik,* the report states that the men who survived the initial massacre "were killed shortly after this event by natives of the Mortlock Islands. An old man named Isak could still remember this fight with the Mortlock natives, in which his father was killed. Since he himself was only a child, he was made captive and was brought to the Mortlock Islands, where he spent the rest of his childhood" (Hahl 1900). Isak appears in genealogies as the son of a Gilbertese woman and the Englishman "Roneid." I recorded an oral account of Roneid's death at the hands of Ewo, the Mortlock Islander hero.

10. The *Blanche*'s 1872 visit is in Brazier 1872 and Simpson 1873:250. For Doane's description, see Doane 1874 and his letter in the *Friend* 23, no. 6 (1874):42. A. A. Sturges also visited Ngatik on this trip and described it in a letter to the Cousins Society in Honolulu (seen at the Hawaiian Mission Children's Society, Honolulu). The 1873 visit of

the *Avola* reports a white man named Hilston and about one hundred Islanders (Riesenberg, pers. comm. 1979).

11. Nahnmwarki Aisikaya governed the islets of Paina and Pikenkarakar for a group called Kehsar; Wasai headed a group named Kedra for Wataluhk, Pikenkeleng, Sirop, and Pikape; and Dauk governed Wad Islet for a group named Kedloh or Keduk.

12. From interviews, scrutiny of documents, genealogies, and land-tenure histories, I suggest this "maximum" listing of the first postmassacre landowners for Ngatik Islet. Some informants say there were fewer original shares but differ in their listings. I have used genealogical information collected in 1979–80 to construct my best guess as to the early resettlement generations:

Aisikaya: an aboriginal survivor, became Nahnmwarki; married Nadoh, the daughter of Sowel (a Pohnpei man) and a Gilbertese woman, Kaweid (Aisikaya's wife is given as "Askina" in the 1890 list of the first church members; I heard the name in genealogies as Aisikaya's mother, but perhaps it is an alternative name for Nadoh, or the name of a previous wife). Aisikaya had no biological children but adopted several, including David, son of a Gilbertese woman (called "Keikei" in genealogies), who became Ngatik's first Nahnken.

Ownahngi: an early immigrant from Pohnpei, perhaps from Madolenihmw; married an aboriginal woman (name unknown) and had three or four children who grew to adulthood.

Pakieh: an aboriginal survivor, given the title of Dauk. He married Limwo, a daughter of Ownahngi, and had four children.

William Brown: variously referred to as "Portuguese" and "Negro"; I think he was an African American. He held the Pohnpei title Isohkeling and was a participant in the massacre and an early immigrant to Ngatik. He married an aboriginal woman, Lipan, and had (or perhaps adopted) a daughter, Ansonia.

"Mister Else": an American from New Jersey, nicknamed "Kehp" ("Carp") for his carpentry skills. He married Meram, whom he brought from Pohnpei along with her sister Emilia/Lisohp (who married Noah's son) and their mother. Ten of their children grew to maturity.

Sowel: a Pohnpei man; I think he arrived with Lass. He was Aisikaya's father-in-law. Sowel married a Gilbertese immigrant (one descendent calls her *mehn Tarawa*), Kawed, and had five children.

"Kaht" (a nickname?): a Pohnpei man who probably also came with Lass; he married Likur, Noah's sister, a woman who was a baby or girl at the time of the massacre (she lived to early Japanese times). Seven of their children grew to adulthood.

Noah: an aboriginal survivor, Noah was Kaht's brother-in-law; he married a Gilbertese immigrant (Lidolehleh) and had two or three children.

Roneid: perhaps John Rodwright, identified as English in oral tradition. He married Nadohd, a Gilbertese woman, and had two children who became adults.

Frazer ("Pirasi" in oral accounts): or perhaps his son Joseph, whose mother was an aboriginal woman.

CHAPTER FOUR: *Conversion and the Colonial Era*

1. Missionary sources begin with the first visit by members of the American Board of Commissioners for Foreign Missions on Pohnpei to Ngatik in January 1874. In December of that year, the mission ship *Morning Star III* made its first visit to Ngatik. Documentary sources for the history of Protestant missions in the Eastern Caroline Islands include papers of the Micronesian Mission–Hawaiian Evangelical Association (Caroline Islands), *Morning Star* documents, missionary letters, and other mission documents at the Hawaiian Mission Children's Society (HMCS), Honolulu; ABCFM microfilm files, letters, and reports, #434 at the Hamilton Library, University of Hawaii, Honolulu; issues of the *Friend*, the *Missionary Herald*, and *Life and Light for Woman*; ABCFM pamphlet "Micronesian Mission, a Condensed Sketch" (Boston, 1907) seen at the HMCS Library; Bliss 1906; Crawford and Crawford 1967; and Gulick 1932. On the Liebenzell Mission and twentieth-century Christian mission activities in the Caroline Islands, Kohl 1971. Studies of mission work on Pohnpei, the politics of conversion, and changes introduced by Christian influence include Coale 1951; Hanlon 1984, 1988; Hezel 1983; and O'Brien 1971; compare Nason 1978 for the Mortlock Islands. Articles in Barker 1990 and Boutelier, Hughes, and Tiffany 1978 provide comparative information from Oceania.

2. Dr. Saul Riesenberg provided me with information on the death of "Ocean Island Jack" on Ngatik about 1882, and on the visits of the *Blanche* (1872), *Avola* (1873), *Palmetto* (1881), and *Bothwell Castle* (1884). On visits of the *Fire Queen* (1872), *Avola* (1873), *Arnolda* (1875), *Helen Mar* (1880), and the wreck of the *Bothwell Castle* (1884), Hezel

1979. The logs of the *Helen Mar* (1880) and *Palmetto* (1881) were seen in the microfilm collection of the Pacific Manuscripts Bureau at the Hamilton Library, University of Hawaii, Honolulu. Summaries of Pohnpei-area colonial history are in Hezel 1983 (covering the period 1521–1885); Hanlon 1984, 1988 (from European contact to 1890); Fischer 1957 (European discovery through postwar U.S. era); Bernart 1977; Fischer, Riesenberg, and Whiting 1977; and U.S. Navy 1944.

3. On Spanish/Catholic–American/Protestant tensions on Pohnpei, Hezel 1970. On Catholic missionaries in the Carolines, see Hernandez 1955; Hezel 1970, 1983; and Wiltgen 1975.

4. Anneliese Eilers, in the report of the 1910 Südsee-Expedition, recounts a legend about an "idol," associating it with the spirit Olpad. At the annual breadfruit harvest, they would take the idol to the sea, anoint and decorate it, then carry it around the island in a canoe. Many pigs were killed at the accompanying celebration; some were eaten, others thrown into the deep water. I am not clear on whether the "idol" of the legend is the same stone figure described in Doane 1874. Eilers describes burial areas for high-ranking persons on Ngatik in 1910, including an identified grave of a Gilbertese couple, and suggests that the place of worship seen by Doane may have been a graveyard (Eilers 1934).

5. See Chapter 3, note 12.

6. On German colonial administration in the Pacific, Hempenstall 1977, 1978. For detail and oral history on German rule on Pohnpei and the Sokehs Rebellion, Ehrlich 1978. Sources for Ngatik in the German era comprise missionary documents (cited above), Eilers 1934, and German colonial publications. Much of the German colonial source material, especially for outer islands, remains unexplored. I thank Heika Rafael for translations.

7. Nahior was Noah's sister's son. If Aisikaya's clan was Dipwinmen toantoal, the clan of Noah and his sister, they may have been related biologically, but this is not clear from genealogies.

8. There are a growing number of sources on Japanese colonial administration in Micronesia, though Japanese sources are still largely unavailable in English. This brief summary relies on Peattie 1984, 1988; Purcell 1967, 1972, 1976; U.S. Navy 1944; and Yanaihara 1940.

9. Francis X. Hezel, S.J., of the Micronesian Seminar, kindly supplied me with copies of translations and notes about early Catholic mission activities on Ngatik. For Fr. Herrera's accounts of his visits, *Cartas de la Provincia de Leon* 3–4 (1923); for results by 1926, an unpublished MS by Bishop de Rego, "Noticias sobre la mision, 1921–1926"; for mention of the pastor's daughter, *El Siglo de las Misiones* 22:11–14 (1935); for 1930s figures, *El Angel de las Carolinas* 49, 65, 75. Unfortunately I am not able to determine the identities of the early Catholics named in Herrera's reports; Islanders at that time often used several names, and the Spanish baptismal names by which Herrera knew them do not appear in genealogies I collected.

10. On World War II on Pohnpei, Denfield 1979, 1981; Falgout 1988, 1989; on Sapwuahfik, Poyer 1989.

11. On the American era in Micronesia and its implications for local economic and political life, Heine 1974; articles in Lutz 1984; McHenry 1975; Nevin 1977; Peoples 1978, 1985. See Richard 1957 on postwar U.S. Navy administration.

CHAPTER FIVE: *Cultural Identity in Context*

1. Portions of this chapter appeared in Poyer 1990, which further discusses Sapwuahfik cultural identity; see also Poyer 1988a on Sapwuahfik-Pohnpei contrasts.

2. *Mehn Sapwuahfik* call this "pidgin English" or "broken English." Sapwuahfik men are known throughout the Eastern Carolines for this type of speech, which they use mostly in work situations, sailing, casual conversation, recreation, and joking. (Although men insist that women do not understand or use it, women occasionally speak pidgin in joking conversation.) On Pohnpei, Sapwuahfik people may teasingly be greeted with the pidgin phrase, "*Whatsmadda you, nan* [fella]?" Kenneth Rehg of the University of Hawaii has investigated this pidgin (Rehg 1979). Trouillot 1988 describes an interestingly similar use of an English pidgin related to local identity in Dominica.

3. American visitors to Sapwuahfik, as to other parts of Micronesia (and indeed, other areas of the world) will also hear many comments about the "stupidity" or inefficiency of local ways compared with the

"good," admired qualities of politically dominant *mehn wai* culture. My field notes contain many such self-deprecatory statements from Sapwuahfik people. Marc Swartz (1961) presents a way to examine such "negative ethnocentrism," which he encountered in Truk.

4. See Barth 1969; Anthony P. Cohen's book *The Symbolic Construction of Community* (1985) elaborates the argument. European examples of the symbolic nature of community boundaries are in Cohen 1982, 1986, including a rather striking similarity between Sapwuahfik and North Yorkshire constructions of identity in Phillips 1986. On the semiotics of cultural oppositions, see Boon 1982, Schwimmer 1972.

5. On how "tradition" develops to serve political and other ends, and examples of the process, see George 1991; Handler 1988; Handler and Linnekin 1984; Herzfeld 1991; Hobsbawm 1983; Jolly 1992; Keesing 1982, 1989; Linnekin 1983, 1990; Shils 1981; Spriggs 1992; Thomas 1989; Wagner 1981; and articles in Hobsbawm and Ranger 1983 and Keesing and Tonkinson 1982.

6. I thank Aram Yengoyan for providing the phrase.

CHAPTER SIX: *The Egalitarian Ethos*

1. I have explored "social equality" on Sapwuahfik in more detail in Poyer 1991, examining social interaction as structural communication of status messages, following Arno 1980, and in Poyer 1993. Woodburn 1982 has discussed egalitarianism as the product of a complex social system, and the concept is reviewed in Flanagan 1989.

2. Taro-garden land is inherited in distinctive ways. A taro plot can exist within or partially within the boundaries of forest or coconut land, but will be owned and inherited separately. The rich, intensively cultivated taro plots are small and nonresidential, and change hands more frequently and casually than other land. For example, some have been given as Christmas gifts or gifts of thanks for help during an illness.

3. Long-term adoptive relationships are not differentiated from biological ties in kin terminology, and adoptive relationships provide additional routes to land, knowledge, cash, and other resources. About half of Sapwuahfik's population has permanent adoptive ties. Of children

younger than eighteen in 1979–80, about one-fourth were described by their parents as adopted. The "ideal" scenario for adoption is permanent adoption of an infant child of a brother or sister, but older children and even adults can be adopted. Even for a young child, ties with biological parents are not broken. The child visits them frequently (or even lives with them intermittently) if they live on Sapwuahfik, brings them food, and may inherit land from them. See Brady 1976 and Carroll 1970 on adoption in the Pacific Islands.

4. I have standardized the spelling of these titles with Riesenberg 1968. (The Rehg and Sohl dictionary [1979] use different spellings.) All but two (B-11, Sedin, and B-13, Lempwei en Isipahu) appear in Riesenberg's listing of Pohnpei titles. The lines match—that is, A-line titles on Sapwuahfik are in the A line of Pohnpei, and the same for B-line titles. The atoll's A line corresponds title for title with Riesenberg's "General" listing of Pohnpei titles, down to #11. The B line of Sapwuahfik corresponds down to #4 with the "General" list and to #6 with one of Riesenberg's Kiti sources (Riesenberg 1968:10–11). The source Riesenberg gives for the "General" list is Luelen, of the district of Kiti. Many of the Pohnpei people who emigrated to Ngatik were Kiti people. The list of Sapwuahfik titles corresponds much less well with Riesenberg's lists for the other districts of Pohnpei. It is interesting that Kiti is regarded by Pohnpei people as being "more conservative and clinging to custom" than other *wehi* (Petersen 1977:37).

5. The term most often used on Sapwuahfik is *keinek,* which on Pohnpei is used to mean more specifically extended family or lineage. The usual Pohnpei terms for exogamous matriclan, *dipw* and *sou,* are also known and used on Sapwuahfik. See Petersen 1977:55–64 for a discussion of descent groups on Pohnpei.

6. Looking at the Eastern Carolines as a region, it is only on Pohnpei that matrilineal clans are active in the process of social life. On Kosrae and on the Micronesian atolls, patrilineal influence in land tenure and title inheritance reduces the importance of matrilineal clans. Glenn Petersen (1977, 1982b) has suggested an explanation of the continued importance of clans on Pohnpei, despite the fact that German, Japanese, and American legal systems have systematically undercut matrilineality in land inheritance. Petersen explains that on Pohnpei matrilineages maintain ties between otherwise isolated communities, because matrikin work together to control titles and manage a complex round of

feasting. Although matrilineages on Pohnpei are not localized, postmarital residence tends to be virilocal, land inheritance patrilineal, and men's role in subsistence agriculture dominant—yet matriliny retains vitality by its involvement in feasting and political activity.

On Sapwuahfik, Mwoakilloa (Mokil), and Pingelap, people do not live in small, potentially isolated communities, and we see a much-diminished role for matrilineages on the atolls. The origin and significance of matrilineal and patrilineal principles on these atolls is a subject of debate (Damas 1979, 1981; Schneider 1980; Weckler 1949). In Chapter 1, I suggested that patrilineal emphasis may have existed on Sapwuahfik aboriginally, but postmassacre conditions and colonial encouragement of patrilineal inheritance might be equally or more responsible for the lesser role of matrilineages in atoll life. To follow Petersen's argument, Sapwuahfik feasts are for the most part organized by households, bilateral kin groups, or the entire community, rather than by matrikin (see also note 9).

7. Weckler 1949 reconstructs the inheritance of the highest titles of Mokil (Mwoakilloa), revealing a complex history. Mokil's importation of Pohnpei titles parallels Sapwuahfik history, as does a period of violent feuding ending with the arrival of missionaries and the transition from sole ownership of land by the nahnmwarki to a division of land among families surviving a typhoon about 1775–80. Mokil has a fairly consistent history of patrilineal inheritance of its highest political titles, and there also have been periods when its "kings" were chosen by the people.

8. The current incumbent is a descendent not of Likur but of Noah (he is Noah's daughter's daughter's son). Noah's children apparently took his Dipwinmen toantoal affiliation, rather than that of his Gilbertese wife. The persistence of Gilbertese clans on Sapwuahfik indicates that this was not the usual case, though according to Morton (1972), nineteenth-century women who immigrated from the Gilbert Islands to Pingelap took local clan affiliations.

9. Fischer (1957:179) suggests that the political systems of Mokil (Mwoakilloa), Pingelap, and Sapwuahfik were shaped in part by Pohnpeian mission teachers and outer islanders who attended mission schools on Pohnpei, who "brought Ponapean ideas about how titles should be bestowed." He characterizes eligibility for titles on Mokil, Pingelap, and Ngatik in the 1950s as father-son inheritance, including a

sentiment that titles are owned by patrilineal extended families (151), with no regular promotion from rank to rank. His information verifies the local characterization of recent title accessions as a "return to the path" of matrilineal clans. However, in a 1974 paper noting changes in the Pohnpei title system, Fischer stated that the son of a deceased Pohnpei titleholder had come to have an equal or better chance of receiving the title as a lineage mate of the dead man. Understanding the relative role of matrilineage membership and patrifiliation in the past and present inheritance of titles on both Pohnpei and the outer islands is complicated as much by recent sociocultural change as by the difficulty of clarifying historical conditions.

10. On several occasions when there was only one Pohnpeian speaker in a group, people shifted to that dialect or addressed questions to the visitor in Pohnpeian. They told me that this was done out of politeness, because the visitor "wouldn't understand" if they spoke Sapwuahfik dialect. (The two are distinctive in phonology, vocabulary, some grammatical variations, and the use of English forms in Sapwuahfik; they are, however, mutually intelligible.) I once listened to a representative of the Historic Preservation Committee, a Pohnpei man, recording old stories told by a Sapwuahfik man—who was narrating them in Pohnpeian for the tape recorder.

CHAPTER SEVEN: *Christian Commitment and Community Identity*

1. I could not confirm the "Pohnleng" reference. Riesenberg (1968:22–23) gives "Pohnauleng" as a Madolenihmw section, but it lies some distance south of Ohwa. John Francis is generally agreed to be a Madolenihmw man, and he attended the mission training school, which was located at Ohwa (see Hanlon 1988).

2. The inside/outside contrast is a common metaphor for understanding selves in central Micronesia. Falgout 1984a:104–6, 1985 analyzes this concept in Pohnpei thought, a discussion relevant to the Sapwuahfik viewpoint. She writes, "For Ponapeans, there is no necessary relationship between this outside appearance (including language and behavior) of a person and his inner content (true feelings, beliefs and capabilities)" (Falgout 1984a:104). See Caughey 1977, Lutz 1988,

and articles in White and Kirkpatrick 1985 for descriptions of Micronesian and other Pacific ethnopsychologies.

3. Black 1978 describes an interestingly similar situation on Tobi Atoll in the Western Caroline Islands, where tragic depopulation left a "cultural vacuum" in which a single visit by a Catholic priest transformed the Tobians into firm Christians. Black describes the conversion of Tobi Atoll as a deliberate act of reasoned choice, based on the priest's single visit in the 1930s. The pre-Christian era of Tobi, like that of Sapwuahfik, is described as "bad." See note 5.

4. One postmassacre immigrant from Pohnpei brought magical knowledge with him and wielded it effectively enough to gain a reputation lasting through the next century. His daughter's son, who died in the mid-1970s, is the man mentioned, whom many spoke of as the last person to know and use indigenous (albeit postmassacre) sorcery. This may be an example of the "escalator" of nostalgic memory (Williams 1973)—important culture elements or values are remembered to have "just recently" disappeared.

5. Letters and diaries of Pacific Islander Christian missionaries, for example, often carry the same tone and phrases as their European and American counterparts, in terms of enlightenment, progress, and the inevitable change of Island peoples toward imported models of social and material life. Black 1978 describes the Tobian memory of the pre-Christian era as a time when "people were both crazy and bad" (1978:328). Like the people of Sapwuahfik, Tobians say that they voluntarily abandoned ancient practices to accept Christianity. Compare Comaroff and Comaroff 1986 on missionary influences on indigenous modes of perception in Africa; Morphy and Morphy 1984 on an Australian "version of history agreed between Aborigine and white in which the present situation was the outcome of a natural progression from 'wild black' to station Aborigine through the acquisition of the English language and new cultural skills and resources" (Morphy and Morphy 1984:476).

Despite the length of Japanese administration, and the evident influence of Japanese economic and military power and cultural influence on island life, I have found no evidence that Japanese ideas about history significantly affected those of Sapwuahfik. Similarly, although a number of *mehn Sapwuahfik* had close personal relationships with Japanese people, and all older Micronesians have opinions about the Japanese as a group, Japan and the Japanese are not usually called *mehn wai,* nor are they described in terms of the *marain/rotorot* scheme described here. I have no explanation for this, but current work on Micronesian oral history of World War II may provide insight.

Conclusion

1. These new questions have been raised directly in relation to historical materials (for example, by Carrier 1987; Dening 1980; Errington 1979; Hanson 1983; Parmentier 1987; Price 1983; Rosaldo 1980; Spear 1981; Webster 1987) and in inquiries into the ongoing construction of "tradition" and cultural identity (see Chapter 5, note 4).

2. I want to repeat here that the contrast of "light" with past "darkness," ideas of history as progress, and ambiguous attitudes toward pre-Christian ancestors and powerful colonizing nations are of course far from unique to Sapwuahfik. They are widespread in the Pacific and in other areas influenced by missionary and colonial activity. In explicating the internal structure and social context of Sapwuahfik beliefs, I am describing one ethnographic case that shares much in content and process with other instances. Nicholas Thomas (1991) has observed that there is a need for "middle-range" work in ethnology, research that connects cases regionally and thematically. Part of the reason that we lack such work is because of a tendency to insist on the uniqueness of each case.

3. People throughout Micronesia, and in many other parts of the world, express a sense of affiliation with Europeans and Americans as powerful foreigners. On Pingelap, Damas (1985:45) writes, "Americans are regarded with special warmth." An interesting parallel is Barnes (1951), who states that the Ngoni of eastern Africa perceive an affinity with whites, saying they are biologically more similar to the English than to their neighbors. The extensive "cargo cult" literature from Melanesia contains other examples of felt affiliation with Americans.

4. The Sapwuahfik proposition that "we are not (or should not be) *mehn Pohnpei*" can also be appreciated in the context of the outer islands/Pohnpei distinction. In the Eastern Carolines, Mwoakilloa, Pingelap, and Sapwuahfik have traditional political systems derived from or influenced by Pohnpei. All are viewed by Pohnpei people and by outer islanders themselves as less-formal, less-elaborate versions of the

original. (The Polynesian islands of Nukuoro and Kapingamarangi are generally thought of as outside this Carolinian cultural system.) Sapwuahfik emphasis on an egalitarian style explicitly identifies them as outer islanders, drawing attention to the geographic separation and the high island–atoll contrast. One would think there would be a certain material advantage for *mehn Sapwuahfik* to identify with politically powerful Pohnpei rather than the outer islands. Some Sapwuahfik individuals do take this tack, emphasizing Sapwuahfik's similarities with Pohnpei and asserting by their actions the plausibility of participating fully in both social worlds. But what value do the majority of Sapwuahfik people see in being affiliated with other outer islands? Recent political activity drawing outer islands together as a special interest voting bloc suggests the alliance's potential usefulness in obtaining political and economic advantages. American bureaucratic processes and values introduced after World War II have facilitated the consolidation of the several island populations as ethnic groups by regarding them in some ways as "minorities" are regarded by the government on the mainland United States. The massive influx of money, projects, and personnel beginning in the 1960s has given weight to American political ideas. But this political strategy is still embryonic, invisible to all except a few leaders. The theme of egalitarianism is aimed not so much at identification with outer islanders—which nonetheless results—as with Americans, who have been and remain the most powerful "neighbors" of Micronesia.

5. Two Pacific examples of the physical embodiment of the past in stones and other markers are Parmentier 1987 on Palau and Kahn 1990 on Papua New Guinea.

6. My thanks to an anonymous reviewer who inquired about the relationship between privately held knowledge and collective identity.

Works Cited

American Board of Commissioners for Foreign Missions (ABCFM)
  1853–1908   *Annual Reports.*

Anderson, Benedict
  1983   *Imagined Communities: Reflections on the Origin and Spread of Nationalism.* London: Verso.

Appadurai, Arjun
  1981   The Past as a Scarce Resource. *Man,* n.s., 6:201–219.

Arno, Andrew
  1980   Fijian Gossip as Adjudication: A Communication Model of Social Control. *Journal of Anthropological Research* 36:343–360.

Bach, John
  1968   The Royal Navy in the Pacific Islands. *Journal of Polynesian History* 3:3–20.

Barker, John, ed.
  1990   *Christianity in Oceania: Ethnographic Perspectives.*

ASAO Monograph no. 12. Lanham, Md.: University Press
of America/Association for Social Anthropology in Oceania.

Barnes, J. A.
1951 The Perception of History in a Plural Society: A Study of a
Ngoni Group in Northern Rhodesia. *Human Relations* 4
(3):295–303.

Barth, Fredrik, ed.
1969 *Ethnic Groups and Boundaries: The Social Organization
of Culture Difference.* Boston: Little, Brown & Co.

Bascom, William R.
1948 Ponapean Prestige Economy. *Southwestern Journal of Anthropology* 4 (2):211–221.
1965 *Ponape: A Pacific Economy in Transition.* University of
California Anthropological Records, no. 22. Berkeley and
Los Angeles: University of California Press.

Behar, Ruth
1986 *Santa María del Monte: The Presence of the Past in a
Spanish Village.* Princeton: Princeton University Press.

Bentley, G. Carter
1987 Ethnicity and Practice. *Comparative Studies in Society
and History* 29 (1):24–55.

Bernart, Luelen
1977 *The Book of Luelen.* J. L. Fischer, S. Riesenberg, and M.
Whiting, eds. Canberra: Australian National University
Press.

Biersack, Aletta
1989 Local Knowledge, Local History: Geertz and Beyond. In
The New Cultural History, L. Hunt, ed. Berkeley and Los
Angeles: University of California Press.

———, ed.
1991 *Clio in Oceania: Toward a Historical Anthropology.*
Washington, D.C.: Smithsonian Institution Press.

Black, Peter W.
1978 The Teachings of Father Marino: Christianity on Tobi

Atoll. In *Mission, Church, and Sect in Oceania.* J. Boutelier, D. Hughes, and S. Tiffany, eds. pp. 307–354. Ann Arbor: University of Michigan Press.

1983   Conflict, Morality and Power in a Western Caroline Society. *Journal of the Polynesian Society* 92 (1):7–30.

Blake, P. L.

1924 [1839]   Report on the Cruise of HMS *Larne* in 1839. *Historical Records of Australia,* series 1, vol. 20:12–28, 654–673.
Library Committee of the Commonwealth Parliament.

Bliss, Theodora Crosby

1906   *Micronesia: Fifty Years in the Island World, A History of
the Mission of the American Board.* Boston: American
Board of Commissioners for Foreign Missions.

Blu, Karen

1980   *The Lumbee Problem: The Making of an American Indian
People.* Cambridge: Cambridge University Press.

Boon, James

1982   *Other Tribes, Other Scribes: Symbolic Anthropology in
the Comparative Study of Cultures, Histories, Religions,
and Texts.* Cambridge: Cambridge University Press.

Borofsky, Robert

1987   *Making History: Pukapukan and Anthropological Constructions of Knowledge.* Cambridge: Cambridge University Press.

Bourdieu, Pierre

1977   *Outline of a Theory of Practice.* Cambridge: Cambridge
University Press.

Boutelier, James A., Daniel T. Hughes, and Sharon W. Tiffany, eds.

1978   *Mission, Church, and Sect in Oceania.* ASAO Monograph
no. 6. Ann Arbor: University of Michigan Press.

Brady, Ivan, ed.

1976   *Transactions in Kinship: Adoption and Fosterage in Oceania.* Honolulu: University Press of Hawaii.

Braroe, Niels

1975   *Indian and White.* Stanford: Stanford University Press.

Brazier, John
　1872　Notes: Cruise of HMS "Blanche" Through the South Sea Islands, May 12–Nov. 15, 1872. MS B512, Mitchell Library, Sydney, Australia.

Brenneis, Donald L., and Fred R. Myers, eds.
　1984　*Dangerous Words: Language and Politics in the Pacific.* New York: New York University Press.

Bryan, E. H.
　1970　*Land in Micronesia and Its Resources: An Annotated Bibliography.* Honolulu: Pacific Science Information Center, Bernice P. Bishop Museum.
　1971　*Guide to Place Names in the Trust Territory of the Pacific Islands.* Honolulu: Pacific Science Information Center, Bernice P. Bishop Museum.

Campbell, I. C.
　1989　*A History of the Pacific Islands.* Berkeley and Los Angeles: University of California Press.

Carrier, James G.
　1987　History and Self-Conception in Ponam Society. *Man,* n.s., 22:111–131.

Carroll, Vern
　1977　Communities and Noncommunities: The Nukuoro on Ponape. In *Exiles and Migrants in Oceania.* M. D. Lieber, ed. pp. 67–79. Honolulu: University Press of Hawaii.

———, ed.
　1970　*Adoption in Eastern Oceania.* ASAO Monograph no. 1. Honolulu: University Press of Hawaii.
　1975　*Pacific Atoll Populations.* ASAO Monograph no. 3. Honolulu: University Press of Hawaii.

Caughey, John L.
　1977　*Fáánakkar, Cultural Values in a Micronesian Society.* Philadelphia: University of Pennsylvania Department of Anthropology.

Chapman, Malcolm, Maryon McDonald, and Elizabeth Tonkin
　1989　Introduction. In *History and Ethnicity.* E. Tonkin, M. Mc-

Donald, and M. Chapman, eds. pp. 1–21. ASA Monograph no. 27. Routledge: London.

Cheyne, Andrew

1852   *A Description of Islands in the Western Pacific Ocean.* London: J. D. Potter.

1977 [1855]   *The Trading Voyages of Andrew Cheyne 1841–44.* D. Shineberg, ed. Honolulu: University Press of Hawaii.

Chowning, Ann

1986   "The Development of Ethnic Identity and Ethnic Stereotypes on Papua New Guinea Plantations." *Journal de la Société des Océanistes* 42:153–162.

Coale, George L.

1951   A Study of Chieftainship, Missionary Contact and Culture Change on Ponape: 1852–1900. Master's thesis, University of Southern California.

Cohen, Anthony P.

1985   *The Symbolic Construction of Community.* London: Tavistock Publications.

———, ed.

1982   *Belonging: Identity and Social Organization in British Rural Cultures.* Manchester: Manchester University Press.

1986   *Symbolizing Boundaries: Identity and Diversity in British Cultures.* Manchester: Manchester University Press.

Cohen, Ronald

1978   Ethnicity: Problem and Focus in Anthropology. *Annual Review of Anthropology* 7:379–403.

Cohn, Bernard S.

1987   *An Anthropologist Among the Historians and Other Essays.* Delhi: Oxford University Press.

Comaroff, Jean

1985   *Body of Power, Spirit of Resistance: The Culture and History of a South African People.* Chicago: University of Chicago Press.

———, and John Comaroff

1986   Christianity and Colonialism in South Africa. *American Ethnologist* 13:1–22.

1992   *Ethnography and the Historical Imagination.* Boulder, Colo.: Westview Press.

Connerton, Paul
    1989   *How Societies Remember.* Cambridge: Cambridge University Press.

Crawford, David, and Leona Crawford
    1967   *Missionary Adventures in the South Pacific.* Rutland: Charles E. Tuttle Co.

Dahlquist, Paul
    1972   *Kohdo Mwenge: The Food Complex in a Changing Ponapean Community.* Ph.D. dissertation, Ohio State University.

Damas, David
    1979   Double Descent in the Eastern Carolines. *Journal of the Polynesian Society* 88 (2):177–198.
    1981   The Keinek of Pingelap and Patrilineal Descent. *Journal of the Polynesian Society* 90 (1):117–122.
    1985   Pingelap Politics and American-Micronesian Relations. *Ethnology* 24 (1):43–55.

Denfield, D. "Colt"
    1979   *Field Survey of Ponape: World War II Features.* Micronesian Archaeological Survey Report No. 6. Saipan: U.S. Trust Territory Historic Preservation Office.
    1981   *Japanese Fortifications and Other Military Structures in the Central Pacific.* Micronesian Archaeological Survey Report No. 9. Saipan: U.S. Trust Territory Historic Preservation Office.

Dening, Greg
    1966   Ethnohistory in Polynesia. *Journal of Pacific History* 1:23–42.
    1980   *Islands and Beaches, Discourse on a Silent Land: Marquesas 1774–1880.* Melbourne: Melbourne University Press.
    1988   *History's Anthropology: The Death of William Gooch.* ASAO Special Publication no. 2. Lanham, Md.: University Press of America.
    1989   History "in" the Pacific. *Contemporary Pacific* 1:134–139.

Doane, Edward T.
　1874　The Caroline Islands. *The Geographical Magazine*
　　　　1:203–205.

Dolgin, Janet L.
　1977　Introduction: "As People Express Their Lives, So
　　　　They Are . . ." In *Symbolic Anthropology*. J. Dolgin,
　　　　D. Kemnitzer, and D. Schneider, eds. pp. 3–45. New
　　　　York: Columbia University Press.

Dominguez, Virginia R.
　1986　*White by Definition: Social Classification in Creole
　　　　Louisiana.* New Brunswick, N.J.: Rutgers University
　　　　Press.

Dunbabin, Thomas
　1926　Shipwreck, Slaughter and Tortoiseshell. *Navy League
　　　　Journal* 6 (11):1–5.

Ehrlich, Paul
　1978　*"The Clothes of Men": Ponape Island and German Colo-
　　　　nial Rule, 1899–1914.* Ph.D. dissertation, State University
　　　　of New York at Stony Brook.

Eilers, Anneliese
　1934　*Inseln um Ponape. Ergebnisse der Südsee-Expedition
　　　　1908–1910.* 2 B, Band 8. G. Thilenius, ed. Hamburg:
　　　　Friederichsen, DeGruyter & Co.

Erdland, August
　1914　*Die Marschall-Insulaner: Leben und Sitte, Sinn und Reli-
　　　　gion Eines Südsee-Volkes.* Band 2, Heft 1. Münster: An-
　　　　thropos Bibliotek.

Errington, Shelly
　1979　Some Comments on Style in the Meanings of the Past.
　　　　Journal of Asian Studies 38:231–244.

Falgout, Suzanne
　1984a　*Persons and Knowledge in Ponape.* Ph.D. dissertation,
　　　　University of Oregon.
　1984b　A Clash of Epistemologies: The Management of Knowl-
　　　　edge in Ponape. Paper presented at American Anthropo-
　　　　logical Association meeting.

1985   The Quiet of the Fierce Barracuda: Anger in Ponape. Paper presented at Association for Social Anthropology in Oceania meeting.

1988   Cultural Encounters: Pohnpei in the Pacific Theatre of World War II. Paper presented at conference, "Cultural Encounters in the Pacific War," East-West Center, Honolulu, May 1988.

1989   From Passive Pawns to Political Strategists: Wartime Lessons for the People of Pohnpei. In *The Pacific Theater; Island Representations of World War II.* G. White and L. Lindstrom, eds. pp. 279–297. Honolulu: University of Hawaii Press.

Feinberg, Richard
1980   History and Structure: A Case of Polynesian Dualism. *Journal of Anthropological Research* 36 (3):361–378.

Fischer, John L.
1957   *The Eastern Carolines.* New Haven: Pacific Science Board in association with HRAF Press.

1958   Contemporary Ponape Island Land Tenure. In *Land Tenure Patterns in the Trust Territory of the Pacific Islands*, vol. 1, pt. 2. J. de Young, ed. Guam: Office of the Staff Anthropologist, U.S. Trust Territory of the Pacific Islands.

1974   The Role of the Traditional Chiefs on Ponape in the American Period. In *Political Development in Micronesia.* D. Hughes and S. Lingenfelter, eds. Columbus: Ohio State University Press.

n.d.   Unpublished notes. Bishop Museum, Honolulu.

———, Saul H. Riesenberg, and Marjorie G. Whiting, transls. and eds.
1977   *Annotations to the Book of Luelen.* Canberra: Australian National University Press.

Flanagan, James G.
1989   Hierarchy in Simple "Egalitarian" Societies. *Annual Review of Anthropology* 18:245–266.

Flinn, Juliana
1990   We Still Have Our Customs: Being Pulapese in Truk. In *Cultural Identity and Ethnicity in the Pacific.* J. Linnekin

and L. Poyer, eds. pp. 103–126. Honolulu: University of Hawaii Press.

Foss, Ida C.
    1901   Letter to American Board of Commissioners for Foreign Missions (ABCFM), 20 October 1901. "Letters and Reports," ABCFM microfilm file #434, Hamilton Library, University of Hawaii.

Foucault, Michel
    1972   *The Archaeology of Knowledge.* New York: Pantheon Books.
    1978   *The History of Sexuality, Volume 1. An Introduction.* New York: Vintage Books.

Fox, Richard G.
    1985   *Lions of the Punjab: Culture in the Making.* Berkeley and Los Angeles: University of California Press.

Fretwell, C. H.
    1892   *The Story of an Ancient Mariner.* London: S. W. Partridge & Co.

Friedman, Jonathan
    1992   The Past in the Future: History and the Politics of Identity. *American Anthropologist* 94 (4):837–859.

Garvin, Paul, and Saul H. Riesenberg
    1952   Respect Behavior on Ponape: An Ethnolinguistic Study. *American Anthropologist* 54 (2):201–220.

Geertz, Clifford
    1973   *The Interpretation of Cultures.* New York: Basic Books.
    1983   *Local Knowledge: Further Essays in Interpretive Anthropology.* New York: Basic Books.

Gellner, Ernest
    1964   *Thought and Change.* Chicago: University of Chicago Press.

George, Kenneth M.
    1991   Headhunting, History and Exchange in Upland Sulawesi. *Journal of Asian Studies* 50:536–564.

Godby, E. P.
  1845   Letter. *Nautical Magazine* 14 (1845): 505–507.

Gorenflo, L. J. and Michael J. Levin
  1992   Regional Demographic Change in Pohnpei State, Federated States of Micronesia. *Pacific Studies* 15:1–49.

Gulick, Addison
  1932   *Evolutionist and Missionary: John Thomas Gulick.* Chicago: University of Chicago Press.

Gunson, Neil
  1978   *Messengers of Grace: Evangelical Missionaries in the South Seas, 1797–1860.* Melbourne: Oxford University Press.

Hahl, Albert
  1900   Besuch der Ngatik-Inseln durch den Kaiserlichen Vice-Gouvernveur. *Deutsches Kolonialblatt* 11 (1 July 1900):505–506.

Handler, Richard
  1988   *Nationalism and the Politics of Culture in Quebec.* Madison: University of Wisconsin Press.

————, and Jocelyn Linnekin
  1984   Tradition, Genuine or Spurious. *Journal of American Folklore* 97:273–290.

Hanlon, David
  1984   God Versus Gods: The First Years of the Micronesian Mission on Ponape, 1852–1859. *Journal of Pacific History* 19:41–59.
  1988   *Upon a Stone Altar: A History of the Island of Ponape to 1890.* Honolulu: University of Hawaii Press.
  1992   The Path Back to Pohnsakar: Luelen Bernart, His Book, and the Practice of History on Pohnpei. *Isla: A Journal of Micronesian Studies* 1 (1):13–36.

Hanson, F. Allan
  1983   Syntagmatic Structures: How the Maoris Make Sense of History. *Semiotica* 46:287–307.

Hassert, Kurt
  1903   *Die Neuen Deutschen Erwerbungen in der Südsee: Die*

Karolinen, Marianen und Samoa-Inseln. Leipzig: Seele & Co.

Heine, Carl
1974   *Micronesia at the Crossroads.* Honolulu: University Press of Hawaii.

Hempenstall, Peter J.
1977   Native Resistance and German Control Policy. In *Germany in the Pacific and the Far East, 1870–1914.* J. Moses, ed. pp. 209–233. St. Lucia, Queensland: University of Queensland Press.
1978   *Pacific Islanders Under German Rule.* Canberra: Australian National University Press.

Hernandez, P. Faustino, S. J.
1955   *Mision de las Islas Carolinas y Marshalls.* Madrid: Graficas Martinez.

Herzfeld, Michael
1991   *A Place in History: Social and Monumental Time in a Cretan Town.* Princeton: Princeton University Press.

Hezel, Francis X., S.J.
1970   Spanish Capuchins in the Caroline Islands. Micronesian Seminar Bulletin. June.
1978   The Role of the Beachcomber in the Carolines. In *The Changing Pacific: Essays in Honor of H. E. Maude.* N. Gunson, ed. Melbourne: Oxford University Press.
1979   *Foreign Ships in Micronesia.* Saipan: U.S. Trust Territory Historic Preservation Office.
1983   *The First Taint of Civilization: A History of the Caroline and Marshall Islands in Pre-Colonial Days, 1521–1885.* Honolulu: University of Hawaii Press.

Hobsbawm, Eric
1983   Introduction: Inventing Traditions. In *The Invention of Tradition.* E. Hobsbawm and T. Ranger, eds. pp. 1–14. Cambridge: Cambridge University Press.

———, and Terence Ranger, eds.
1983   *The Invention of Tradition.* Cambridge: Cambridge University Press.

Howard, Alan
  1990   Cultural Paradigms, History, and the Search for Identity in
          Oceania. In *Cultural Identity and Ethnicity in the Pacific.*
          J. Linnekin and L. Poyer, eds. pp. 259–279. Honolulu: Uni-
          versity of Hawaii Press.

———, and Irwin Howard
  1977   Rotumans in Fiji: The Genesis of an Ethnic Group. In *Ex-
          iles and Migrants in Oceania.* M. Lieber, ed. pp. 161–194.
          Honolulu: University Press of Hawaii.

Howe, K. R.
  1984   *Where the Waves Fall: A New South Sea Islands History
          from First Settlement to Colonial Rule.* Honolulu: Univer-
          sity of Hawaii Press.

Hughes, Daniel T.
  1969   Reciprocal Influence of Traditional and Democratic Lead-
          ership Roles on Ponape. *Ethnology* 8 (3):278–291.
  1970   *Political Conflict and Harmony on Ponape.* New Haven:
          HRAF.
  1972   Integration of the Role of Territorial Congressman into
          Ponapean Society. *Oceania* 43 (2):140–152.
  1974   Obstacles to the Integration of the District Legislature
          into Ponapean Society. In *Political Development in Mi-
          cronesia.* D. T. Hughes and S. G. Lingenfelter, eds. pp.
          93–109.
  1982   Continuity of Indigenous Social Structure and Stratifica-
          tion. *Oceania* 53 (1):5–18.

Isaacs, Harold R.
  1975   *Idols of the Tribe: Group Identity and Political Change.*
          New York: Harper and Row.

Jolly, Margaret
  1992   Specters of Inauthenticity. *Contemporary Pacific* 4:49–72.

Kahn, Miriam
  1990   Stone-Faced Ancestors: The Spatial Anchoring of Myth in
          Wamira, Papua New Guinea. *Ethnology* 29:51–66.

Keesing, Roger M.
  1982   Kastom in Melanesia: An Overview. *Mankind* 13:297–301.

1989   Creating the Past: Custom and Identity in the Contemporary Pacific. *The Contemporary Pacific* 1:19–42.

———, and Peter Corris
1980   *Lightning Meets the West Wind: The Malaita Massacre.* Melbourne: Oxford University Press.

———, and Robert Tonkinson, eds.
1982   Reinventing Traditional Culture: The Politics of Kastom in Island Melanesia. *Mankind,* Special Issue, 13(4).

Kirtley, Bacil F.
1971   *A Motif-Index of Traditional Polynesian Narrative.* Honolulu: University of Hawaii Press.

Kohl, Manfred W.
1971   *Lagoon in the Pacific: The Story of Truk.* Schooley's Mountain, N.J.: Publications Committee of the Liebenzell Mission USA.

Krämer, Augustin, and Hans Nevermann
1938   Ralik-Ratak (Marschall Inseln). *Ergebnisse der Südsee-Expedition, 1908–1910.* 2, B. G. Thilenius, ed. Hamburg: Friederichsen, DeGruyter. (University of Hawaii Pacific Islands Studies Program translation.)

Krech, Shepard
1991   The State of Ethnohistory. *Annual Reviews in Anthropology* 20:345–75.

Lederman, Rena
1984   Who Speaks Here? Formality and the Politics of Gender in Mendi, Highland Papua New Guinea. In *Dangerous Words: Language and Politics in the Pacific.* D. Brenneis and F. Myers, eds. pp. 85–107. New York: New York University Press.

Lessa, William A., and Carlos G. Velez-I.
1978   Bwang, a Martial Art of the Caroline Islands. *Micronesica* 14 (2):139–176.

LeVine, Robert A., and Donald T. Campbell
1972   *Ethnocentrism: Theories of Conflict, Ethnic Attitudes, and Group Behavior.* New York: John Wiley and Sons.

Lieber, Michael D.

1977a The Processes of Change in Two Kapingamarangi Communities. In *Exiles and Migrants in Oceania.* M. Lieber, ed. Honolulu: University Press of Hawaii.

1984 Strange Feast: Negotiating Identities on Ponape. *Journal of the Polynesian Society* 93:141–189.

1990 Lamarckian Definitions of Identity on Kapingamarangi and Pohnpei. In *Cultural Identity and Ethnicity in the Pacific.* J. Linnekin and L. Poyer, eds. pp. 71–101. Honolulu: University of Hawaii Press.

———, ed.

1977b *Exiles and Migrants in Oceania.* Honolulu: University Press of Hawaii.

Lindstrom, Lamont

1990 *Knowledge and Power in a South Pacific Society.* Washington, D.C.: Smithsonian Institution Press.

Linnekin, Jocelyn

1983 Defining Tradition: Variations on the Hawaiian Identity. *American Ethnologist* 10:241–252.

1985 *Children of the Land: Exchange and Status in a Hawaiian Community.* New Brunswick, N.J.: Rutgers University Press.

1990 The Politics of Culture in the Pacific. In *Cultural Identity and Ethnicity in the Pacific.* J. Linnekin and L. Poyer, eds. pp. 149–173. Honolulu: University of Hawaii Press.

———, and Lin Poyer

1990a Introduction. In *Cultural Identity and Ethnicity in the Pacific.* J. Linnekin and L. Poyer, eds. pp. 1–16. Honolulu: University of Hawaii Press.

———, eds.

1990b *Cultural Identity and Ethnicity in Oceania.* Honolulu: University of Hawaii Press.

Lundsgaarde, Henry P., ed.

1974 *Land Tenure in Oceania.* Honolulu: University Press of Hawaii.

Lütke, Fedor P.
    1971 [1835] *Voyage Autour du Monde,* vol. 2. Amsterdam: N. Is-
                rael.

Lutz, Catherine
    1988 *Unnatural Emotions: Everyday Sentiments on a Microne-
           sian Atoll and Their Challenge to Western Theory.* Chica-
           go: University of Chicago Press.

———, ed.
    1984 Micronesia as a Strategic Colony: The Impact of U.S. Poli-
           cy on Micronesian Health and Culture. *Cultural Survival
           Occasional Papers,* vol. 12.

Marcus, George E.
    1984 Three Perspectives on Role Distance in Conversations Be-
           tween Tongan Nobles and Their "People." In *Dangerous
           Words: Language and Politics in the Pacific.* D. Brenneis
           and F. Myers, eds. pp. 243–265. New York: New York Uni-
           versity Press.

Marshall, Mac
    1975 Changing Patterns of Marriage and Migration on
           Namoluk Atoll. In *Pacific Atoll Populations.* V. Carroll,
           ed. pp. 160–211. Honolulu: University Press of Hawaii.

———, and Leslie B. Marshall
    1976 Holy and Unholy Spirits: The Effects of Missionization on
           Alcohol Use in Eastern Micronesia. *Journal of Pacific His-
           tory* 3–4:135–166.

Maude, H. E.
    1968 *Of Islands and Men: Studies in Pacific History.* Mel-
           bourne: Oxford University Press.

McDowell, Nancy
    1985 Past and Future: The Nature of Episodic Time in Bun. In
           *History and Ethnohistory in Papua New Guinea. Oceania
           Monograph* no. 28. D. Gewertz and E. Schieffelin, eds. pp.
           26–39.

McHenry, Donald F.
    1975 *Micronesia: Trust Betrayed.* New York: Carnegie Endow-
           ment for International Peace.

Meller, Norman
    1969   *The Congress of Micronesia.* Honolulu: University of
            Hawaii Press.

Mercer, P. M.
    1979   Oral Traditions in the Pacific: Problems of Investigation.
            Journal of Pacific History 14:130–153.

Mitchell, Roger
    1968   Genre and Function in Eastern Carolinian Narrative.
            Asian Folklore Studies 27 (2):1–15.
    1970   Oral Tradition and Micronesian History. *Journal of Pacific*
            History 5:33–41.

Morphy, Howard, and Frances Morphy
    1984   The "Myths" of Ngalakan History: Ideology and Images of
            the Past in Northern Australia. *Man,* n.s., 19 (3):459–478.

Morton, N. E.
    1972   Pingelap and Mokil Atolls: Clans and Cognatic Frequen-
            cies. *American Journal of Human Genetics* 24:290–298.

Muga, David
    1984   Academic Sub-cultural Theory and the Problematic of
            Ethnicity: A Tentative Critique. *Journal of Ethnic Studies*
            12:1–52.

Munger, James F.
    1967 [1852]   *Two Years in the Pacific, Arctic Ocean and China: A*
            Journal of . . . a Whaling Voyage. Fairfield, Wash.: Ye
            Galleon Press.

Nason, James D.
    1975   The Strength of the Land: Community Perception of Pop-
            ulation on Etal Atoll. In *Pacific Atoll Populations.* V. Car-
            roll, ed. pp. 117–159. Honolulu: University Press of Hawaii.
    1978   Civilizing the Heathen: Missionaries and Social Change in
            the Mortlock Islands. In *Mission, Church, and Sect in*
            Oceania. J. Boutelier, D. Hughes, and S. Tiffany, eds. pp.
            109–37.

Nevin, David
    1977   *The American Touch in Micronesia.* New York: W. W.
            Norton.

Nisbet, Robert A.
    1969   *Social Change and History: Aspects of the Western Theory of Development.* New York: Oxford University Press.

O'Brien, Ilma E.
    1971   Missionaries on Ponape: Induced Social and Political Change. *Australia National University Historical Journal* 8:53–64.

O'Brien, Jay, and William Roseberry, eds.
    1991   *Golden Ages, Dark Ages: Imagining the Past in Anthropology and History.* Berkeley and Los Angeles: University of California Press.

Oliver, Douglas
    1989   *The Pacific Islands.* 3d ed. Honolulu: University of Hawaii Press.

Ortner, Sherry
    1973   On Key Symbols. *American Anthropologist* 75:1338–1346.
    1984   Theory in Anthropology Since the Sixties. *Comparative Studies in Society and History* 26:126–166.

Parmentier, Richard J.
    1987   *The Sacred Remains: Myth, History, and Polity in Belau.* Chicago: University of Chicago Press.

Peattie, Mark
    1984   The Nan'yo: Japan in the South Pacific, 1885–1945. In *The Japanese Colonial Empire, 1895–1945.* R. Myers and M. Peattie, eds. Princeton: Princeton University Press.
    1988   *Nan'yo: The Rise and Fall of the Japanese in Micronesia, 1885–1945.* Honolulu: University of Hawaii Press.

Peel, J. D. Y.
    1989   The Cultural Work of Yoruba Ethnogenesis. In *History and Ethnicity.* E. Tonkin, M. McDonald, and M. Chapman, eds. pp. 198–215. London: Routledge.

Peoples, James G.
    1978   Dependence in a Micronesian Economy. *American Ethnologist* 5 (3):535–552.
    1985   *Island in Trust: Culture Change and Dependence in a Micronesian Economy.* Boulder, Colo.: Westview Press.

Petersen, Glenn T.

1977   *Ponapean Agriculture and Economy.* Ph.D. dissertation,
         Columbia University, New York.

1979   External Politics, Internal Economics, and Ponapean So-
         cial Formation. *American Ethnologist* 6:25–40.

1982a   *One Man Cannot Rule a Thousand: Fission in a Ponapean
         Chiefdom.* Ann Arbor: University of Michigan Press.

1982b   Ponapean Matriliny: Production, Exchange, and the Ties
         That Bind. *American Ethnologist* 9 (1):129–144.

Phillips, Scott K.

1986   Natives and Incomers: The Symbolism of Belonging in
         Muker Parish, North Yorkshire. In *Symbolizing Bound-
         aries: Identity and Diversity in British Cultures.* A. P. Co-
         hen, ed. pp. 141–154.

Poyer, Lin

1983   *The Ngatik Massacre: History and Identity on a Microne-
         sian Atoll.* Ph.D. dissertation, University of Michigan,
         Ann Arbor, Michigan.

1985   The Ngatik Massacre: Documentary and Oral Traditional
         Accounts. *Journal of Pacific History* 20:4–22.

1988a   Maintaining "Otherness": Sapwuahfik Cultural Identity.
         American Ethnologist 15 (3):472–485.

1988b   History, Identity and Christian Evangelism: The Sapwuah-
         fik Massacre. *Ethnohistory* 35 (3):209–233.

1989   Echoes of Massacre: Recollections of World War II on Sap-
         wuahfik (Ngatik Atoll). In *The Pacific Theater: Island
         Representations of World War II.* G. White and L. Lind-
         strom, eds. pp. 97–115. Honolulu: University of Hawaii
         Press.

1990   Being Sapwuahfik: Cultural and Ethnic Identity in a Mi-
         cronesian Society. In *Cultural Identity and Ethnicity in
         the Pacific.* J. Linnekin and L. Poyer, eds. pp. 127–147.
         Honolulu: University of Hawaii Press.

1991   Maintaining Egalitarianism: Social Equality on a Microne-
         sian Atoll. In *Between Bands and States.* S. Gregg, ed. pp.
         359–375. Carbondale: Center for Archaeological Investiga-
         tion, Southern Illinois University.

1993   Egalitarianism in the Face of Hierarchy. *Journal of An-
         thropological Research* 49 (2). In press.

Price, Richard
    1983   *First-Time: The Historical Vision of an Afro-American People.* Baltimore: Johns Hopkins University Press.

Purcell, David C., Jr.
    1967   *Japanese Expansion in the South Pacific, 1890–1935.* Ph.D. dissertation, University of Pennsylvania.
    1972   Japanese Entrepreneurs. In *East Across the Pacific.* H. Conry and T. Miyakawa, eds. Santa Barbara, Calif.: Clio Press.
    1976   The Economics of Exploitation: The Japanese in the Mariana, Caroline and Marshall Islands, 1915–1940. *Journal of Pacific History* 11:189–211.

Ralston, Caroline
    1978   *Grass Huts and Warehouses: Pacific Beach Communities of the Nineteenth Century.* Honolulu: University Press of Hawaii.

Rand, Frank E.
    1889   The *Morning Star*'s Report to Her Stockholders for 1888–89. *Missionary Herald* 85:261–264.

Rebel, Hermann
    1989   Cultural Hegemony and Class Experience: A Critical Reading of Recent Ethnological-Historical Approaches. (Pts. 1 and 2). *American Ethnologist* 16:117–136; 350–365.

Rehg, Kenneth L.
    1979   A Linguistic History of Ngatikese. Paper presented at Linguistic Society of Hawaii Fifth Annual Oceanic Linguistics Festival.

———, and Damian G. Sohl
    1979   *Ponapean-English Dictionary.* Honolulu: University Press of Hawaii.

Reminick, Ronald A.
    1983   *Theory of Ethnicity: An Anthropologist's Perspective.* Lanham, Md.: University Press of America.

Richard, Dorothy
    1957   *United States Naval Administration of the Trust Territory of the Pacific Islands.* 3 vols. Washington, D.C.: Office of the Chief of Naval Operations.

Riesenberg, Saul H.
1948   Magic and Medicine in Ponape. *Southwestern Journal of Anthropology* 4 (2):406–429.
1965   Table of Voyages Affecting Micronesian Islands. *Oceania* 36:155–170.
1966   The Ngatik Massacre. *Micronesian Reporter* 14 (5):9–12, 29–30.
1968   *The Native Polity of Ponape.* Smithsonian Contributions to Anthropology, Vol. 10. Washington, D.C.: Smithsonian Institution Press.
1974   Six Pacific Island Discoveries. *American Neptune* 34:249–257.

Rosaldo, Renato
1980   *Ilongot Headhunting 1882–1974: A Study in Society and History.* Stanford: Stanford University Press.

Roseberry, William
1989   *Anthropologies and Histories: Essays in Culture, History, and Political Economy.* New Brunswick, N.J.: Rutgers University Press.

Sahlins, Marshall D.
1958   *Social Stratification in Polynesia.* Seattle: University of Washington Press.
1981a   The Stranger-king, or Dumezil Among the Fijians. *Journal of Pacific History* 15:107–132.
1981b   *Historical Metaphors and Mythical Realities: Structure in the Early History of the Sandwich Islands Kingdom.* Ann Arbor: University of Michigan Press.
1985   *Islands of History.* Chicago: University of Chicago Press.

Schneider, David M.
1968   *American Kinship: A Cultural Account.* Englewood Cliffs, N.J.: Prentice-Hall.
1976   Notes Toward a Theory of Culture. In *Meaning in Anthropology.* K. Basso and H. Selby, eds. pp. 197–220. Albuquerque: University of New Mexico Press.
1980   Is There Really Double Descent in Pingelap? On Damas 1979 (vol. 88:177–98). *Journal of the Polynesian Society* 89:525–528.

1984   *A Critique of the Study of Kinship.* Ann Arbor: University of Michigan Press.

Schwimmer, E. G.
   1972   Symbolic Competition. *Anthropologica* 14:117–155.

Sharp, Andrew
   1960   *The Discovery of the Pacific Islands.* Oxford: Clarendon.

Shils, Edward
   1981   *Tradition.* Chicago: University of Chicago Press.

Shimizu, Akitoshi
   1982   Chiefdom and the Spatial Classification of the Life-world: Everyday Life, Subsistence and the Political System on Ponape. In *Islanders and Their Outside World.* M. Aoyagi, ed. pp. 153–215. Tokyo: Committee for Micronesian Research, St. Paul's (Rikkyo) University.
   1987   Feasting as a Socio-political Process of Chieftainship on Ponape, Eastern Carolines. In *Cultural Uniformity and Diversity in Micronesia,* Senri Ethnological Studies, No. 21. I. Ushijima and K. Sudo, eds. Osaka: National Museum of Ethnology.

Shore, Bradd
   1982   *Sala'ilua: A Samoan Mystery.* New York: Columbia University Press.

Sider, Gerald M.
   1986   *Culture and Class in Anthropology and History: A Newfoundland Illustration.* Cambridge: Cambridge University Press.

Silverman, Martin G.
   1967   The Historiographic Implications of Social and Cultural Change: Some Banaban Examples. *Journal of Pacific History* 2:137–147.
   1969   Maximize Your Options: A Study in Symbols, Values, and Social Structure. In *Forms of Symbolic Action.* R. Spencer, ed. pp. 97–115. Seattle: University of Washington Press.
   1971   *Disconcerting Issue: Meaning and Struggle in a Resettled Pacific Community.* Chicago: University of Chicago Press.

Simpson, C. H.
> 1873   Report on the Proceedings of H.M.S. *Blanche;* 15 Novem-
>   ber 1872. *Parliamentary Papers of the South Sea Islands*
>   50:191–204.

Smith, Anthony D.
> 1986   *The Ethnic Origin of Nations.* Oxford: Basil Blackwell.

Spate, O. H. K.
> 1983   *Monopolists and Freebooters. The Pacific Since Magellan,*
>   *Vol. II.* Minneapolis: University of Minnesota Press.
> 1988   *Paradise Found and Lost. The Pacific Since Magellan, Vol.*
>   *III.* Minneapolis: University of Minnesota Press.

Spear, Thomas
> 1981   Oral Traditions: Whose History? *Journal of Pacific History*
>   16:133–148.

Spicer, Edward H.
> 1980   *The Yaquis: A Cultural History.* Tucson: University of
>   Arizona Press.

Spriggs, Matthew
> 1992   Alternative Prehistories for Bougainville: Regional,
>   National, or Micronational. *The Contemporary Pacific*
>   4:269–298.

Swartz, Marc J.
> 1961   Negative Ethnocentrism. *Journal of Conflict Resolution*
>   5:75–81.

Thomas, Nicholas
> 1989   The Inversion of Tradition. *American Ethnologist*
>   19:213–23
> 1990   Partial Texts: Representation, Colonialism and Agency in
>   Pacific History. *Journal of Pacific History* 25 (2):139–158.
> 1991   *Entangled Objects: Exchange, Material Culture, and*
>   *Colonialism in the Pacific.* Cambridge: Harvard Universi-
>   ty Press.

Thompson, Seth
> 1966   A Charter Trip to Ngatik. *Micronesian Reporter* 14 (Janu-
>   ary–March): 12–13, 18–19.

Tonkin, Elizabeth, Maryon McDonald, and Malcolm Chapman, eds.
   1989   *History and Ethnicity.* London: Routledge.

Tonkinson, Myrna Ewart
   1990   Is It in the Blood? Australian Aboriginal Identity. In *Cultural Identity and Ethnicity in the Pacific.* J. Linnekin and L. Poyer, eds. pp. 191–218. Honolulu: University of Hawaii Press.

Trouillot, Michel-Rolph
   1988   *Peasants and Capital: Dominica in the World Economy.* Baltimore: Johns Hopkins University Press.

U.S. Navy, Office of the Chief of Naval Operations
   1944   *Civil Affairs Handbook: East Caroline Islands.* Washington, D.C.: Navy Department.

Useem, John
   1945   The American Pattern of Military Government in Micronesia. *American Journal of Sociology* 51 (2):93–102.

Vansina, Jan
   1961   *Oral Tradition: A Study in Historical Methodology.* Transl. by H. M. Wright. Chicago: Aldine Publishing.
   1985   *Oral Tradition as History.* Madison: University of Wisconsin Press.

von Kittlitz, Friedrich H.
   1858   *Denkwürdigkeiten einer Riese nach dem russischen Amerika, nach Mikronesien, und durch Kamtschatka.* Zweiter Band. Gotha: Verlag von Justus Berthes.

Wagner, Roy
   1981   *The Invention of Culture.* Chicago: University of Chicago Press.

Ward, Martha
   1975   Alive and Well: A View of the Contemporary Ponapean Title System. Paper presented at Association for Social Anthropology meeting.
   1989   *Nest in the Wind: Adventures in Anthropology on a Tropical Island.* Prospect Heights, Ill.: Waveland Press.

Ward, R. Gerard, ed.
    1967   *American Activities in the Central Pacific, 1870–1970.* 8
            vols. Ridgewood, N.J.: Gregg Press.

Ward, Roger L.
    1977   *Curing on Ponape: A Medical Ethnography.* Ph.D. disser-
            tation, Tulane University.

Warren, Kay B.
    1978   *The Symbolism of Subordination: Indian Identity in a
            Guatemalan Town.* Austin: University of Texas Press.

Watanabe, John M.
    1990   From Saints to Shibboleths: Image, Structure, and Identity
            in Maya Religious Syncretism. *American Ethnologist* 17
            (1):131–150.

Watson, James B.
    1990   Other People Do Other Things: Lamarckian Identities in
            Kainantu Subdistrict, Papua New Guinea. In *Cultural
            Identity and Ethnicity in the Pacific.* J. Linnekin and L.
            Poyer, eds. pp. 17–41. Honolulu: University of Hawaii
            Press.

Webster, Steven
    1987   Structuralist Historicism and the History of Structural-
            ism: Sahlins, the Hansons' *Counterpoint in Maori Cul-
            ture,* and Postmodernist Ethnographic Form. *The Journal
            of the Polynesian Society* 96:27–65.

Weckler, Joseph E.
    1949   *Land and Livelihood on Mokil, An Atoll in the Eastern
            Carolines.* Coordinated Investigation of Micronesian An-
            thropology Report No. 11, pt. 1. Los Angeles: University
            of Southern California.

Westwood, John
    1905   *Island Stories: Being Extracts from the Papers of Mr. John
            Westwood, Mariner, of London and Shanghai.* Shanghai:
            North China Herald.

White, Geoffrey M.
    1991   *Identity through History: Living Stories in a Solomon Is-
            lands Society.* Cambridge: Cambridge University Press.

————, and John Kirkpatrick, eds.

　1985　*Person, Self, and Experience: Exploring Pacific Ethnopsy-chologies.* Berkeley and Los Angeles: University of California Press.

Williams, Raymond

　1973　*The Country and the City.* New York: Oxford University Press.

Wiltgen, Ralph M.

　1975　*The Founding of the Roman Catholic Church in Oceania 1825 to 1850.* Canberra: Australian National University Press.

Woodburn, James

　1982　Egalitarian Societies. *Man,* n.s., 17:431–451.

Yanaihara, Tadao

　1940　*Pacific Islands Under Japanese Mandate.* New York: Oxford University Press.

Yinger, J. Milton

　1985　Ethnicity. *Annual Review of Sociology* 11:151–180.

Zelenietz, Martin, and David Kravits

　1974　Absorption, Trade and Warfare: Beachcombers on Ponape, 1830–1854. *Ethnohistory* 21 (3):223–249.

Zonabend, Françoise

　1984　*The Enduring Memory: Time and History in a French Village.* Transl. Anthony Forster. Manchester: Manchester University Press.

Index

Aisikaya, 92, 111, 258n12; accepts Christianity, 102; clan of, 179; encounter with German governor, 109; land division by, 94, 95; selected as nahnmwarki, 88–89

Americans: Pohnpei view of, 232–33; post–World War II administration by, 122–24; Sapwuahfik view of, 75–76, 226, 231, 233–34; World War II contact with, 120–22

Bernart, Luelen, 49, 224–25

Blake, P. L.: investigation of Ngatik Massacre, 3, 55, 63, 65–66, 67–68, 73, 80–81

Brown, William, 84, 258n12

Christianity: Catholic mission, 108, 114–15; early missionaries, 100–104, 208–9; and identity, 234; influence on historical view, 223–27; introduction of, 97–98, 207–8; modern church groups, 210–13; and protection from disasters, 222–23; as repayment for massacre, 76

Copra trade, 89, 106–7, 110

Doane, Edward T., 93–94, 102

Eilers, Anneliese. *See* Südsee-Expedition

Ethnicity, 24–25. *See also* Identity, cultural

Falcon tragedy, 2, 60–62

Falgout, Suzanne, 174, 233, 265n2

Fischer, John, 180, 189–90, 199, 264–65n9

Francis, John, 100–101, 102, 103, 208–9

295

Index

Index prepared by Andrew L. Christenson